THE BERNARD SHAW LIBRARY

PLAYS EXTRAVAGANT

Bernard Shaw was born in Dublin in 1856. Essentially shy, he yet created the persona of G.B.S., the showman, satirist, controversialist, critic, pundit, wit, intellectual buffoon and dramatist. Commentators brought a new adjective into English: Shavian, a term used to embody all his brilliant qualities.

After his arrival in London in 1876 he became an active Socialist and a brilliant platform speaker. He wrote on many social aspects of the day; on *Common Sense about the War* (1914), *How to Settle the Irish Question* (1917) and *The Intelligent Woman's Guide to Socialism and Capitalism* (1928). He undertook his own education at the British Museum and consequently became keenly interested in cultural subjects. Thus his prolific output included music, art and theatre reviews, which were collected into several volumes published as *Music in London 1890–1894* (3 vols., 1931); *Pen Portraits and Reviews* (1931); and *Our Theatres in the Nineties* (3 vols., 1931). Among his five novels, *Cashel Byron's Profession* and some shorter fiction including *The Black Girl in Search of God and Some Lesser Tales* are published in Penguins.

He conducted a strong attack on the London theatre and was closely associated with the intellectual revival of British theatre. His many plays fall into several categories: his 'Plays Pleasant'; 'Plays Unpleasant'; comedies; chronicle-plays; 'metabiological Pentateuch' (*Back to Methuselah*, a series of plays) and 'political extravaganzas'. G.B.S. died in 1950.

BERNARD SHAW

PLAYS EXTRAVAGANT

TOO TRUE TO BE GOOD
THE SIMPLETON
OF THE UNEXPECTED ISLES
THE MILLIONAIRESS

DEFINITIVE TEXT
UNDER THE EDITORIAL
SUPERVISION OF
DAN H. LAURENCE

PENGUIN BOOKS

PENGUIN BOOKS

Published by the Penguin Group
Penguin Books Ltd, 27 Wrights Lane, London W8 5TZ, England
Penguin Putnam Inc., 375 Hudson Street, New York, New York 10014, USA
Penguin Books Australia Ltd, Ringwood, Victoria, Australia
Penguin Books Canada Ltd, 10 Alcorn Avenue, Toronto, Ontario, Canada M4V 3B2
Penguin Books (NZ) Ltd, Private Bag 102902, NSMC, Auckland, New Zealand

Penguin Books Ltd, Registered Offices: Harmondsworth, Middlesex, England

This collection first published in Penguin Books 1981

7

Contents

TOO TRUE TO BE GOOD:

A POLITICAL EXTRAVAGANZA

with

Preface

First presented by the Theatre Guild at the National Theatre, Boston, on 29 February 1932.

THE MONSTER	Julius Evans
THE PATIENT (MISS MOPPLY)	Hope Williams
THE ELDERLY LADY (MRS MOPPLY)	Minna Phillips
THE DOCTOR	Alexander Clark, Jr
THE NURSE (SUSAN 'SWEETIE' SIMPKINS, *alias* THE COUNTESS VALBRIONI)	Beatrice Lillie
THE BURGLAR ('POPSY,' *alias* THE HONORABLE AUBREY BAGOT)	Hugh Sinclair
COLONEL TALLBOYS, V.C., D.S.O.	Ernest Cossart
PRIVATE NAPOLEON ALEXANDER TROTSKY MEEK	Leo G. Carroll
SERGEANT FIELDING	Frank Shannon
THE ELDER	Claude Rains

Period – The Present

ACT I: *One of the Best Bedrooms in one of the Best Surburban Villas in one of the Richest Cities in England*

ACT II: *A Sea Beach in a Mountainous Country*

ACT III: *A Narrow Gap leading down to the Beach*

Preface

CONTENTS

MONEY AND HAPPINESS

SOMEHOW my play, Too True To Be Good, has in performance excited an animosity and an enthusiasm which will hardly be accounted for by the printed text. Some of the spectators felt that they had had a divine revelation, and overlooked the fact that the eloquent gentleman through whose extremely active mouth they had received it was the most hopeless sort of scoundrel: that is, one whose scoundrelism consists in the absence of conscience rather than in any positive vices, and is masked by good looks and agreeable manners. The less intellectual journalist critics sulked as they always do when their poverty but not their will consents to their witnessing a play of mine; but over and above the resultant querulousness to which I have long been accustomed I thought I detected an unusual intensity of resentment, as if I had hit them in some new and unbearably sore spot.

Where, then, was the offence that so exceedingly disgruntled these unhappy persons? I think it must have been the main gist and moral of the play, which is not, as usual, that our social system is unjust to the poor, but that it is cruel to the rich. Our revolutionary writers have dwelt on the horrors of poverty. Our conventional and romantic writers have ignored those horrors, dwelling pleasantly on the elegances of an existence free from pecuniary care. The poor have been pitied for miseries which do not, unfortunately, make them unbearably miserable. But who has pitied the idle rich or really believed that they have a worse time of it than those who have to live on ten shillings a day or less, and earn it? My play is a story of three reckless young people who come into possession of, for the moment, unlimited riches, and set out to have a thoroughly good time with all the modern machinery of pleasure to aid them. The result is that they get nothing for their money but a multitude of worries and a maddening dissatisfaction.

THE VAMPIRE AND THE CALF

I doubt whether this state of things is ever intentionally produced. We see a man apparently slaving to place his children in the position of my three adventurers; but on closer investigation we generally find that he does not care twopence for his children, and is wholly wrapped up in the fascinating game of making money. Like other games it is enjoyable only by people with an irresistible and virtually exclusive fancy for it, and enough arithmetical ability and flair for market values to play it well; but with these qualifications the poorest men can make the most astounding fortunes. They accumulate nothing but powers of extracting money every six months from their less acquisitive neighbors; and their children accumulate nothing but obligations to spend it. As between these two processes of bleeding and being bled, bleeding is the better fun. The vampire has a better time than the calf hung up by the heels with its throat cut. The moneygetter spends less on his food, clothes, and amusements than his clerks do, and is happy. His wife and sons and daughters, spending fabulous sums on themselves, are no happier than their housemaids, if so happy; for the routine of fashion is virtually as compulsory as the routine of a housemaid, its dressing is as much dictated as her uniform, its snubbings are as humiliating, and its monotony is more tedious because more senseless and useless, not to mention that it must be pleasanter to be tipped than to tip. And, as I surmise, the housemaid's day off or evening off is really off: in those hard earned hours she ceases to be a housemaid and can be herself; but the lady of fashion never has a moment off: she has to be fashionable even in her little leisure, and dies without ever having had any self at all. Here and there you find rich ladies taking up occupations and interests which keep them so busy doing professional or public work that they might as well have five hundred a year as fifty thousand 'for all the good it does them' as the poor say in their amazement when they see people who could afford to be fashionable and extravagant working hard and dressing rather plainly. But that requires a personal endowment of tastes and talents quite out of the common run.

I remember a soldier of the old never-do-well type drifting into a little Socialist Society which I happened to be addressing more than fifty years ago. As he had evidently blundered into the wrong shop and was half drunk, some of the comrades began to chaff him, and finally held me up to him as an example of the advantages of teetotalism. With the most complete conviction he denounced me as a hypocrite and a liar, affirming it to be a wellknown and inexorable law of nature that no man with money in his pocket could pass a public house without going in for a drink.

THE OLD SOLDIER AND THE PUBLIC HOUSE

I have never forgotten that soldier, because his delusion, in less crude forms, and his conception of happiness, seem to afflict everybody in England more or less. When I say less crude forms I do not mean truer forms; for the soldier, being half drunk, was probably happier than he would have been if quite sober, whereas the plutocrat who has spent a hundred pounds in a day in the search for pleasure is not happier than if he had spent only five shillings. For it must be admitted that a private soldier, outside that surprising centre of culture, the Red Army of Russia, has so little to be happy about when sober that his case is hardly a fair one. But it serves to illustrate the moral of my play, which is, that our capitalistic system, with its golden exceptions of idle richery and its leaden rule of anxious poverty, is as desperate a failure from the point of view of the rich as of the poor. We are all amazed and incredulous, like the soldier, when we hear of the multimillionaire passing the public house without going in and drinking himself silly; and we envy his sons and daughters who do go in and drink themselves silly. The vulgar pub may be in fact a Palace Hotel, and the pints of beer or glasses of whisky an elaborate dinner with many courses and wines culminating in cigars and liqueurs; but the illusion and the results are cognate.

I therefore plead for a science of happiness to cure us of the miserable delusion that we can achieve it by becoming richer than our neighbors. Modern colossal fortunes have demonstrated its vanity. When country parsons were 'passing rich with forty pounds a year' there was some excuse for believing that to be rich was to be happy, as the conception of riches did not venture beyond enough to pay for the necessities of a cultivated life. A hundred years ago Samuel Warren wrote a famous novel about a man who became enormously rich. The title of the novel was Ten Thousand a Year; and this, to any resident Irish family in my boyhood, represented an opulence beyond which only Lords Lieutenant and their like could aspire. The scale has changed since then. I have just seen in the papers a picture of the funeral of a shipping magnate whose income, if the capital value of the property left by him be correctly stated, must have been over four thousand pounds a day or a million and a half a year. If happiness is to be measured by riches he must have been fourteen thousand times as happy as the laborer lucky enough to be earning two pounds a week. Those who believe that riches are the reward of virtue are bound to conclude that he was also fourteen thousand times as sober, honest, and industrious, which would lead to the quaint conclusion that if he drank a bottle of wine a day the laborer must have drunk fourteen thousand.

THE UNLOADING MILLIONAIRES

This is so obviously monstrous that it may now be dismissed as an illusion of the poor who know nothing of the lives of the rich. Poverty, when it involves continual privation and anxiety, is, like toothache, so painful that the victim can desire nothing happier than the cessation of the pain. But it takes no very extraordinary supply of money to enable a humble person to say 'I want for nothing'; and when that modest point is reached the power of money to produce happiness vanishes, and the trouble which an excess of it brings begins to assert itself, and finally reaches a point at which the multi-millionaires are seen frantically unloading on charitable, educational, scientific, religious, and even (though rarely) artistic and political 'causes' of all kinds, mostly without stopping to examine whether the causes produce any effects, and if so what effects. And far from suffering a loss of happiness every time they give away a thousand pounds, they find themselves rather in the enviable state of mind of the reveller in

The Pilgrim's Progress with his riddle 'There was a man, though some did think him mad, the more he gave away the more he had.'

DELUSIONS OF POVERTY

The notion that the rich must be happy is complemented by the delusion that the poor must be miserable. Our society is so constituted that most people remain all their lives in the condition in which they were born, and have to depend on their imagination for their notions of what it is like to be in the opposite condition. The upstarts and the downstarts, though we hear a great deal about them either as popular celebrities or criminals, are exceptional. The rich, it is said, do not know how the poor live; but nobody insists on the more mischievous fact that the poor do not know how the rich live. The rich are a minority; and they are not consumed with envy of the poor. But the poor are a huge majority and they are so demoralized by the notion that they would be happy if only they were rich, that they make themselves poorer, if hopefuller, by backing horses and buying sweepstake tickets on the chance of realizing their daydreams of unearned fortunes. Our penny newspapers now depend for their circulation, and consequently for their existence, on the sale of what are virtually lottery coupons. The real opposition to Socialism comes from the fear (well founded) that it would cut off the possibilities of becoming rich beyond those dreams of avarice which our capitalist system encourages. The odds against a poor person becoming a millionaire are of astronomical magnitude; but they are sufficient to establish and maintain the Totalisator as a national institution, and to produce unlimited daydreams of bequests from imaginary long lost uncles in Australia or a lucky ticket in the Calcutta or Irish Sweeps.

TRYING IT FOR AN HOUR

Besides, even quite poor people save up for holidays during which they can be idle and rich, if not for life, at least for an hour, an afternoon, or even a week. And for the poor these moments derive such a charm from the change from the monotony of daily toil and servitude, that the most intolerable hardships and discomforts and fatigues in excursion trains and overcrowded lodgings seem delightful, and leave the reveller with a completely false notion of what a lifetime of such revelry would be.

I maintain that nobody with a sane sense of values can feel that the sole prize which our villainous capitalist system has to offer, the prize of admission to the ranks of the idle rich, can possibly confer either happiness or health or freedom on its winner. No one can convict me of crying sour grapes; for during the last thirty-five years I have been under no compulsion to work, nor had any material privation or social ostracism to fear as a consequence of not working. But, like all the intelligent rich people of my acquaintance, I have worked as hard, ate and drunk no more, and dressed no better than when I had to work or starve. When my pockets were empty I did not buy any of the luxuries in the London shops because I had no money to buy them with. When, later on, I had enough to buy anything that London could tempt me with, the result was the same: I returned home day after day without having made a single purchase. And I am no ascetic: no man alive is freer than I from the fancy that selfmortification will propitiate a spiteful deity or increase my balance in a salvation bank in a world beyond the grave. I would and could live the life of the idle rich if I liked it; and my sole reason for not living it is that I dont like it. I have every opportunity of observing it both in its daily practice and its remoter results; and I know that a year of it would make me more unhappy than anything else of an accepted kind that I can imagine.

For, just as the beanfeaster can live like a lord for an afternoon, and the Lancashire factory operative have a gorgeous week at Blackpool when the wakes are on, so I have had my afternoons as an idle rich man, and know only too well what it is like. It makes me feel suicidal.

You may say that I am an exceptional man. So I am, in respect of being able to write plays and books; but as everybody is exceptional in respect of being able to do something that most other people cannot do, there is nothing in that. Where I am really a little exceptional is in respect of my having experienced both poverty and riches, servitude and selfgovernment, and also having for some reason or other (possibly when I was assured in my infancy that some nasty medicine was delicious) made up my mind early in life never to let myself be persuaded that I am enjoying myself gloriously when I am, as a matter of fact, being bored and pestered and plundered and worried and tired. You cannot humbug me on this point: I understand perfectly why Florence Nightingale fled from fashionable society in London to the horrors of the Crimean hospitals rather than behave like a lady, and why my neighbor Mr Apsley Cherry-Garrard, the sole survivor of what he calls with good reason 'the worst journey in the world' through the Antarctic winter, was no poor sailorman driven by his need for daily bread to make a hard living before the mast, but a country gentleman opulent enough to choose the best that London society could offer him if he chose. Better the wards of the most terrible of field hospitals than a drawingroom in Mayfair: better the South Pole at its blackest six months winter night and its most murderous extremities of cold than Sunday by the Serpentine in the height of the season.

CONSOLATIONS OF THE LANDED GENTRY

To some extent this misery of riches is a new thing. Anyone who has the run of our country houses, with their great parks and gardens, their staffs of retainers, indoor and outdoor, and the local public work that is always available for the resident landed gentry, will at once challenge the unqualified assertion that the rich, in a lump, are miserable. Clearly they are nothing of the sort, any more than the poor in a lump. But then they are neither idle nor free. A lady with a big house to manage, and the rearing of a family to supervise, has a reasonably busy time of it even without counting her share in the routine of sport and entertainment and occasional travel which to people brought up to it is a necessary and important part of a well ordered life. The landed gentry have enough exercise and occupation and sense of social importance and utility to keep them on very good terms with themselves and their neighbors. If you suddenly asked them whether they really enjoyed their routine and whether they would not rather be Communists in Russia they would be more sincerely scandalized than if you had turned to them in Church and asked them whether they really believed every clause in the Apostles' Creed. When one of their ugly ducklings becomes a revolutionist it is not because country-house life is idle, but because its activities are uncongenial and because the duckling has tastes or talents which it thwarts, or a faculty for social criticism which discovers that the great country house is not built on the eternal rock but on the sandy shore of an ocean of poverty which may at any moment pass from calm to tempest. On the whole, there is no reason why a territorial lady should not be as happy as her dairymaid, or her husband be as happy as his gamekeeper. The riches of the county families are attached to property; and the only miserable county people are those who will not work at their job.

MISERIES OF THE VAGRANT ROOTLESS RICH

But the new thing is riches detached from real property: that is, detached from work, from responsibility, from tradition, and from every sort of prescribed routine, even from the routine of going to the village church every Sunday, paying and receiving calls, and having every month set apart for the killing of some particular bird or animal. It means being a tramp without the daily recurrent obligation to beg or steal your dinner and the price of your bed. Instead, you have the daily question 'What shall I do? Where shall I go?' and the daily answer 'Do what you please: go where you like: it doesnt matter what you do or where you go.' In short, the perfect liberty of which slaves dream because they have no experience of its horrors. Of course the answer of outraged Nature is drowned for a time by the luxury merchants shouting 'Come and shop, whether you need anything or not. Come to our palace hotels. Come round the world in our liners. Come and wallow in our swimming pools. Come and see our latest model automobile: we have changed the inventor's design for-better-for-worse solely to give you an excuse for buying a new one and selling your old one at scrap iron prices. Come and buy our latest fashions in dress: you cannot possibly be seen in last season's garments.' And so on and so forth. But the old questions come home to the rich tourists in the palace hotels and luxury liners just as they do to the tramps on the high-road. They come up when you have the latest car and the latest wardrobe and all the rest of it. The only want that money can satisfy without satiating for more than a few hours is the need for food and drink and sleep. So from one serious meal a day and two very minor ones you go on to three serious meals a day and two minor ones. Then you work another minor one between breakfast and lunch 'to sustain you'; and you soon find that you cannot tackle any meal without a cocktail, and that you cannot sleep. That obliges you to resort to the latest soporific drug, guaranteed in the advertisements to have none of the ruinous effects of its equally guaranteed forerunner. Then comes the doctor, with his tonics, which are simply additional cocktails, and his sure knowledge that if he tells you the truth about yourself and refuses to prescribe the tonics and the drugs, his children will starve. If you indulge in such a luxury as a clerical spiritual adviser it is his duty to tell you that what is the matter with you is that you are an idle useless glutton and drunkard and that you are going to hell; but alas! he, like the doctor, cannot afford this, as he may have to ask you for a subscription tomorrow to keep his church going. And that is 'Liberty: thou choicest treasure.'

This sort of life has been made possible, and indeed inevitable, by what William Cobbett, who had a sturdy sense of vital values, denounced as The Funding System. It was a product of war, which obliged belligerent governments to obtain enormous sums from all and sundry by giving them in exchange the right to live for nothing on the future income of the country until their money was returned: a system now so popular among people with any money to spare that they can be induced to part with it only on condition that the Government promises not to repay it before a certain more or less remote day. When joint stock companies were formed to run big industrial concerns with money raised on the still more tempting terms that the money is never to be repaid, the system became so extensive that the idle upstart rich became a definitely mischievous and miserable class quite different in character from the old feudal rich.

THE REDEMPTION FROM PROPERTY

When I propose the abolition of our capitalistic system to redeem mankind from the double curse of poverty and riches, loud wailings arise. The most articulate sounds in the hubbub are to the effect that the wretched slaves of the curse will lose their liberty if they are forced to earn their living honorably. The retort that they have nothing to lose but their chains, with the addition that the gold chains are as bad as the iron ones, cannot silence them, because they think they are free, and have been brought up to believe that unless the country remains the private property of irresponsible owners maintaining a parliament to make any change impossible, with

21

churches, schools and universities to inculcate the sacredness of private property and party government disguised as religion, education and democracy, civilization must perish. I am accused of every sort of reactionary extravagance by the people who think themselves advanced, and of every sort of destructive madness by people who thank God they are no wiser than their fathers.

Now I cannot profitably discuss politics, religion and economics with terrified ignoramuses who understand neither what they are defending nor what they are attacking. But it happens that Mr Gilbert Chesterton, who is not an ignoramus and not in the least terrified, and whose very interesting conversion to Roman Catholicism has obliged him to face the problem of social organization fundamentally, discarding the Protestant impostures on English history which inspired the vigorous Liberalism of his salad days, has lately taken me to task for the entirely imaginary offence of advocating government by a committee of celebrities. To clear up the matter I have replied to Mr Chesterton very fully and in Catholic terms. Those who have read my reply in the magazines in which it appeared need read no further, unless they wish, as I should advise, to read it twice. For the benefit of the rest, and to put it on permanent record, here it is.

FUNDAMENTAL NATURAL CONDITIONS OF HUMAN SOCIETY

1. Government is necessary wherever two or three are gathered together – or two or three billions – for keeps.

2. Government is neither automatic nor abstract: it must be performed by human rulers and agents as best they can.

3. The business of the rulers is to check disastrously selfish or unexpected behavior on the part of individuals in social affairs.

4. This business can be done only by devizing and enforcing rules of social conduct codifying the greatest common

measure of agreement as to the necessary sacrifice of individual liberty to the good of the community.

5. The paradox of government is that as the good of the community involves a maximum of individual liberty for all its members the rulers have at the same time to enslave everyone ruthlessly and to secure for everyone the utmost possible freedom.

6. In primitive communities people feed and lodge themselves without bothering the Government. In big civilizations this is impossible; so the first business of the Government is to provide for the production and distribution of wealth from day to day and the just sharing of the labor and leisure involved. Thus the individual citizen has to be compelled not only to behave himself properly, but to work productively.

7. The moral slavery of the compulsion to behave properly is a whole-time compulsion admitting of no liberty; but the personal slavery of the compulsion to work lasts only as many hours daily as suffice to discharge the economic duties of the citizen, the remaining hours (over and above those needed for feeding, sleeping, locomotion, etc.) being his leisure.

8. Leisure is the sphere of individual liberty: labor is the sphere of slavery.

9. People who think they can be honestly free all the time are idiots: people who seek whole-time freedom by putting their share of productive work on others are thieves.

10. The use of the word slavery to denote subjection to public government has grown up among the idiots and thieves, and is resorted to here only because it is expedient to explain things to fools according to their folly.

So much for the fundamental natural conditions of social organization. They are as completely beyond argument as the precession of the equinoxes; but they present different problems to different people. To the thief, for instance, the problem is how to evade his share in the labor of production, to increase his share in the distribution of the product, and to corrupt the Government so that it may protect and glorify his chicaneries instead of liquidating him. To Mr Chesterton the Distributist (or Extreme Left Communist) and Catholic (or Equalitarian Internationalist) it is how to select rulers who will govern righteously and impartially in accordance with the fundamental natural conditions.

The history of civilization is the history of the conflict between these rival views of the situation. The Pirate King, the Robber Baron, and the Manchester Man produced between them a government which they called the Empire, the State, the Realm, the Republic, or any other imposing name that did not give away its central purpose. The Chestertonians produced a government which they called The Church; and in due time the Last of the Chestertons joined this Catholic Church, like a very large ship entering a very small harbor, to the great peril of its many rickety old piers and wharves, and the swamping of all the small craft in its neighborhood. So let us see what the Catholic Church made of its governmental problem.

THE CATHOLIC SOLUTION

To begin with, the Church, being catholic, was necessarily democratic to the extent that its aim was to save the souls of all persons without regard to their age, sex, nationality, class, or color. The nobleman who felt that God would not lightly damn a man of his quality received no countenance from the Church in that conviction. Within its fold all souls were equal before God.

But the Church did not draw the ridiculous conclusion that all men and women are equally qualified or equally desirous to legislate, to govern, to administer, to make decisions, to manage public affairs or even their own private affairs. It faced the fact that only about five per cent. of the population are capable of exercising these powers, and are certain to be corrupted by them unless they have an irresistible religious vocation for public work and a faith in its beneficence which will induce them to take vows to abstain from any profit that is not shared by all the rest, and from all indulgences which might blunt their consciences or subject them to the family influences so bitterly deprecated by Jesus.

This natural 'called' minority was never elected in the scandalous way we call democratic. Its members were in the first instance self-elected: that is, they voluntarily lived holy lives and devoted themselves to the public welfare in obedience to the impulse of the Holy Ghost within them. This impulse was their vocation. They were called from above, not chosen by the uncalled. To protect themselves and obtain the necessary power, they organized themselves, and called their organization The Church. After that, the genuineness and sufficiency of the vocation of the new recruits were judged by The Church. If the judgment was favorable, and the candidates took certain vows, they were admitted to the official priesthood and set to govern as priests in the parish and spiritual directors in the family, all of them being eligible, if they had the requisite ability, for promotion to the work of governing the Church itself as bishops or cardinals, or to the supreme rank of Pope or Vicar of Christ on earth. And all this without the smallest reference to the opinions of the uncalled and unordained.

NEED FOR A COMMON FAITH

Now comes the question, why should persons of genuine vocation be asked to take vows before being placed in authority? Is not the vocation a sufficient guarantee of their wisdom?

No. Before priests can govern they must have a common faith as to the fundamental conditions of a stable human society. Otherwise the result might be an assembly of random men of genius unable to agree on a single legislative measure or point of policy. An ecumenical council consisting of Einstein and Colonel Lynch, Aquinas and Francis Bacon, Dante and Galileo, Lenin and Lloyd George, could seldom come to a unanimous decision, if indeed to any decision except in the negative against a minority of one, on any point beyond the capacity of a coroner's jury. The Pope must not be an eccentric genius presiding over a conclave of variously disposed cardinals: he must have an absolutely closed mind on what Herbert Spencer called Social Statics; and in this the cardinals must resemble and agree with him. What is more, they must to some extent represent the conscience of the common people; for it is evident that if they made laws and gave personal directions which would produce general horror or be taken as proofs of insanity their authority would collapse. Hence the need for vows committing all who take them to definite articles of faith on social statics, and to their logical consequences in law and custom. Such vows automatically exclude revolutionary geniuses, who, being uncommon, are not representative, more especially scientific geniuses, with whom it is a point of honor to have unconditionally open minds even on the most apparently sacred subjects.

RUSSIA REDISCOVERS THE CHURCH SYSTEM

A tremendous importance is given to a clear understanding of the Catholic system at this moment by the staggering fact that the biggest State in the modern world, having made a clean sweep of its Church by denouncing its religion as dope, depriving its priests and bishops of any greater authority than a quack can pick up at a fair, encouraging its most seriously minded children to form a League of the Godless, shooting its pious Tsar, turning its cathedrals into historical museums illustrating the infamies of ecclesiastical history and expressly entitling them anti-religious: in short, addressing itself solemnly and implacably to a root-and-branch extermination of everything that we associate with priesthood, has, under pressure of circumstances, unconsciously and spontaneously established as its system of government an as-close-as-possible reproduction of the hierarchy of the Catholic Church. The nomenclature is changed, of course: the Church is called the Communist Party; and the Holy Office and its familiars are known as the Komintern and the Gay Pay Oo. There is the popular safeguard of having the symptoms of the priestly vocation verified in the first instance by the group of peasants or industrial workers with whom the postulant's daily life has been passed, thus giving a genuine democratic basis to the system; and the hierarchy elected on this basis is not only up to date for the moment, but amenable to the daily lessons of trial and error in its practical operations and in no way pledged against change and innovation as such. But essentially the system is that of the old Christian Catholic Church, even to its fundamental vow of Communism and the death penalty on Ananias and Sapphira for violating it.

If our newspapers knew what is really happening in the world, or could discriminate between the news value of a bicycle accident in Clapham and that of a capsize of civilization, their columns would be full of this literally epoch-making event. And the first question they would address to Russia would be 'Why, seeing that the Christian system has been such a hopeless failure, do you go back to it, and invite us to go back to it?'

WHY THE CHRISTIAN SYSTEM FAILED

The answer is that the Christian system failed, not because it was wrong in its psychology, its fundamental postulate of equality, or its anticipation of Lenin's principle that the rulers must be as poor as the ruled so that they can raise themselves only by raising their people, but because the old priests' ignorance of economics and political science blinded them to the mischief latent in the selfishness of private property in the physical earth. Before the Church knew where it was (it has not quite located itself yet) it found itself so prodigiously rich that the Pope was a secular Italian prince with armies and frontiers, enjoying not only the rent of Church lands, but selling salvation on such a scale that when Torquemada began burning Jews instead of allowing them to ransom their bodies by payments to the Roman treasury, and leaving their souls to God, a first-rate quarrel between the Church and the Spanish Inquisition was the result.

But the riches of the Church were nothing compared to the riches of the Church's great rival, the Empire. And the poverty of the priest was opulence compared to the poverty of the proletarian. Whilst the Church was being so corrupted by its own property, and by the influence on it of the lay proprietors, that it lost all its moral prestige, the warriors and robbers of the Empire had been learning from experience that a pirate ship needs a hierarchy of officers and an iron discipline even more than police boats, and that the work of robbing the poor all the time involves a very elaborate system of government to ensure that the poor shall, like bees, continue to produce not only their own subsistence but the surplus that can be robbed from them without bringing on them the doom of the goose that lays the golden eggs. Naked coercion is so expensive that it became necessary to practise on the imaginations of the poor to the extent of making them believe that it is a pious duty to be robbed, and that their moment of life in this world is only a prelude to an eternity in which the poor will be blest and happy, and the rich horribly tortured.

Matters at last reached a point at which there was more law and order in the Empire than in The Church. Emperor Philip of Spain was enormously more respectable and pious, if less amiable, than Pope Alexander Borgia. The Empire gained moral prestige as The Church lost it until the Empire, virtuously indignant, took it on itself to reform The Church, all the more readily as the restoration of priestly poverty was a first-rate excuse for plundering it.

Now The Church could not with any decency allow itself to be reformed by a plutocracy of pirate kings, robber barons, commercial adventurers, moneylenders, and deserters from its own ranks. It reformed itself from within by its own saints and the Orders they founded, and thus 'dished' the Reformation; whilst the Reformers set up national Churches and free Churches of their own under the general definition of Protestants, and thereby found themselves committed to a curious adulteration of their doctrine of Individualism, or the right of private judgment, with most of the ecclesiastical corruptions against which they had protested. And as neither Church nor Empire would share the government of mankind with the other nor allow the common people any say in the matter, the Catholics and Protestants set to work to exterminate one another with rack and stake, fire, sword, and gunpowder, aided by the poison gas of scurrilous calumny, until the very name of religion began to stink in the nostrils of all really charitable and faithful people.

GOVERNMENT BY EVERYBODY

The moral drawn from all this was that as nobody could be trusted to govern the people the people must govern themselves, which was nonsense. Nevertheless it was assumed that by inscribing every man's name on a register of voters we could realize the ideal of every man his own Solon and his own Plato, as to which one could only ask why not every man his own Shakespear and his own Einstein? But this assumption suited the plutocrats very well, as they had only to master the easy art of stampeding elections by their newspapers to do anything they liked in the name of the people. Votes for everybody (called for short, Democracy) ended in government neither of the best nor of the worst, but in an official government which could do nothing but talk, and an actual government of landlords, employers, and financiers at war with an Opposition of trade unionists, strikers, pickets, and – occasionally – rioters. The resultant disorder, indiscipline, and breakdown of distribution, produced a reaction of pure disappointment and distress in which the people looked wildly round for a Savior, and were ready to give a hopeful trial to anyone bold enough to assume dictatorship and kick aside the impotent official government until he had completely muzzled and subjugated it.

FAILURE ALL ROUND

That is the history of Catholicism and Protestantism, Church and Empire, Liberalism and Democracy, up to date. Clearly a ghastly failure, both positively as an attempt to solve the problem of government and negatively as an attempt to secure freedom of thought and facility of change to keep pace with thought.

Now this does not mean in the least that the original Catholic plan was wrong. On the contrary, all the disasters to which it has led have been demonstrations of the eternal need for it. The alternative to vocational government is a mixture of a haporth of very incompetent official government with an intolerable deal of very competent private tyranny. Providence, or Nature if you prefer that expression, has not ordained that all men shall have a vocation for being 'servants of all the rest' as saints or rulers. Providence knows better than to provide armies consisting exclusively of commanders-in-chief or factories staffed exclusively with managing directors; and to that inexorable natural fact we shall always have to come back, just as the Russian revolutionists, who were reeking with Protestant Liberal superstitions at the beginning, have had to come back to it. But we have now thought out much more carefully than St Peter the basic articles of faith, without which the vocation of the priest is inevitably pushed out by the vocation of the robbers and the racketeers, self-elected as gentlemen and ladies. We know that private property distributes wealth, work, and leisure so unevenly that a wretchedly poor and miserably overworked majority are forced to maintain a minority inordinately rich and passionately convinced that labor is so disgraceful to them that they dare not be seen carrying a parcel down Bond

Street. We know that the strains set up by such a division of interests also destroy peace, justice, religion, good breeding, honor, reasonable freedom, and everything that government exists to secure, and that all this iniquity arises automatically when we thoughtlessly allow a person to own a thousand acres of land in the middle of London much more completely than he owns the pair of boots in which he walks over it; for he may not kick me out of my house into the street with his boots; but he may do so with his writ of ejectment. And so we are driven to the conclusion that the modern priesthood must utterly renounce, abjure, abhor, abominate and annihilate private property as the very worst of all the devil's inventions for the demoralization and damnation of mankind. Civilized men and women must live by their ordered and equal share in the work needed to support the community, and must find their freedom in their ordered and equal share of the leisure produced by scientific economy in producing that support. It still takes some conviction to repudiate an institution so well spoken of as private property; but the facts must be faced: our clandestine methods of violating it by income tax and surtax, which mean only 'What a thief stole steal thou from the thief,' will no longer serve; for a modern government, as the Russians soon found out, must not take money, even from thieves, until it is ready to employ it productively. To throw it away in doles as our governing duffers do, is to burn the candle at both ends and precipitate the catastrophe they are trying to avert.

OBSOLETE VOWS

As to the vows, some of the old ones must go. The Catholic Church and our Board of Education insist on celibacy, the one for priests and the other for schoolmistresses. That is a remnant of the cynical superstition of original sin. Married people have a right to married rulers; mothers have a right to have their children taught and handled by mothers; and priests and pastors who meddle with family affairs should know what they are talking about.

Another important modern discovery is that government is not a whole-time job for all its agents. A council of peasants derives its ancient wisdom from its normal day's work on the land, without which it would be a council of tramps and village idiots. It is not desirable that an ordinary parish priest should have no other occupation, nor an abnormal occupation, even that of a scholar. Nor is it desirable that his uniform should be too sacerdotal; for that is the method of idolatry, which substitutes for rational authority the superstitious awe produced by a contrived singularity. St Vincent de Paul knew thoroughly well what he was about when he constituted his Sisterhood of Charity on the rule that the sister should not be distinguishable from an ordinary respectable woman. Unfortunately, the costume prescribed under this rule has in the course of the centuries become as extraordinary as that of the Bluecoat boy; and St Vincent's idea is consequently lost; but modern industrial experience confirms it; for the latest rediscovery of the Vincentian principle has been made by Mr Ford, who has testified that if you want a staff of helpful persons who will turn their hands to anything at need you must not give them either title, rank, or uniform, as the immediate result will be their partial disablement by the exclusion from their activities of many of the most necessary jobs as beneath their dignity.

Another stipulation made by St Vincent, who already in the sixteenth century was far ahead of us, was that no sister may pledge herself for longer than a year at a time, however often she may renew her vows. Thus the sisters can never lose their freedom nor suffer from cold feet. If he were alive today St Vincent would probably propose a clean sweep of all our difficulties about marriage and divorce by forbidding people to marry for longer than a year, and make them renew their vows every twelve months. In Russia the members of the Communist Party cannot dedicate themselves eternally: they can drop out into the laity when they please, and if they do not please and nevertheless have become slack in their ministry, they are pushed out.

SUPERNATURAL PRETENSIONS

Furthermore, modern priests must not make supernatural pretensions. They must not be impostors. A vocation for politics, though essentially a religious vocation, must be on the same footing as a vocation for music or mathematics or cooking or nursing or acting or architecture or farming or billiards or any other born aptitude. The authority which must attach to all public officials and councils must rest on their ability and efficiency. In the Royal Navy every mishap to a ship involves a court martial on the responsible officer: if the officer makes a mistake he forfeits his command unless he can convince the court that he is still worthy it. In no other way can our hackneyed phrase 'responsible government' acquire any real meaning. When a Catholic priest goes wrong (or too right) he is silenced: when a Russian Commissar goes wrong, he is expelled from the Party. Such responsibility necessarily makes official authority very authoritative and frightens off the unduly nervous. Stalin and Mussolini are the most responsible statesmen in Europe because they have no hold on their places except their efficiency; and their authority is consequently greater than that of any of the monarchs, presidents, and prime ministers who have to deal with them. Stalin is one of the higher functionaries with whom governing is necessarily a whole-time job. But he is no richer than his neighbors, and can 'better himself' only by bettering them, not by buttering them like a British demagogue.

ECLECTIC DEMOCRACY

I think my views on intellectual aristocracy and democracy and all the rest of it are now plain enough. As between the intentions of The Church and the intentions of The Empire (unrealized ideals both) I am on the side of The Church. As to the evil done by The Church with the best intentions and the good done by The Empire with the worst, I am an Eclectic: there is much to be learnt from each. I harp on Russia because the Moscow experiment is the only really new departure from Tweedledum and Tweedledee: Fascism is still wavering between Empire and Church, between private property and Communism. Years ago, I said that what democracy needed was a trustworthy anthropometric machine for the selection of qualified rulers. Since then I have elaborated this by demanding the formation of panels of tested persons eligible for the different grades in the governmental hierarchy. Panel A would be for diplomacy and international finance, Panel B for national affairs, Panel C for municipal and county affairs, Panel D for the village councils and so forth. Under such a panel system the voters would lose their present liberty to return such candidates as the late Horatio Bottomley to parliament by enormous majorities; but they would gain the advantage of at least knowing that their rulers know how to read and write, which they do not enjoy at present.

Nobody ventured to disagree with me when I urged the need for such panels; but when I was challenged to produce my anthropometric machine or my endocrine or phrenological tests, I was obliged to confess that they had not yet been invented, and that such existing attempts at them as competitive examinations are so irrelevant and misleading as to be worse than useless as tests of vocation. But the Soviet system, hammered out under the sternest pressure of circumstances, supplies an excellent provisional solution, which turns out to be the solution of the old Catholic Church purged of supernatural pretension, assumption of final perfection, and the poison of private property with its fatal consequences. Mr Stalin is not in the least like an Emperor, nor an Archbishop, nor a Prime Minister, nor a Chancellor; but he would be strikingly like a Pope, claiming for form's sake an apostolic succession from Marx, were it not for his frank method of Trial and Error, his entirely human footing, and his liability to removal at a moment's notice if his eminence should upset his mental balance. At the other end of the scale are the rank and file of the Communist Party, doing an ordinary day's work with the common folk, and giving only their leisure to the Party. For their election as representatives of the commons they must depend on the votes of their intimate and equal neighbors and workmates. They have no incentive to seek election except the vocational incentive; for success, in the first instance, means, not release from the day's ordinary work, but the sacrifice of all one's leisure to politics, and, if promotion to the whole-time-grades be achieved, a comparatively ascetic discipline and virtually no pecuniary gain.

If anyone can suggest a better practically tested plan, now is the time to do it; for it is all up with the old Anarchist–Liberal parliamentary systems in the face of thirty millions of unemployed, and World Idiotic Conferences at which each nation implores all the others to absorb its unemployed by a revival of international trade. Mr Chesterton says truly that a government, if it is to govern, 'cannot select one ruler to do something and another to undo it, one intellectual to restore the nation and another to ruin the nation.' But that is precisely what our parliamentary party system does. Mr Chesterton has put it in a nutshell; and I hope he will appreciate the sound Catholicism with which I have cracked it.

Ayot St Lawrence, 1933

ACT I

Night. One of the best bedrooms in one of the best suburban villas in one of the richest cities in England. A young lady with an unhealthy complexion is asleep in the bed. A small table at the head of the bed, convenient to her right hand, and crowded with a medicine bottle, a measuring glass, a pill box, a clinical thermometer in a glass of water, a half read book with the place marked by a handkerchief, a powder puff and handmirror, and an electric bell handle on a flex, shews that the bed is a sick bed and the young lady an invalid.

The furniture includes a very handsome dressing table with silver-backed hairbrushes and toilet articles, a dainty pincushion, a stand of rings, a jewel box of black steel with the lid open and a rope of pearls heaped carelessly half in and half out, a Louis Quinze writing table and chair with inkstand, blotter, and cabinet of stationery, a magnificent wardrobe, a luxurious couch and a tall screen of Chinese workmanship which, like the expensive carpet and everything else in the room, proclaims that the owner has money enough to buy the best things at the best shops in the best purchaseable taste.

The bed is nearly in the middle of the room, so that the patient's nurses can pass freely between the wall and the head of it. If we contemplate the room from the foot of the bed, with the patient's toes pointing straight at us, we have the door (carefully sandbagged lest a draught of fresh air should creep underneath) level with us in the righthand wall, the couch against the same wall farther away, the window (every ray of moonlight excluded by closed curtains and a dark green spring blind) in the middle of the left wall with the wardrobe on its right and the writing table on its left, the screen at right angles to the wardrobe, and the dressing table against the wall facing us halfway between the bed and the couch.

Besides the chair at the writing table there is an easy chair at the medicine table, and a chair at each side of the dressing table.

The room is lighted by invisible cornice lights, and by two mirror lights on the dressing table and a portable one on the writing table; but these are now switched off; and the only light in action is another portable one on the medicine table, very carefully subdued by a green shade.

The patient is sleeping heavily. Near her, in the easy chair, sits a Monster. In shape and size it resembles a human being; but in substance it seems to be made of a luminous jelly with a visible skeleton of short black rods. It droops forward in the chair with its head in its hands, and seems in the last degree wretched.

THE MONSTER. Oh! Oh!! Oh!!! I am so ill! so miserable! Oh, I wish I were dead. Why doesnt she die and release me from my sufferings? What right has she to get ill and make me ill like this? Measles: thats what she's got. Measles! German measles! And she's given them to me, a poor innocent microbe that never did her any harm. And she says that *I* gave them to her. Oh, is this justice? Oh, I feel so rotten. I wonder what my temperature is: they took it from under her tongue half an hour ago. [*Scrutinizing the table and discovering the thermometer in the glass*]. Here's the thermometer: theyve left it for the doctor to see instead of shaking it down. If it's over a hundred I'm done for: I darent look. Oh, can it be that I'm dying? I must look. [*It looks, and drops the thermometer back into the glass with a gasping scream*]. A hundred and three! It's all over. [*It collapses*].

The door opens; and an elderly lady and a young doctor come in. The lady steals along on tiptoe, full of the deepest concern for the invalid. The doctor is indifferent, but keeps up his bedside manner carefully, though he evidently does not think the case so serious as the lady does. She comes to the bedside on the invalid's left. He comes to the other side of the bed and looks attentively at his patient.

THE ELDERLY LADY [*in a whisper sibilant enough to wake the dead*] She is asleep.

THE MONSTER. I should think so. This fool here, the doctor, has given her a dose of the latest fashionable opiate that would keep a cock asleep til half past eleven on a May morning.

THE ELDERLY LADY. Oh doctor, do you think there is any chance? Can she possibly survive this last terrible complication.

THE MONSTER. Measles! He mistook it for influenza.

THE ELDERLY LADY. It was so unexpected! such a crushing blow! And I have taken such care of her. She is my only surviving child: my pet: my precious one. Why do they all die? I have never neglected the smallest symptom of illness. She has had doctors in attendance on her almost constantly since she was born.

THE MONSTER. She has the constitution of a horse or she'd have died like the others.

THE ELDERLY LADY. Oh, dont you think, dear doctor – of course you know best; but I am so terribly anxious – dont you think you ought to change the prescription? I had such hopes of that last bottle; but you know it was after that that she developed measles.

THE DOCTOR. My dear Mrs Mopply, you may rest assured that the bottle had nothing to do with the measles. It was merely a gentle tonic –

THE MONSTER. Strychnine!

THE DOCTOR. – to brace her up.

THE ELDERLY LADY. But she got measles after it.

THE DOCTOR. That was a specific infection: a germ, a microbe.

THE MONSTER. Me! Put it all on me.

THE ELDERLY LADY. But how did it get in? I keep the windows closed so carefully. And there is a sheet steeped in carbolic acid always hung over the door.

THE MONSTER. [in tears] Not a breath of fresh air for me!

THE DOCTOR. Who knows? It may have lurked here since the house was built. You never can tell. But you must not worry. It is not serious: a light rubeola: you can hardly call it measles. We shall pull her through, believe me.

THE ELDERLY LADY. It is such a comfort to hear you say so, doctor. I am sure I shall never be able to express my gratitude for all you have done for us.

THE DOCTOR. Oh, that is my profession. We do what we can.

THE ELDERLY LADY. Yes; but some doctors are dreadful.

There was that man at Folkstone: he was impossible. He tore aside the curtain and let the blazing sunlight into the room, though she cannot bear it without green spectacles. He opened the windows and let in all the cold morning air. I told him he was a murderer; and he only said 'One guinea, please'. I am sure he let in that microbe.

THE DOCTOR. Oh, three months ago! No: it was not that.

THE ELDERLY LADY. Then what was it? Oh, are you quite quite sure that it would not be better to change the prescription?

THE DOCTOR. Well, I have already changed it.

THE MONSTER. Three times!

THE ELDERLY LADY. Oh, I know you have, doctor: nobody could have been kinder. But it really did not do her any good. She got worse.

THE DOCTOR. But, my dear lady, she was sickening for measles. That was not the fault of my prescription.

THE ELDERLY LADY. Oh, of course not. You mustnt think that I ever doubted for a moment that everything you did was for the best. Still —

THE DOCTOR. Oh, very well, very well: I will write another prescription.

THE ELDERLY LADY. Oh, thank you, thank you: I felt sure you would. I have so often known a change of medicine work wonders.

THE DOCTOR. When we have pulled her through this attack I think a change of air —

THE ELDERLY LADY. Oh no: dont say that. She must be near a doctor who knows her constitution. Dear old Dr Newland knew it so well from her very birth.

THE DOCTOR. Unfortunately, Newland is dead.

THE ELDERLY LADY. Yes: but you bought his practice. I should never be easy in my mind if you were not within call. You persuaded me to take her to Folkstone: and see what happened! No: never again.

THE DOCTOR. Oh, well! [*He shrugs his shoulders resignedly, and goes to the bedside table*]. What about the temperature?

THE ELDERLY LADY. The day nurse took it. I havnt dared to look.

THE DOCTOR [*looking at the thermometer*] Hm!

THE ELDERLY LADY [*trembling*] Has it gone up? Oh, doctor!

THE DOCTOR [*hastily shaking the mercury down*] No. Nothing. Nearly normal.

THE MONSTER. Liar!

THE ELDERLY LADY. What a relief!

THE DOCTOR. You must be careful, though. Dont fancy she's well yet: she isnt. She must not get out of bed for a moment. The slightest chill might be serious.

THE ELDERLY LADY. Doctor: are you sure you are not concealing something from me? Why does she never get well in spite of the fortune I have spent on her illnesses? There must be some deep-rooted cause. Tell me the worst: I have dreaded it all my life. Perhaps I should have told you the whole truth; but I was afraid. Her uncle's stepfather died of an enlarged heart. Is that what it is?

THE DOCTOR. Good gracious, NO! What put that into your head?

THE ELDERLY LADY. But even before this rash broke out there were pimples.

THE MONSTER. Boils! Too many chocolate creams.

THE DOCTOR. Oh, that! Nothing. Her blood is not quite what it should be. But we shall get that right.

THE ELDERLY LADY. You are sure it is not her lungs?

THE DOCTOR. My good lady, her lungs are as sound as a seagull's.

THE ELDERLY LADY. Then it must be her heart. Dont deceive me. She has palpitations. She told me the other day that it stopped for five minutes when that horrid nurse was rude to her.

THE DOCTOR. Nonsense! She wouldnt be alive now if her

heart had stopped for five seconds. There is nothing con-
stitutionally wrong. A little below par: that is all. We shall
feed her up scientifically. Plenty of good fresh meat. A half
bottle of champagne at lunch and a glass of port after
dinner will make another woman of her. A chop at
breakfast, rather underdone, is sometimes very helpful.

THE MONSTER. I shall die of overfeeding. So will she too:
thats one consolation.

THE DOCTOR. Dont worry about the measles. It's really
quite a light case.

THE ELDERLY LADY. Oh, you can depend on me for
that. Nobody can say that I am a worrier. You wont forget
the new prescription?

THE DOCTOR. I will write it here and now [*he takes out his
pen and book, and sits down at the writing table*].

THE ELDERLY LADY. Oh, thank you. And I will go and
see what the new night nurse is doing. They take so long
with their cups of tea [*she goes to the door and is about to go out
when she hesitates and comes back*]. Doctor: I know you dont
believe in inoculations; but I cant help thinking she ought
to have one. They do so much good.

THE DOCTOR [*almost at the end of his patience*] My dear Mrs
Mopply: I never said that I dont believe in inoculations.
But it is no use inoculating when the the patient is already
fully infected.

THE ELDERLY LADY. But I have found it so necessary
myself. I was inoculated against influenza three years ago;
and I have had it only four times since. My sister has it
every February. Do, to please me, give her an inoculation.
I feel such a responsibility if anything is left undone to cure
her.

THE DOCTOR. Oh very well, very well: I will see what can
be done. She shall have both an inoculation and a new
prescription. Will that set your mind at rest?

THE ELDERLY LADY. Oh, thank you. You have lifted

such a weight from my conscience. I feel sure they will do her the greatest good. And now excuse me a moment while I fetch the nurse. [*She goes out*].

THE DOCTOR. What a perfectly maddening woman!

THE MONSTER [*rising and coming behind him*] Yes: aint she?

THE DOCTOR [*starting*] What! Who is that?

THE MONSTER. Nobody but me and the patient. And you have dosed her so that she wont speak again for ten hours. You will overdo that some day.

THE DOCTOR. Rubbish! She thought it was an opiate; but it was only an aspirin dissolved in ether. But who am I talking to? I must be drunk.

THE MONSTER. Not a bit of it.

THE DOCTOR. Then who are you? What are you? Where are you? Is this a trick?

THE MONSTER. I'm only an unfortunate sick bacillus.

THE DOCTOR. A sick bacillus!

THE MONSTER. Yes. I suppose it never occurs to you that a bacillus can be sick like anyone else.

THE DOCTOR. Whats the matter with you?

THE MONSTER. Measles.

THE DOCTOR. Rot! The microbe of measles has never been discovered. If there is a microbe it cannot be measles: it must be parameasles.

THE MONSTER. Great Heavens! what are parameasles?

THE DOCTOR. Something so like measles that nobody can see any difference.

THE MONSTER. If there is no measles microbe why did you tell the old girl that her daughter caught measles from a microbe?

THE DOCTOR. Patients insist on having microbes nowadays. If I told her there is no measles microbe she wouldnt believe me; and I should lose my patient. When there is no microbe I invent one. Am I to understand that you are the missing microbe of measles, and that you have given them to this patient here?

THE MONSTER. No: she gave them to me. These humans are full of horrid diseases: they infect us poor microbes with them; and you doctors pretend that it is we that infect them. You ought all to be struck off the register.

THE DOCTOR. We should be, if we talked like that.

THE MONSTER. Oh, I feel so wretched! Please cure my measles.

THE DOCTOR. I cant. I cant cure any disease. But I get the credit when the patients cure themselves. When she cures herself she will cure you too.

THE MONSTER. But she cant cure herself because you and her mother wont give her a dog's chance. You wont let her have even a breath of fresh air. I tell you she's naturally as strong as a rhinoceros. Curse your silly bottles and inoculations! Why dont you chuck them and turn faith healer?

THE DOCTOR. I am a faith healer. You dont suppose I believe the bottles cure people? But the patient's faith in the bottle does.

THE MONSTER. Youre a humbug: thats what you are.

THE DOCTOR. Faith is humbug. But it works.

THE MONSTER. Then why do you call it science?

THE DOCTOR. Because people believe in science. The Christian Scientists call their fudge science for the same reason.

THE MONSTER. The Christian Scientists let their patients cure themselves. Why dont you?

THE DOCTOR. I do. But I help them. You see, it's easier to believe in bottles and inoculations than in oneself and in that mysterious power that gives us our life and that none of us knows anything about. Lots of people believe in the bottles and wouldnt know what you were talking about if you suggested the real thing. And the bottles do the trick. My patients get well as often as not. That is, unless their number's up. Then we all have to go.

THE MONSTER. No girl's number is up until she's worn

out. I tell you this girl could cure herself and cure me if youd let her.

THE DOCTOR. And I tell you that it would be very hard work for her. Well, why should she work hard when she can afford to pay other people to work for her? She doesnt black her own boots or scrub her own floors. She pays somebody else to do it. Why should she cure herself, which is harder work than blacking boots or scrubbing floors, when she can afford to pay the doctor to cure her? It pays her and it pays me. That's logic, my friend. And now, if you will excuse me, I shall take myself off before the old woman comes back and provokes me to wring her neck. [*Rising*] Mark my words: someday somebody will fetch her a clout over the head. Somebody who can afford to. Not the doctor. She has driven me mad already: the proof is that I hear voices and talk to them. [*He goes out*].

THE MONSTER. Youre saner than most of them, you fool. They think I have the keys of life and death in my pocket; but I have nothing but a horrid headache. Oh dear! oh dear!

The Monster wanders away behind the screen. The patient, left alone, begins to stir in her bed. She turns over and calls querulously for somebody to attend to her.

THE PATIENT. Nurse! Mother! Oh, is anyone there? [*Crying*] Selfish beasts! to leave me like this. [*She snatches angrily at the electric bell which hangs within her reach and presses the button repeatedly*].

The Elderly Lady and the night nurse come running in. The nurse is young, quick, active, resolute, and decidedly pretty. Mrs Mopply goes to the bedside table, the nurse going to the patient's left.

THE ELDERLY LADY. What is it, darling? Are you awake? Was the sleeping draught no good? Are you worse? What has happened? What has become of the doctor?

THE PATIENT. I am in the most frightful agony. I have been lying here ringing for ages and ages, and no one has come to attend to me. Nobody cares whether I am alive or dead.

THE ELDERLY LADY. Oh, how can you say such things, darling? I left the doctor here. I was away only for a minute. I had to receive the new night nurse and give her instructions. Here she is. And oh, do cover up your arm, darling. You will get a chill; and then it will be all over. Nurse: see that she is never uncovered for a moment. Do you think it would be well to have another hot water bottle against her arm until it is quite warm again? Do you feel it cold, darling?

THE PATIENT [*angrily*] Yes, deadly cold.

THE ELDERLY LADY. Oh dont say that. And there is so much pneumonia about. I wish the doctor had not gone. He could sound your lungs —

NIGHT NURSE [*feeling the patient's arm*] She is quite warm enough.

THE PATIENT [*bursting into tears*] Mother: take this hateful woman away. She wants to kill me.

THE ELDERLY LADY. Oh no, dear: she has been so highly recommended. I cant get a new nurse at this hour. Wont you try, for my sake, to put up with her until the day nurse comes in the morning?

THE NURSE. Come! Let me arrange your pillows and make you comfortable. You are smothered with all this bedding. Four thick blankets and an eiderdown! No wonder you feel irritable.

THE PATIENT [*screaming*] Dont touch me. Go away. You want to murder me. Nobody cares whether I am alive or dead.

THE ELDERLY LADY. Oh, darling, dont keep on saying that. You know it's not true; and it does hurt me so.

THE NURSE. You must not mind what a sick person says, madam. You had better go to bed and leave the patient to me. You are quite worn out. [*She comes to Mrs Mopply and takes her arm coaxingly but firmly*].

THE ELDERLY LADY. I know I am: I am ready to drop. How sympathetic of you to notice it! But how can I leave her at such a moment?

THE NURSE. She ought not to have more than one person in the room at a time. You see how it excites and worries her.

THE ELDERLY LADY. Oh, thats very true. The doctor said she was to be kept as quiet as possible.

THE NURSE [*leading her to the door*] You need a good night's sleep. You may trust me to do what is right and necessary.

THE ELDERLY LADY [*whispering*] I will indeed. How kind of you! You will let me know if anything –

THE NURSE. Yes, yes. I promise to come for you and wake you if anything happens. Good night, madam.

THE ELDERLY LADY [*sotto voce*] Good night. [*She steals out*].

The nurse, left alone with her patient, pays no attention to her, but goes to the window. She opens the curtains and raises the blind, admitting a flood of moonlight. She unfastens the sash and throws it right up. She then makes for the door, where the electric switch is.

THE PATIENT [*huddling herself up in the bedclothes*] What are you doing? Shut that window and pull down that blind and close those curtains at once. Do you want to kill me?

The nurse turns all the lights full on.

THE PATIENT [*hiding her eyes*] Oh! Oh! I cant bear it: turn it off.

The nurse switches the lights off.

THE PATIENT. So inconsiderate of you!

The nurse switches the lights on again.

THE PATIENT. Oh, please, please. Not all that light.

The nurse switches off.

THE PATIENT. No, no. Leave me something to read by. My bedside lamp is not enough, you stupid idiot.

The nurse switches on again, and calmly returns to the bedside.

THE PATIENT. I cant imagine how anyone can be so thoughtless and clumsy when I am so ill. I am suffering horribly. Shut that window and switch off half those lights at once: do you hear?

46

The nurse snatches the eiderdown and one of the pillows rudely from the bed, letting the patient down with a jerk, and arranges them comfortably in the bedside chair.

THE PATIENT. How dare you touch my pillow? The audacity!

The nurse sits down; takes out a leaf from an illustrated journal; and proceeds to study it attentively.

THE PATIENT. Well! How much longer are you going to sit there neglecting me? Shut that window instantly.

THE NURSE [*insolently, in her commonest dialect*] Oh go to – to sleep [*she resumes her study of the document*].

THE PATIENT. Dont dare address me like that. I dont believe you are a properly qualified nurse.

THE NURSE [*calmly*] I should think not. I wouldnt take five thousand a year to be a nurse. But I know how to deal with you and your like, because I was once a patient in a hospital where the women patients were a rough lot, and the nurses had to treat them accordingly. I kept my eyes open there, and learnt a little of the game. [*She takes a paper packet from her pocket and opens it on the bedside table. It contains about half a pound of kitchen salt*]. Do you know what that is and what it's for?

THE PATIENT. Is it medicine?

THE NURSE. Yes. It's a cure for screaming and hysterics and tantrums. When a woman starts making a row, the first thing she does is to open her mouth. A nurse who knows her business just shoves a handful of this into it. Common kitchen salt. No more screaming. Understand?

THE PATIENT [*hardily*] No I dont [*she reaches for the bell*].

THE NURSE [*intercepting her quickly*] No you dont. [*She throws the bell cord with its button away on the floor behind the bed*]. Now we shant be disturbed. No bell. And if you open your mouth too wide, youll get the salt. See?

THE PATIENT. And do you think I am a poor woman in a hospital whom you can illtreat as you please? Do you know what will happen to you when my mother comes in the morning?

THE NURSE. In the morning, darling, I shall be over the hills and far away.

THE PATIENT. And you expect me, sick as I am, to stay here alone with you!

THE NURSE. We shant be alone. I'm expecting a friend.

THE PATIENT. A friend!

THE NURSE. A gentleman friend. I told him he might drop in when he saw the lights switched off twice.

THE PATIENT. So that was why –

THE NURSE. That was why.

THE PATIENT. And you calmly propose to have your young man here in my room to amuse yourself all night before my face.

THE NURSE. You can go to sleep.

THE PATIENT. I shall do nothing of the sort. You will have to behave yourself decently before me.

THE NURSE. Oh, dont worry about that. He's coming on business. He's my business partner, in fact: not my best boy.

THE PATIENT. And can you not find some more suitable place for your business than in my room at night?

THE NURSE. You see, you dont know the nature of the business yet. It's got to be done here and at night. Here he is, I think.

A burglar, well dressed, wearing rubber gloves and a small white mask over his nose, clambers in. He is still in his early thirties, and quite goodlooking. His voice is disarmingly pleasant.

THE BURGLAR. All right, Sweetie?

THE NURSE. All right, Popsy.

The burglar closes the window softly; draws the curtains; and comes past the nurse to the bedside.

THE BURGLAR. Damn it, she's awake. Didnt you give her a sleeping draught?

THE PATIENT. Do you expect me to sleep with you in the room? Who are you? and what are you wearing that mask for?

THE BURGLAR. Only so that you will not recognize me if we should happen to meet again.

THE PATIENT. I have no intention of meeting you again. So you may just as well take it off.

THE NURSE. I havnt broken to her what we are here for, Popsy.

THE PATIENT. I neither know nor care what you are here for. All I can tell you is that if you dont leave the room at once and send my mother to me, I will give you both measles.

THE BURGLAR. We have both had them, dear invalid. I am afraid we must intrude a little longer. [*To the nurse*] Have you found out where it is?

THE NURSE. No: I havnt had time. The dressing table's over there. Try that.

The burglar crosses to the other side of the bed, coming round by the foot of it, and is making for the dressing table when —

THE PATIENT. What do you want at my dressing table?

THE BURGLAR. Obviously, your celebrated pearl necklace.

THE PATIENT [*escaping from her bed with a formidable bound and planting herself with her back to the dressing table as a bulwark for the jewel case*] Not if I know it, you shant.

THE BURGLAR [*approaching her*] You really must allow me.

THE PATIENT. Take that.

Holding on to the table edge behind her, she lifts her foot vigorously waist high, and shoots it hard into his solar plexus. He curls up on the bed with an agonized groan and rolls off on to the carpet at the other side. The nurse rushes across behind the head of the bed and tackles the patient. The patient swoops at her knees; lifts her; and sends her flying. She comes down with a thump flat on her back on the couch. The patient pants hard; sways giddily; staggers to the bed and falls on it, exhausted. The nurse, dazed by the patient's very unexpected athleticism, but not hurt, springs up.

THE NURSE. Quick, Popsy: tie her feet. She's fainted.

THE BURGLAR [*utters a lamentable groan and rolls over on his face*]!!

THE NURSE. Be quick, will you?

THE BURGLAR [*trying to rise*] Ugh! Ugh!

THE NURSE [*running to him and shaking him*] My God, you are a fool, Popsy. Come and help me before she comes to. She's too strong for me.

THE BURGLAR. Ugh! Let me die.

THE NURSE. Are you going to lie there for ever? Has she killed you?

THE BURGLAR [*rising slowly to his knees*] As nearly as doesnt matter. Oh, Sweetie, why did you tell me that this heavyweight champion was a helpless invalid?

THE NURSE. Shut up. Get the pearls.

THE BURGLAR [*rising with difficulty*] I dont seem to want any pearls. She got me just in the wind. I am sorry to have been of so little assistance: but oh, my Sweetie-Weetie, Nature never intended us to be burglars. Our first attempt has been a hopeless failure. Let us apologize and withdraw.

THE NURSE. Fathead! Dont be such a coward. [*Looking closely at the patient*] I say, Popsy: I believe she's asleep.

THE BURGLAR. Let her sleep. Wake not the lioness's wrath.

THE NURSE. You maddening fool, dont you see that we can tie her feet and gag her before she wakes, and get away with the pearls. It's quite easy if we do it quick together. Come along.

THE BURGLAR. Do not deceive yourself, my pet: we should have about as much chance as if we tried to take a female gorilla to the Zoo. No: I am not going to steal those jewels. Honesty is the best policy. I have another idea, and a much better one. You leave this to me. [*He goes to the dressing table. She follows him*].

THE NURSE. Whatever have you got into your silly head now?

THE BURGLAR. You shall see. [*Handling the jewel case*] One of these safes that open by a secret arrangement of letters. As they are as troublesome as an automatic telephone nobody ever locks them. Here is the necklace. By Jove! If they are all real, it must be worth about twenty thousand pounds. Gosh! here's a ring with a big blue diamond in it. Worth four thousand pounds if it's worth a penny. Sweetie: we are on velvet for the rest of our lives.

THE NURSE. What good are blue diamonds to us if we dont steal them?

THE BURGLAR. Wait. Wait and see. Go and sit down in that chair and look as like a nice gentle nurse as you can.

THE NURSE. But –

THE BURGLAR. Do as you are told. Have faith – faith in your Popsy.

THE NURSE [*obeying*] Well, I give it up. Youre mad.

THE BURGLAR. I was never saner in my life. Stop. How does she call people? Hasnt she an electric bell? Where is it?

THE NURSE [*picking it up*] Here. I chucked it out of her reach when she was grabbing at it.

THE BURGLAR. Put it on the bed close to her hand.

THE NURSE. Popsy: youre off your chump. She –

THE BURGLAR. Sweetie: in our firm I am the brains: you are the hand. This is going to be our most glorious achievement. Obey me instantly.

THE NURSE [*resignedly*] Oh, very well. [*She places the handle of the bell as desired*]. I wash my hands of this job. [*She sits down doggedly*].

THE BURGLAR [*coming to the bedside*] By the way, she is hardly a success as The Sleeping Beauty. She has a wretched complexion: and her breath is not precisely ambrosial. But if we can turn her out to grass she may put up some good looks. And if her punch is anything like her kick she will be an invaluable bodyguard for us two weaklings – if I can persuade her to join us.

THE NURSE. Join us! What do you mean?

THE BURGLAR. Shshshshsh. Not too much noise: we must wake her gently. [*He stoops to the patient's ear and whispers*] Miss Mopply.

THE PATIENT [*in a murmur of protest*] Mmmmmmmmmmmmmmmmm.

THE NURSE. What does she say?

THE BURGLAR. She says, in effect, 'You have waked me too soon: I must slumber again.' [*To the patient, more distinctly*] It is not your dear mother, Miss Mopply: it is the burglar. [*The patient springs half up, threateningly. He falls on his knees and throws up his hands*]. Kamerad, Miss Mopply: Kamerad! I am utterly at your mercy. The bell is on your bed, close to your hand: look at it. You have only to press the button to bring your mother and the police in upon me [*she seizes the handle of the bell*] and be a miserable invalid again for the rest of your life. [*She drops the bell thoughtfully*]. Not an attractive prospect, is it? Now listen. I have something to propose to you of the greatest importance: something that may make another woman of you and change your entire destiny. You can listen to me in perfect security: at any moment you can ring your bell, or throw us out of the window if you prefer it. I ask you for five minutes only.

THE PATIENT [*still dangerously on guard*] Well?

THE BURGLAR [*rising*] Let me give you one more proof of my confidence. [*He takes off his mask*]. Look. Can you be afraid of such a face? Do I look like a burglar?

THE PATIENT [*relaxing, and even shewing signs of goodhumor*] No: you look like a curate.

THE BURGLAR [*a little hurt*] Oh, not a curate. I hope I look at least like a beneficed clergyman. But it is very clever of you to have found me out. The fact is, I am a clergyman. But I must ask you to keep it a dead secret: for my father, who is an atheist, would disinherit me if he knew. I was secretly ordained when I was up at Oxford.

THE PATIENT. Oh, this is ridiculous. I'm dreaming. It must be that new sleeping draught the doctor gave me. But it's delicious, because I'm dreaming that I'm perfectly well. Ive never been so happy in my life. Go on with the dream, Pops: the nicest part of it is that I am in love with you. My beautiful Pops, my own, my darling, you are a perfect film hero, only more like an English gentleman. [*She waves him a kiss*].

THE NURSE. Well I'll be da –

THE BURGLAR. Shshshshsh. Break not the spell.

THE PATIENT [*with a deep sigh of contentment*] Let nobody wake me. I'm in heaven. [*She sinks back blissfully on her pillows*]. Go on, Pops. Tell me another.

THE BURGLAR. Splendid. [*He takes a chair from beside the dressing table and seats himself comfortably at the bedside*]. We are going to have an ideal night. Now listen. Picture to yourself a heavenly afternoon in July: a Scottish loch surrounded by mirrored mountains, and a boat – may I call it a shallop? –

THE PATIENT [*ecstatically*] A shallop! Oh, Popsy!

THE BURGLAR. – with Sweetie sitting in the stern, and I stretched out at full length with my head pillowed on Sweetie's knees.

THE PATIENT. You can leave Sweetie out, Pops. Her amorous emotions do not interest me.

THE BURGLAR. You misunderstand. Sweetie's thoughts were far from me. She was thinking about you.

THE PATIENT. Just like her impudence! How did she know about me?

THE BURGLAR. Simply enough. In her lily hand was a copy of The Lady's Pictorial. It contained an illustrated account of your jewels. Can you guess what Sweetie said to me as she gazed at the soft majesty of the mountains and bathed her soul in the beauty of the sunset?

THE PATIENT. Yes. She said 'Popsy: we must pinch that necklace.'

THE BURGLAR. Exactly. Word for word. But now can you guess what *I* said?

53

THE PATIENT. I suppose you said 'Right you are, Sweetie' or something vulgar like that.

THE BURGLAR. Wrong. I said, 'If that girl had any sense she'd steal the necklace herself.'

THE PATIENT. Oh! This is getting interesting. How could I steal my own necklace?

THE BURGLAR. Sell it; and have a glorious spree with the price. See life. Live. You dont call being an invalid living, do you?

THE PATIENT. Why shouldnt I call it living? I am not dead. Of course when I am awake I am terribly delicate –

THE BURGLAR. Delicate! It's not five minutes since you knocked me out, and threw Sweetie all over the room. If you can fight like that for a string of pearls that you never have a chance of wearing, why not fight for freedom to do what you like, with your pocket full of money and all the fun in the wide world at your command? Hang it all, dont you want to be young and goodlooking and have a sweet breath and be a lawn tennis champion and enjoy everything that is to be enjoyed instead of frowsting here and being messed about by your silly mother and all the doctors that live on her folly? Have you no conscience, that you waste God's gifts so shamefully? You think you are in a state of illness. Youre not: youre in a state of sin. Sell the necklace and buy your salvation with the proceeds.

THE PATIENT. Youre a clergyman all right, Pops. But I dont know how to sell the necklace.

THE BURGLAR. I do. Let me sell it for you. You will of course give us a fairly handsome commission on the transaction.

THE PATIENT. Theres some catch in this. If I trust you with it how do I know that you will not keep the whole price for yourself?

THE BURGLAR. Sweetie: Miss Mopply has the makings of a good business woman in her. [*To the patient*] Just reflect,

Mops (Let us call one another Mops and Pops for short). If I steal that necklace, I shall have to sell it as a burglar to a man who will know perfectly well that I have stolen it. I shall be lucky if I get a fiftieth of its value. But if I sell it on the square, as the agent of its lawful owner, I shall be able to get its full market value. The payment will be made to you; and I will trust you to pay me the commission. Sweetie and I will be more than satisfied with fifty per cent.

THE PATIENT. Fifty! Oh!

THE BURGLAR [*firmly*] I think you will admit that we deserve it for our enterprise, our risk, and the priceless boon of your emancipation from this wretched home. Is it a bargain, Mops?

THE PATIENT. It's a monstrous overcharge; but in dreamland generosity costs nothing. You shall have your fifty. Lucky for you that I'm asleep. If I wake up I shall never get loose from my people and my social position. It's all very well for you two criminals: you can do what you like. If you were ladies and gentlemen, youd know how hard it is not to do what everybody else does.

THE BURGLAR. Pardon me; but I think you will feel more at ease with us if I inform you that we are ladies and gentlemen. My own rank – not that I would presume on it for a moment – is, if you ask Burke or Debrett, higher than your own. Your people's money was made in trade: my people have always lived by owning property or governing Crown Colonies. Sweetie would be a woman of the highest position but for the unfortunate fact that her parents, though united in the sight of Heaven, were not legally married. At least so she tells me.

THE NURSE [*hotly*] I tell you what is true. [*To the patient*] Popsy and I are as good company as ever you kept.

THE PATIENT. No, Sweetie: you are a common little devil and a liar. But you amuse me. If you were a real lady you wouldnt amuse me. Youd be afraid to be so unladylike.

THE BURGLAR. Just so. Come! confess! we are better fun

55

than your dear anxious mother and the curate and all the sympathizing relatives, arnt we? Of course we are.

THE PATIENT. I think it perfectly scandalous that you two, who ought to be in prison, are having all the fun while I, because I am respectable and a lady, might just as well be in prison.

THE BURGLAR. Dont you wish you could come with us?

THE PATIENT [*calmly*] I fully intend to come with you. I'm going to make the most of this dream. Do you forget that I love you, Pops. The world is before us. You and Sweetie have had a week in the land of the mountain and the flood for seven guineas, tips included. Now you shall have an eternity with your Mops in the loveliest earthly paradise we can find, for nothing.

THE NURSE. And where do I come in?

THE PATIENT. You will be our chaperone.

THE NURSE. Chaperone! Well, you have a nerve, you have.

THE PATIENT. Listen. You will be a Countess. We shall go abroad, where nobody will know the difference. You shall have a splendid foreign title. The Countess Valbrioni: doesnt that tempt you?

THE NURSE. Tempt me hell! I'll see you further first.

THE BURGLAR. Stop. Sweetie: I have another idea. A regular dazzler. Lets stage a kidnap.

THE NURSE. What do you mean? stage a kidnap.

THE BURGLAR. It's quite simple. We kidnap Mops: that is, we shall hide her in the mountains of Corsica or Istria or Dalmatia or Greece or in the Atlas or where you please that is out of reach of Scotland Yard. We shall pretend to be brigands. Her devoted mother will cough up five thousand to ransom her. We shall share the ransom fifty-fifty: fifty for Mops, twentyfive for you, twentyfive for me. Mops: you will realize not only the value of the pearls, but of yourself. What a stroke of finance!

THE PATIENT [*excited*] Greece! Dalmatia! Kidnapped!

Brigands! Ransomed! [*Collapsing a little*] Oh, dont tantalize me, you two fools: you have forgotten the measles.

The Monster suddenly reappears from behind the screen. It is transfigured. The bloated moribund Caliban has become a dainty Ariel.

THE MONSTER [*picking up the last remark of the patient*] So have you. No more measles: that scrap for the jewels cured you and cured me. Ha ha! I am well, I am well, I am well. [*It bounds about ecstatically, and finally perches on the pillows and gets into bed beside the patient*].

THE NURSE. If you could jump out of bed to knock out Popsy and me you can jump out to dress yourself and hop it from here. Wrap yourself up well: we have a car waiting.

THE BURGLAR. It's no worse than being taken to a nursing home, Mops. Strike for freedom. Up with you!

They pull her out of bed.

THE PATIENT. But I cant dress myself without a maid.

THE NURSE. Have you ever tried?

THE BURGLAR. We will give you five minutes. If you are not ready we go without you [*he looks at his watch*].

The patient dashes at the wardrobe and tears out a fur cloak, a hat, a walking dress, a combination, a pair of stockings, black silk breeches, and shoes, all of which she flings on the floor. The nurse picks up most of them; the patient snatches up the rest; the two retire behind the screen. Meanwhile the burglar comes forward to the foot of the bed and comments oratorically, half auctioneer, half clergyman.

THE BURGLAR. Fur cloak. Seal. Old fashioned but worth forty-five guineas. Hat. Quiet and ladylike. Tailor made frock. Combination: silk and wool. Real silk stockings without ladders. Knickers: how daringly modern! Shoes: heels only two inches but no use for the mountains. What a theme for a sermon! The well brought up maiden revolts against her respectable life. The aspiring soul escapes from home, sweet home, which, as a wellknown author has said, is the girl's prison and the woman's workhouse. The

intrusive care of her anxious parents, the officious concern
of the family clergyman for her salvation and of the family
doctor for her health, the imposed affection of uninteresting
brothers and sisters, the outrage of being called by her
Christian name by distant cousins who will not keep their
distance, the invasion of her privacy and independence at
every turn by questions as to where she has been and what
she has been doing, the whispering behind her back about
her chances of marriage, the continual violation of that
sacred aura which surrounds every living soul like the halo
surrounding the heads of saints in religious pictures: against
all these devices for worrying her to death the innermost
uppermost life in her rises like milk in a boiling saucepan
and cries 'Down with you! away with you! henceforth my
gates are open to real life, bring what it may. For what sense
is there in this world of hazards, disasters, elations and
victories, except as a field for the adventures of the life
everlasting? In vain do we disfigure our streets with scrawls
of Safety First: in vain do the nations clamor for Security,
security, security. They who cry Safety First never cross the
street: the empires which sacrifice life to security find it in
the grave. For me Safety Last; and Forward, Forward,
always For —'

THE NURSE [*coming from behind the screen*] Dry up, Popsy:
she's ready.

*The patient, cloaked, hatted, and shoed, follows her breathless,
and comes to the burglar, on his left.*

THE PATIENT. Here I am, Pops. One kiss; and then —
Lead on.

THE BURGLAR. Good. Your complexion still leaves something to be desired; but [*kissing her*] your breath is sweet:
you breathe the air of freedom.

THE MONSTER. Never mind her complexion: look at mine!

THE BURGLAR [*releasing the patient and turning to the nurse*]
Did you speak?

THE NURSE. No. Hurry up, will you.

58

THE BURGLAR. It must have been your mother snoring, Mops. It will be long before you hear that music again. Drop a tear.

THE PATIENT. Not one. A woman's future is not with her mother.

THE NURSE. If you are going to start preaching like Popsy, the milkman will be here before we get away. Remember, I have to take off this uniform and put on my walking things downstairs. Popsy: there may be a copper on his beat outside. Spy out and see. Safety First [*she hurries out*].

THE BURGLAR. Well, for just this once, safety first [*he makes for the window*].

THE PATIENT [*stopping him*] Idiot: the police cant touch you if I back you up. It's I who run the risk of being caught by my mother.

THE BURGLAR. True. You have an unexpectedly powerful mind. Pray Heaven that in kidnapping you I am not biting off more than I can chew. Come along. [*He runs out*].

THE PATIENT. He's forgotten the pearls!!! Thank Heaven he's a fool, a lovely fool: I shall be able to do as I like with him. [*She rushes to the dressing table; bundles the jewels into their case; and carries it out*].

THE MONSTER [*sitting up*] The play is now virtually over; but the characters will discuss it at great length for two acts more. The exit doors are all in order. Goodnight. [*It draws up the bedclothes round its neck and goes to sleep*].

ACT II

A sea beach in a mountainous country. Sand dunes rise to a brow which cuts off the view of the plain beyond, only the summits of the distant mountain range which bounds it being visible. An army hut on the hither side, with a klaxon electric horn projecting from a board on the wall, shews that we are in a military cantonment. Opposite the hut is a particolored canvas bathing pavilion with a folding stool beside the entrance. As seen from the sand dunes the hut is on the right and the pavilion on the left. From the neighborhood of the hut a date palm throws a long shadow; for it is early morning.

In this shadow sits a British colonel in a deck chair, peacefully reading the weekly edition of The Times, but with a revolver in his equipment. A light cane chair for use by his visitors is at hand by the hut. Though well over fifty, he is still slender, handsome, well set up, and every inch a commanding officer. His full style and title is Colonel Tallboys V.C., D.S.O. He won his cross as a company-officer, and has never looked back since then.

He is disturbed by a shattering series of explosions announcing the approach of a powerful and very imperfectly silenced motor bicycle from the side opposite to the huts.

TALLBOYS. Damn that noise!

The unseen rider dismounts and races his engine with a hideous clatter.

TALLBOYS [*angrily*] Stop that motorbike, will you?

The noise stops; and the bicyclist, having hoiked his machine up on to its stand, taken off his goggles and gloves, and extracted a letter from his carrier, comes past the pavilion into the colonel's view with the letter in his hand.

He is an insignificant looking private soldier, dusty as to his clothes and a bit gritty as to his windbeaten face. Otherwise there is nothing to find fault with: his tunic and puttees are smart and correct, and his speech ready and rapid. Yet the colonel, already irritated by the racket of the bicycle and the interruption to his newspaper, contemplates him with stern disfavor; for there is something exasperatingly and inexplicably wrong about him. He wears a pith helmet with a pagri; and in profile this pagri suggests a shirt which he has forgotten to tuck in behind, whilst its front view as it falls on his shoulders gives a feminine air of having ringlets and a veil which is in the last degree unsoldierly. His figure is that of a boy of seventeen; but he seems to have borrowed a long head and Wellingtonian nose and chin from somebody else for the express purpose of annoying the colonel. Fortunately for him these are offences which cannot be stated on a charge sheet and dealt with by the provo-marshal; and of this the colonel is angrily aware. The dispatch rider seems conscious of his incongruities; for, though very prompt, concise, and soldierly in his replies, he somehow suggests that there is an imprescriptible joke somewhere by an invisible smile which unhappily produces at times an impression of irony.

He salutes; hands the letter to the colonel; and stands at attention.

TALLBOYS [*taking the letter*] Whats this?

THE RIDER. I was sent with a letter to the headman of the native village in the mountains, sir. That is his answer, sir.

TALLBOYS. I know nothing about it. Who sent you?

THE RIDER. Colonel Saxby, sir.

TALLBOYS. Colonel Saxby has just returned to the base, seriously ill. I have taken over from him. I am Colonel Tallboys.

THE RIDER. So I understand, sir.

TALLBOYS. Well, is this a personal letter to be sent on to him, or is it a dispatch?

THE RIDER. Dispatch, sir. Service document, sir. You may open it.

TALLBOYS [*turning in his chair and concentrating on him with fierce sarcasm*] Thank you. [*He surveys him from his instep to his nose*]. What is your name?

THE RIDER. Meek, sir.

TALLBOYS [*with disgust*] What!

THE RIDER. Meek, sir. M, double e, k.

The colonel looks at him with loathing, and tears open the letter. There is a painful silence whilst he puzzles over it.

TALLBOYS. In dialect. Send the interpreter to me.

MEEK. It's of no consequence, sir. It was only to impress the headman.

TALLBOYS. INNdeed. Who picked you for this duty?

MEEK. Sergeant, sir.

TALLBOYS. He should have selected a capable responsible person, with sufficient style to impress the native headman to whom Colonel Saxby's letter was addressed. How did he come to select you?

MEEK. I volunteered, sir.

TALLBOYS. Did you indeed? You consider yourself an impressive person, eh? You think you carry about with you the atmosphere of the British Empire, do you?

MEEK. No, sir. I know the country. I can speak the dialects a little.

TALLBOYS. Marvellous! And why, with all these accomplishments, are you not at least a corporal?

MEEK. Not educationally qualified, sir.

TALLBOYS. Illiterate! Are you not ashamed?

MEEK. No, sir.

TALLBOYS. Proud of it, eh?

MEEK. Cant help it, sir.

TALLBOYS. Where did you pick up your knowledge of the country?

MEEK. I was mostly a sort of tramp before I enlisted, sir.

TALLBOYS. Well, if I could get hold of the recruiting sergeant who enlisted you, I'd have his stripes off. Youre a disgrace to the army.

MEEK. Yessir.

TALLBOYS. Go and send the interpreter to me. And dont come back with him. Keep out of my sight.

MEEK [hesitates] Er –

TALLBOYS [peremptorily] Now then! Did you hear me give you an order? Send me the interpreter.

MEEK. The fact is, Colonel –

TALLBOYS [outraged] How dare you say Colonel and tell

62

me that the fact is? Obey your order and hold your tongue.

MEEK. Yessir. Sorry, sir. *I am the interpreter.*

> *Tallboys bounds to his feet; towers over Meek, who looks smaller than ever; and folds his arms to give emphasis to a terrible rejoinder. On the point of delivering it, he suddenly unfolds them again and sits down resignedly.*

TALLBOYS [*wearily and quite gently*] Very well. If you are the interpreter you had better interpret this for me. [*He proffers the letter*].

MEEK [*not accepting it*] No need, thank you, sir. The headman couldnt compose a letter, sir. I had to do it for him.

TALLBOYS. How did you know what was in Colonel Saxby's letter?

MEEK. I read it to him, sir.

TALLBOYS. Did he ask you to?

MEEK. Yessir.

TALLBOYS. He had no right to communicate the contents of such a letter to a private soldier. He cannot have known what he was doing. You must have represented yourself as being a responsible officer. Did you?

MEEK. It would be all the same to him, sir. He addressed me as Lord of the Western Isles.

TALLBOYS. You! You worm! If my letter was sent by the hands of an irresponsible messenger it should have contained a statement to that effect. Who drafted it?

MEEK. Quartermaster's clerk, sir.

TALLBOYS. Send him to me. Tell him to bring his note of Colonel Saxby's instructions. Do you hear? Stop making idiotic faces; and get a move on. Send me the quartermaster's clerk.

MEEK. The fact is –

TALLBOYS [*thundering*] Again!!

MEEK. Sorry, sir. *I am the quartermaster's clerk.*

TALLBOYS. What! You wrote both the letter and the headman's answer?

MEEK. Yessir.

TALLBOYS. Then either you are lying now or you were lying when you said you were illiterate. Which is it?

MEEK. I dont seem to be able to pass the examination when they want to promote me. It's my nerves, sir, I suppose.

TALLBOYS. Your nerves! What business has a soldier with nerves? You mean that you are no use for fighting, and have to be put to do anything that can be done without it.

MEEK. Yessir.

TALLBOYS. Well, next time you are sent with a letter I hope the brigands will catch you and keep you.

MEEK. There are no brigands, sir.

TALLBOYS. No brigands! Did you say no brigands?

MEEK. Yessir.

TALLBOYS. You are acquainted with the Articles of War, are you not?

MEEK. I have heard them read out, sir.

TALLBOYS. Do you understand them?

MEEK. I think so, sir.

TALLBOYS. You think so! Well, do a little more thinking. You are serving on an expeditionary force sent out to suppress brigandage in this district and to rescue a British lady who is being held for ransom. You know that. You dont think it: you know it, eh?

MEEK. So they say, sir.

TALLBOYS. You know also that under the Articles of War any soldier who knowingly does when on active service any act calculated to imperil the success of his Majesty's forces or any part thereof shall be liable to suffer death. Do you understand? Death!

MEEK. Yessir. Army Act, Part One, Section Four, Number Six. I think you mean Section Five, Number Five, sir.

TALLBOYS. Do I? Perhaps you will be good enough to quote Section Five, Number Five.

MEEK. Yessir. 'By word of mouth spreads reports calculated to create unnecessary alarm or despondency.'

TALLBOYS. It is fortunate for you, Private Meek, that the Act says nothing about private soldiers who create despondency by their personal appearance. Had it done so your life would not be worth half an hour's purchase.

MEEK. No, sir. Am I to file the letter and the reply with a translation, sir?

TALLBOYS [*tearing the letter to pieces and throwing them away*] Your folly has made a mockery of both. What did the headman say?

MEEK. Only that the country has very good roads now, sir. Motor coaches ply every day all the year round. The last active brigand retired fifteen years ago, and is ninety years old.

TALLBOYS. The usual tissue of lies. That headman is in league with the brigands. He takes a turn himself occasionally, I should say.

MEEK. I think not, sir. The fact is –

TALLBOYS. Did I hear you say 'The fact is'?

MEEK. Sorry, sir. That old brigand was the headman himself. He is sending you a present of a sheep and six turkeys.

TALLBOYS. Send them back instantly. Take them back on your damned bicycle. Inform him that British officers are not orientals, and do not accept bribes from officials in whose districts they have to restore order.

MEEK. He wont understand, sir. He wont believe you have any authority unless you take presents. Besides, they havnt arrived yet.

TALLBOYS. Well, when his messengers arrive pack them back with their sheep and their turkeys and a note to say that my favor can be earned by honesty and diligence, but not purchased.

MEEK. They wont dare take back either the presents or the note, sir. Theyll steal the sheep and turkeys and report gracious messages from you. Better keep the meat and the birds, sir: they will be welcome after a long stretch of regulation food.

TALLBOYS. Private Meek.

MEEK. Yessir.

TALLBOYS. If you should be at any future time entrusted with the command of this expedition you will no doubt give effect to your own views and moral standards. For the present will you be good enough to obey my orders without comment?

MEEK. Yessir. Sorry, sir.

As Meek salutes and turns to go, he is confronted by the nurse, who, brilliantly undressed for bathing under a variegated silk wrap, comes from the pavilion, followed by the patient in the character of a native servant. All traces of the patient's illness have disappeared: she is sunburnt to the color of terra cotta; and her muscles are hard and glistening with unguent. She is disguised en belle sauvage *by headdress, wig, ornaments, and girdle proper to no locality on earth except perhaps the Russian ballet. She carries a sun umbrella and a rug.*

TALLBOYS [*rising gallantly*] Ah, my dear Countess, delighted to see you. How good of you to come!

THE COUNTESS [*giving him her finger tips*] How do, Colonel? Hot, isnt it? [*Her dialect is now a spirited amalgamation of the foreign accents of all the waiters she has known*].

TALLBOYS. Take my chair. [*He goes behind it and moves it nearer to her*].

THE COUNTESS. Thanks. [*She throws of her wrap, which the patient takes, and flings herself with careless elegance into the chair, calling*] Mr Meek. Mr Mee-e-e-eek!

Meek returns smartly, and touches the front of his cap.

THE COUNTESS. My new things from Paris have arrived at last. If you would be so very sweet as to get them to my bungalow somehow. Of course I will pay anything necessary. And could you get a letter of credit cashed for me. I'd better have three hundred pounds to go on with.

MEEK [*quite at his ease: unconsciously dropping the soldier and assuming the gentleman*] How many boxes, Countess?

66

THE COUNTESS. Six, I am afraid. Will it be a lot of trouble?

MEEK. It will involve a camel.

THE COUNTESS. Oh, strings of camels if necessary. Expense is no object. And the letter of credit?

MEEK. Sorry, Countess: I have only two hundred on me. You shall have the other hundred tomorrow. [*He hands her a roll of notes; and she gives him the letter of credit*].

THE COUNTESS. You are never at a loss. Thanks. So good of you.

TALLBOYS. Chut! Dismiss.

Meek comes to attention, salutes, left-turns, and goes out at the double.

TALLBOYS [*who has listened to this colloquy in renewed stupefaction*] Countess: that was very naughty of you.

THE COUNTESS. What have I done?

TALLBOYS. In camp you must never forget discipline. We keep it in the background; but it is always there and always necessary. That man is a private soldier. Any sort of social relation – any hint of familiarity with him – is impossible for you.

THE COUNTESS. But surely I may treat him as a human being.

TALLBOYS. Most certainly not. Your intention is natural and kindly; but if you treat a private soldier as a human being the result is disastrous to himself. He presumes. He takes liberties. And the consequence of that is that he gets into trouble and has a very bad time of it until he is taught his proper place by appropriate disciplinary measures. I must ask you to be particularly careful with this man Meek. He is only half-witted: he carries all his money about with him. If you have occasion to speak to him, make him feel by your tone that the relation between you is one of a superior addressing a very distant inferior. Never let him address you on his own initiative, or call you anything but 'my lady.' If there is anything we can do for you we

67

shall be delighted to do it; but you must always ask me.

The patient, greatly pleased with the colonel for snubbing Sweetie, deposits her rug and umbrella on the sand, and places a chair for him on the lady's right with grinning courtesy. She then seats herself on the rug, and listens to them, hugging her knees and her umbrella, and trying to look as indigenous as possible.

TALLBOYS. Thank you. [*He sits down*].

THE COUNTESS. I am so sorry. But if I ask anyone else they only look helpless and say 'You had better see Meek about it.'

TALLBOYS. No doubt they put everything on the poor fellow because he is not quite all there. Is it understood that in future you come to me, and not to Meek?

THE COUNTESS. I will indeed, Colonel. I am so sorry, and I thoroughly understand. I am scolded and forgiven, arnt I?

TALLBOYS [*smiling graciously*] Admonished, we call it. But of course it is not your fault: I have no right to scold you. It is I who must ask your forgiveness.

THE COUNTESS. Granted.

THE PATIENT [*in waiting behind them, coughs significantly*]!!

THE COUNTESS [*hastily*] A vulgar expression, Colonel, isnt it? But so simple and direct. I like it.

TALLBOYS. I didnt know it was vulgar. It is concise.

THE COUNTESS. Of course it isnt really vulgar. But a little lower middle class, if you follow me.

THE PATIENT [*pokes the chair with the sun umbrella*]!

THE COUNTESS [*as before*] Any news of the brigands, Colonel?

TALLBOYS. No; but Miss Mopply's mother, who is in a distracted condition – very naturally of course, poor woman! – has actually sent me the ransom. She implores me to pay it and release her child. She is afraid that if I make the slightest hostile demonstration the brigands will cut off the girl's fingers and send them in one by one until the ransom is paid. She thinks they may even begin with her ears, and disfigure her for life. Of course that is a possibility: such things have been done; and the poor lady points out very justly that I cannot replace her daughter's ears by exterminating the brigands afterwards, as I shall most certainly do if they dare lay a hand on a British lady. But I cannot countenance such a concession to deliberate criminality as the payment of a ransom. [*The two conspirators exchange dismayed glances*]. I have sent a message to the old lady by wireless to say that the payment of a ransom is out of the question, but that the British Government is offering a substantial reward for information.

THE COUNTESS [*jumping up excitedly*] Wotjesoy? A reward on top of the ransom?

THE PATIENT [*pokes her savagely with the umbrella*]!!!

TALLBOYS [*surprised*] No. Instead of the ransom.

THE COUNTESS [*recollecting herself*] Of course. How silly of me! [*She sits down and adds, reflectively*] If this native girl could find out anything would she get the reward?

TALLBOYS. Certainly she would. Good idea that: what?

THE COUNTESS. Yes, Colonel, isnt it?

TALLBOYS. By the way, Countess, I met three people yesterday who know you very well.

THE PATIENT [*forgetting herself and scrambling forward to her knees*] But you –

THE COUNTESS [*stopping her with a backhand slap on the mouth*] Silence, girl. How dare you interrupt the colonel? Go back to your place and hold your tongue.

The Patient obeys humbly until the Colonel delicately turns his head away, when she shakes her fist threateningly at the smiter.

TALLBOYS. One of them was a lady. I happened to mention your brother's name; and she lit up at once and said 'Dear Aubrey Bagot! I know his sister intimately. We were all three children together.'

THE COUNTESS. It must have been dear Florence Dorchester. I hope she wont come here. I want to have an absolute holiday. I dont want to see anybody – except you, Colonel.

TALLBOYS. Haw! Very good of you to say so.

*The Burglar comes from the bathing tent, very elegant in black
and white bathing costume and black silken wrap with white silk
lapels: a clerical touch.*

TALLBOYS [*continuing*] Ah, Bagot! Ready for your dip? I
was just telling the Countess that I met some friends of
yours yesterday. Fancy coming on them out here of all
places! Shews how small the world is, after all. [*Rising*] And
now I am off to inspect stores. There is a shortage of
maroons that I dont understand.

THE COUNTESS. What a pity! I love maroons. They have
such nice ones at that confectioner's near the Place Ven-
dôme.

TALLBOYS. Oh, youre thinking of marrons glacés. No:
maroons are fireworks: things that go off with a bang. For
signalling.

THE COUNTESS. Oh! the things they used to have in the
war to warn us of an air raid?

TALLBOYS. Just so. Well, au revoir.

THE COUNTESS. Au revoir. Au revoir.

*The Colonel touches his cap gallantly and bustles off past the hut
to his inspection.*

THE PATIENT [*rising vengefully*] You dare smack me in the
face again, my girl, and I'll lay you out flat, even if I have
to give away the whole show.

THE COUNTESS. Well, you keep that umbrella to yourself
next time. What do you suppose I'm made of? Leather?

AUBREY [*coming between them*] Now! now! now! Children!
children! Whats wrong?

THE PATIENT. This silly bitch –

AUBREY. Oh no, no, no, Mops. Damn it, be a lady. Whats
the matter, Sweetie?

THE COUNTESS. You shouldnt talk like that, dearie. A low
girl might say a thing like that; but youre expected to know
better.

AUBREY. Mops: youve shocked Sweetie.

THE PATIENT. Well: do you think she never shocks me? She's a walking earthquake. And now what are we to do if these people the colonel has met turn up? There must be a real Countess Valbrioni.

THE COUNTESS. Not much there isnt. Do you suppose we three are the only liars in the world? All you have to do is to give yourself a swell title, and all the snobs within fifty miles will swear that you are their dearest friend.

AUBREY. The first lesson a crook has to learn, darling, is that nothing succeeds like lying. Make any statement that is so true that it has been staring us in the face all our lives, and the whole world will rise up and passionately contradict you. If you dont withdraw and apologize, it will be the worse for you. But just tell a thundering silly lie that everyone knows is a lie, and a murmur of pleased assent will hum up from every quarter of the globe. If Sweetie had introduced herself as what she obviously is: that is, an ex-hotel chambermaid who became a criminal on principle through the preaching of an ex-army chaplain – me! – with whom she fell in love deeply but transitorily, nobody would have believed her. But she has no sooner made the impossible statement that she is a countess, and that the ex-chaplain is her half stepbrother the Honorable Aubrey Bagot, than clouds of witnesses spring up to assure Colonel Tallboys that it is all gospel truth. So have no fear of exposure, darling; and do you, my Sweetie, lie and lie and lie until your imagination bursts.

THE PATIENT [*throwing herself moodily into the deck chair*] I wonder are all crooks as fond of preaching as you are.

AUBREY [*bending affectionately over her*] Not all, dearest. I dont preach because I am a crook, but because I have a gift – a divine gift – that way.

THE PATIENT. Where did you get it? Is your father a bishop?

AUBREY [*straightening himself up to declaim*] Have I not told you that he is an atheist, and, like all atheists, an inflexible moralist? He said I might become a preacher if I believed what I preached. That, of course, was nonsense: my gift of preaching is not confined to what I believe: I can preach anything, true or false. I am like a violin, on which you can play all sorts of music, from jazz to Mozart. [*Relaxing*] But the old man never could be brought to see it. He said the proper profession for me was the bar. [*He snatches up the rug; replaces it on the patient's left; and throws himself down lazily on it*].

THE COUNTESS. Aint we going to bathe?

AUBREY. Oh, dash it, dont lets go into the water. Lets sunbathe.

THE COUNTESS. Lazy devil! [*She takes the folding stool from the pavilion, and sits down discontentedly*].

THE PATIENT. Your father was right. If you have no conscience about what you preach, your proper job is at the bar. But as you have no conscience about what you do, you will probably end in the dock.

AUBREY. Most likely. But I am a born preacher, not a pleader. The theory of legal procedure is that if you set two liars to expose one another, the truth will emerge. That would not suit me. I greatly dislike being contradicted; and the only place where a man is safe from contradiction is in the pulpit. I detest argument: it is unmannerly, and obscures the preacher's message. Besides, the law is too much concerned with crude facts and too little with spiritual things; and it is in spiritual things that I am interested: they alone call my gift into full play.

THE PATIENT. You call preaching things you dont believe spiritual, do you?

AUBREY. Put a sock in it, Mops. My gift is divine: it is not limited by my petty personal convictions. It is a gift of lucidity as well as of eloquence. Lucidity is one of the most precious of gifts: the gift of the teacher: the gift of explanation. I can explain anything to anybody; and I love doing it. I feel I must do it if only the doctrine is beautiful and subtle and exquisitely put together. I may feel instinctively that it is the rottenest nonsense. Still, if I can get a moving dramatic effect out of it, and preach a really splendid sermon about it, my gift takes possession of me and obliges me to sail in and do it. Sweetie: go and get me a cushion for my head: there's a dear.

THE PATIENT. Do nothing of the kind, Sweetie. Let him wait on himself.

THE COUNTESS [rising] He'd only mess everything about looking for it. I like to have my rooms left tidy. [She goes into the pavilion].

THE PATIENT. Isnt that funny, Pops? She has a conscience as a chambermaid and none as a woman.

AUBREY. Very few people have more than one point of honor, Mops. And lots of them havnt even one.

THE COUNTESS [returning with a silk cushion, which she hurls hard at Aubrey's head] There! And now I give you both notice. I'm getting bored with this place.

AUBREY [making himself comfortable with his cushion] Oh, you are always getting bored.

THE PATIENT. I suppose that means that you are tired of Tallboys.

THE COUNTESS [moving restlessly about] I am fed up with him to that degree that I sometimes feel I could almost marry him, just to put him on the list of the inevitables that I must put up with willynilly, like getting up in the morning, and washing and dressing and eating and drinking: things you darent let yourself get tired of because if you did theyd drive you mad. Lets go and have a bit of real life somewhere.

THE PATIENT. Real life! I wonder where thats to be found! Weve spent nearly six thousand pounds in two months looking for it. The money we got for the necklace wont last for ever.

AUBREY. Sweetie: you will have to stick it in this spot until we touch that ransom; and that's all about it.

THE COUNTESS. I'll do as I like, not what you tell me.

And I tell you again – the two of you – you can take a week's notice. I'm bored with this business. I need a change.

AUBREY. What are we to do with her, Mops? Always change! change! change!

THE COUNTESS. Well, I like to see new faces.

AUBREY. I could be happy as a Buddha in a temple, eternally contemplating my own middle and having the same old priest to polish me up every day. But Sweetie wants a new face every fortnight. I have known her fall in love with a new face twice in the same week. [*Turning to her*] Woman: have you any sense of the greatness of constancy?

THE COUNTESS. I might be constant if I were a real countess. But I'm only a hotel chambermaid; and a hotel chambermaid gets so used to new faces that at last they become a necessity. [*She sits down on the stool*].

AUBREY. And the oftener the faces change the more the tips come to, eh?

THE COUNTESS. Oh, it's not that, though of course that counts. The real secret of it is that though men are awfully nice for the first few days, it doesnt last. You get the best out of men by having them always new. What I say is that a love affair should always be a honeymoon. And the only way to make sure of that is to keep changing the man; for the same man can never keep it up. In all my life I have known only one man that kept it up til he died.

THE PATIENT [*interested*] Ah! Then the thing is possible?

THE COUNTESS. Yes: it was a man that married my sister: that was how I came to know about it.

AUBREY. And his ardor never palled? Day in and day out, until death did them part, he was the same as on the wedding day? Is that really true, Sweetie?

THE COUNTESS. It is. But then he beat her on their wedding day; and he beat her just as hard every day afterwards. I made her get a separation order; but she went back to him because nobody else paid her any attention.

AUBREY. Why didnt you tell me that before? I'd have beaten you black and blue sooner than lose you. [*Sitting up*] Would you believe it, Mops, I was in love with this woman: madly in love with her. She was not my intellectual equal; and I had to teach her table manners. But there was an extraordinary sympathy between our lower centres; and when after ten days she threw me over for another man I was restrained from murder and suicide only by the most resolute exercise of my reasoning powers, my determination to be a civilized man, and fear of the police.

THE COUNTESS. Well, I gave you a good time for the ten days, didnt I? Lots of people dont get that much to look back on. Besides, you know it was for your own good, Popsy. We werent really suited, were we?

AUBREY. You had acquired an insatiable taste for commercial travellers. You could sample them at the rate of three a week. I could not help admiring such amazing mobility of the affections. I had heard operatic tenors bawling Woman is Fickle; but it always seemed to me that what was to be dreaded in women was their implacable constancy. But you! Fickle! I should think so.

THE COUNTESS. Well, the travellers were just as bad, you know.

AUBREY. Just as bad! Say just as good. Fickleness means simply mobility, and mobility is a mark of civilization. You should pride yourself on it. If you dont you will lose your self-respect; and I cannot endure a woman who has no self-respect.

THE COUNTESS. Oh, whats the use of us talking about self-respect? You are a thief and so am I. I go a little further than that, myself; and so would you if you were a woman. Dont you be a hypocrite, Popsy: at least not with me.

AUBREY. At least not with you! Sweetie: that touch of concern for my spiritual welfare almost convinces me that you still love me.

THE COUNTESS. Not me. Not much. I'm through with you, my lad. And I cant quite fancy the colonel: he's too old, and too much the gentleman.

AUBREY. He's better than nobody. Who else is there?

THE COUNTESS. Well, there's the sergeant. I daresay I have low tastes; but he's my sort, and the colonel isnt.

THE PATIENT. Have you fallen in love with Sergeant Fielding, Sweetie?

THE COUNTESS. Well, yes; if you like to call it that.

AUBREY. May I ask have you sounded him on the subject?

THE COUNTESS. How can I? I'm a countess; and he's only a sergeant. If I as much as let on that I'm conscious of his existence I give away the show to the colonel. I can only look at him. And I cant do even that when anyone else is looking. And all the time I want to hug him [*she breaks down in tears*].

AUBREY. Oh for Heaven's sake dont start crying.

THE PATIENT. For all you know, Sweetie, the sergeant may be a happily married man.

THE COUNTESS. What difference does that make to my feelings? I am so lonely. The place is so dull. No pictures. No dances. Nothing to do but be ladylike. And the one really lovable man going to waste! I'd rather be dead.

THE PATIENT. Well, it's just as bad for me.

THE COUNTESS. No it isnt. Youre a real lady: youre broken in to be dull. Besides, you have Popsy. And youre supposed to be our servant. That gives you the run of the whole camp when youre tired of him. You can pick up a private when you like. Whats to prevent you?

THE PATIENT. My ladylike morals, I suppose.

THE COUNTESS. Morals your grandmother! I thought youd left all that flapdoodle behind you when you came away with us.

THE PATIENT. I meant to. Ive tried to. But you shock me in spite of myself every second time you open your mouth.

THE COUNTESS. Dont you set up to be a more moral woman than I am, because youre not.

THE PATIENT. I dont pretend to be. But I may tell you that my infatuation for Popsy, which I now see was what really nerved me to this astonishing breakaway, has been, so far, quite innocent. Can you believe that, you clod?

THE COUNTESS. Oh yes I can: Popsy's satisfied as long as you let him talk. What I mean is – and I tell it to you straight – that with all my faults I'm content with one man at a time.

THE PATIENT. Do you suggest that I am carrying on with two men?

THE COUNTESS. I dont suggest anything. I say what I mean straight out; and if you dont like it you can lump it. You may be in love with Popsy; but youre interested in Private Meek, though what you see in that dry little worm beats me.

THE PATIENT. Have you noticed, my Sweetie, that your big strapping splendid sergeant is completely under the thumb of that dry little worm?

THE COUNTESS. He wont be when I get him under my thumb. But you just be careful. Take this tip from me: one man at a time. I am advising you for your good, because youre only a beginner; and what you think is love, and interest, and all that, is not real love at all: three quarters of it is only unsatisfied curiosity. Ive lived at that address myself; and I know. When I love a man now it's all love and nothing else. It's the real thing while it lasts. I havnt the least curiosity about my lovely sergeant: I know just what he'll say and what he'll do. I just want him to do it.

THE PATIENT [*rising, revolted*] Sweetie: I really cannot bear any more of this. No doubt it's perfectly true. It's quite right that you should say it frankly and plainly. I envy and admire the frightful coolness with which you plump it all out. Perhaps I shall get used to it in time. But at present it knocks me to pieces. I shall simply have to go away if you pursue the subject. [*She sits down in the cane chair with her back to them*].

AUBREY. Thats the worst of Sweetie. We all have – to put it as nicely as I can – our lower centres and our higher centres. Our lower centres act: they act with a terrible power that sometimes destroys us; but they dont talk. Speech belongs to the higher centres. In all the great poetry and literature of the world the higher centres speak. In all respectable conversation the higher centres speak, even when they are saying nothing or telling lies. But the lower centres are there all the time: a sort of guilty secret with every one of us, though they are dumb. I remember asking my tutor at college whether, if anyone's lower centres began to talk, the shock would not be worse than the one Balaam got when his donkey began talking to him. He only told me half a dozen improper stories to shew how open-minded he was. I never mentioned the subject again until I met Sweetie. Sweetie is Balaam's ass.

THE COUNTESS. Keep a civil tongue in your head, Popsy. I —

AUBREY [*springing to his feet*] Woman: I am paying you a compliment: Balaam's ass was wiser than Balaam. You should read your Bible. That is what makes Sweetie almost superhuman. Her lower centres speak. Since the war the lower centres have become vocal. And the effect is that of an earthquake. For they speak truths that have never been spoken before — truths that the makers of our domestic institutions have tried to ignore. And now that Sweetie goes shouting them all over the place, the institutions are rocking and splitting and sundering. They leave us no place to live, no certainties, no workable morality, no heaven, no hell, no commandments, and no God.

THE PATIENT. What about the light in our own souls that you were so eloquent about the day before yesterday at lunch when you drank a pint of champagne?

AUBREY. Most of us seem to have no souls. Or if we have them, they have nothing to hang on to. Meanwhile, Sweetie goes on shouting. [*He takes refuge in the deck chair*].

THE COUNTESS [*rising*] Oh, what are you gassing about? I am not shouting. I should be a good woman if it wasnt so dull. If youre goodnatured, you just get put upon. Who are the good women? Those that enjoy being dull and like being put upon. Theyve no appetites. Life's thrown away on them: they get nothing out of it.

THE PATIENT. Well, come, Sweetie! What do you get out of it?

THE COUNTESS. Excitement: thats what I get out of it. Look at Popsy and me! We're always planning robberies. Of course I know it's mostly imagination; but the fun is in the planning and the expectation. Even if we did them and were caught, there would be the excitement of being tried and being in all the papers. Look at poor Harry Smiler that murdered the cop in Croydon! When he came and told us what he'd done Popsy offered to go out and get him some cyanide to poison himself; for it was a dead sure thing that he'd be caught and bumped off. 'What!' says Harry; 'and lose the excitement of being tried for my life! I'd rather be hanged' he says; and hanged he was. And I say it must have been almost worth it. After all, he'd have died anyhow: perhaps of something really painful. Harry wasnt a bad man really; but he couldnt bear dullness. He had a wonderful collection of pistols that he had begun as a boy: he picked up a lot in the war. Just for the romance of it, you know: he meant no harm. But he'd never shot anyone with them; and at last the temptation was too great and he went out and shot the cop. Just for nothing but the feeling that he'd fired the thing off and done somebody in with it. When Popsy asked him why he'd done it, all he could say was that it was a sort of fulfilment. But it gives you an idea, doesnt it, of what I mean? [*She sits down again, relieved by her outburst*].

AUBREY. All it means is a low vitality. Here is a man with all the miracles of the universe to stagger his imagination and all the problems of human destiny to employ his mind, and he goes out and shoots an innocent policeman because he can think of nothing more interesting to do. Quite right to hang him. And all the people who can find nothing more exciting to do than to crowd into the court to watch him being sentenced to death should have been hanged too. You will be hanged someday, Sweetie, because you have not what people call a richly stored mind. I have tried to educate you –

THE COUNTESS. Yes: you gave me books to read. But I couldnt read them: they were as dull as ditchwater. Ive tried crossword puzzles to occupy my mind and keep me off planning robberies; but what crossword puzzle is half the fun and excitement of picking somebody's pocket, let alone that you cant live by it? You wanted me to take to drink to keep me quiet. But I dont like being drunk; and what would become of my good looks if I did? Ten bottles of champagne couldnt make you feel as you do when you walk past a policeman who has only to stop you and search you to put you away for three years.

THE PATIENT. Pops: did you really try to set her drinking? What a thoroughpaced blackguard you are!

AUBREY. She is much better company when she's half drunk. Listen to her now, when she is sober!

THE PATIENT. Sweetie: are you really having such a jolly time after all? You began by threatening to give up our exciting enterprise because it is so dull.

AUBREY. She is free. There is the sergeant. And there is always the hope of something turning up and the sense of being ready for it without having to break all the shackles and throw down all the walls that imprison a respectable woman.

THE PATIENT. Well, what about me?

AUBREY [*puzzled*] Well, what about you? You are free, arnt you?

THE PATIENT [*rising very deliberately, and going behind him to his left hand, which she picks up and fondles as she sermonizes, seated on the arm of his chair*] My angel love, you have rescued me from respectability so completely that I have for a month past been living the life of a mountain goat. I have got rid of my anxious worrying mother as completely as a weaned kid, and I no longer hate her. My slavery to cooks stuffing me with long meals of fish, flesh, and fowl is a thing of the miserable past: I eat dates and bread and water and raw onions when I can get them; and when I cant get them I fast, with the result that I have forgotten what illness means; and if I ran away from you two neither of you could catch me; and if you did I could fight the pair of you with one hand tied behind me. I revel in all your miracles of the universe: the delicious dawns, the lovely sunsets, the changing winds, the cloud pictures, the flowers, the animals and their ways, the birds and insects and reptiles. Every day is a day of adventure with its cold and heat, its light and darkness, its cycles of exultant vigor and exhaustion, hunger and satiety, its longings for action that change into a longing for sleep, its thoughts of heavenly things that change so suddenly into a need for food.

AUBREY. What more could any mortal desire?

THE PATIENT [*seizing him by the ears*] Liar.

AUBREY. Thank you. You mean, I presume, that these things do not satisfy you: you want me as well.

THE PATIENT. You!! You!!! you selfish lazy sugary tongued blackguard. [*Releasing him*] No: I included you with the animals and their ways, just as I included Sweetie and the sergeant.

THE COUNTESS. You let Sweetie and her sergeant alone: d'y'hear? I have had enough of that joke on me.

THE PATIENT [*rising and taking her by the chin to turn her face up*] It is no joke, Sweetiest: it is the dead solemn earnest. I called Pops a liar, Sweetie, because all this is not enough. The glories of nature dont last any decently active person a week, unless theyre professional naturalists or mathematicians or a painter or something. I want something sensible to do. A beaver has a jolly time because it has to build its dam and bring up its family. I want my little job like the beaver. If I do nothing but contemplate the universe there is so much in it that is cruel and terrible and wantonly evil, and so much more that is oppressively astronomical and endless and inconceivable and impossible, that I shall just go stark raving mad and be taken back to my mother with straws in my hair. The truth is, I am free; I am healthy; I am happy; and I am utterly miserable. [*Turning on Aubrey*] Do you hear? Utterly miserable.

AUBREY [*losing his temper*] And what do you suppose I am? Here with nothing to do but drag about two damn' silly women and talk to them.

THE COUNTESS. It's worse for them. They have to listen to you.

THE PATIENT. I despise you. I hate you. You – you – you – you gentleman thief. What right has a thief to be a gentleman? Sweetie is bad enough, heaven knows, with her vulgarity and her low cunning: always trying to get the better of somebody or to get hold of a man; but at least she's a woman; and she's real. Men are not real: theyre all talk, talk, talk –

THE COUNTESS [*half rising*] You keep a civil tongue in your head: do you hear?

THE PATIENT. Another syllable of your cheek, Sweetie; and I'll give you a hiding that will keep you screaming for half an hour. [*Sweetie subsides*]. I want to beat somebody: I want to kill somebody. I shall end by killing the two of you. What are we, we three glorious adventurers? Just three inefficient fertilizers.

AUBREY. What on earth do you mean by that?

THE PATIENT. Yes: inefficient fertilizers. We do nothing but convert good food into bad manure. We are walking factories of bad manure: thats what we are.

THE COUNTESS [*rising*] Well, I am not going to sit here and listen to that sort of talk. You ought to be ashamed of yourself.

AUBREY [*rising also, shocked*] Miss Mopply: there are certain disgusting truths that no lady would throw in the teeth of her fellow creatures –

THE PATIENT. I am not a lady: I am free now to say what I please. How do you like it?

THE COUNTESS [*relenting*] Look here, dearie. You mustnt go off at the deep end like this. You – [*The patient turns fiercely on her: she screams*]. Ah-a-a-ah! Popsy: she's mad. Save me. [*She runs away, out past the pavilion*].

AUBREY. What is the matter with you? Are you out of your senses? [*He tries to hold her; but she sends him sprawling*].

THE PATIENT. No. I am exercising my freedom. The freedom you preached. The freedom you made possible for me. You dont like to hear Sweetie's lower centres shouting. Well, now you hear my higher centres shouting. You dont seem to like it any better.

AUBREY. Mops: youre hysterical. You felt splendid an hour ago; and you will feel splendid again an hour from now. You will always feel splendid if you keep yourself fit.

THE PATIENT. Fit for what? A lost dog feels fit: thats what makes him stray; but he's the unhappiest thing alive. I am a lost dog: a tramp, a vagabond. Ive got nothing to do. Ive got nowhere to go. Sweetie's miserable; and youre miserable; and I'm miserable; and I shall just kick you and beat you to a jelly.

She rushes at him. He dodges her and runs off past the hut. At that moment Tallboys returns with Meek past the other side of the hut; and the patient, unable to check herself, crashes into his arms.

TALLBOYS [*sternly*] Whats this? What are you doing here? Why are you making this noise? Dont clench your fists in my presence. [*She droops obsequiously*]. Whats the matter?

THE PATIENT [*salaaming and chanting*] Bmal elttil a dah yram, Tuan.

TALLBOYS. Can you speak English?

THE PATIENT. No Engliss.

TALLBOYS. Or French?

THE PATIENT. No Frennss, Tuan. Wons sa etihw saw eceelf sti.

TALLBOYS. Very well: dont do it again. Now off with you.

She goes out backward into the pavilion, salaaming. Tallboys sits down in the deck chair.

TALLBOYS [*to Meek*] Here, you. You say youre the inter-preter. Did you understand what that girl said to me?

MEEK. Yessir.

TALLBOYS. What dialect was it? It didnt sound like what the natives speak here.

MEEK. No sir. I used to speak it at school. English back slang, sir.

TALLBOYS. Back slang? What do you mean?

MEEK. English spelt backwards. She reversed the order of the words too, sir. That shews that she has those two little speeches off by heart.

TALLBOYS. But how could a native girl do such a thing? I couldnt do it myself.

MEEK. That shews that she's not a native girl, sir.

TALLBOYS. But this must be looked into. Were you able to pick up what she said?

MEEK. Only bmal elttil, sir. That was quite easy. It put me on to the rest.

TALLBOYS. But what does bmal elttil mean?

MEEK. Little lamb, sir.

TALLBOYS. She called me a little lamb!

MEEK. No sir. All she said was 'Mary had a little lamb.' And when you asked her could she speak French she said, of course, 'Its fleece was white as snow.'

TALLBOYS. But that was insolence.

MEEK. It got her out of her difficulty, sir.

TALLBOYS. This is very serious. The woman is passing her-self off on the Countess as a native servant.

MEEK. Do you think so, sir?

TALLBOYS. I dont think so: I know so. Dont be a fool, man. Pull yourself together, and dont make silly answers.

MEEK. Yessir. No sir.

TALLBOYS [*angrily bawling at him*] 'Ba Ba black sheep:

have you any wool? Yes sir, no sir, three bags full.' Dont say yessir no sir to me.

MEEK. No sir.

TALLBOYS. Go and fetch that girl back. Not a word to her about my finding her out, mind. When I have finished with her you will explain to me about those maroons.

MEEK. Yessir. [*He goes into the pavilion*].

TALLBOYS. Hurry up. [*He settles himself comfortably and takes out his cigaret case*].

The Countess peers round the corner of the pavilion to see whether she may safely return. Aubrey makes a similar reconnaissance round the corner of the hut.

THE COUNTESS. Here I am again, you see. [*She smiles fascinatingly at the Colonel and sits down on her stool*].

AUBREY. Moi aussi. May I – [*he stretches himself on the rug*].

TALLBOYS [*sitting up and putting the cigaret case back in his pocket*] Just in the nick of time. I was about to send for you. I have made a very grave discovery. That native servant of yours is not a native. Her lingo is a ridiculous fraud. She is an Englishwoman.

AUBREY. You dont say so!

THE COUNTESS. Oh, impossible.

TALLBOYS. Not a doubt of it. She's a fraud: take care of your jewels. Or else – and this is what I suspect – she's a spy.

AUBREY. A spy! But we are not at war.

TALLBOYS. The League of Nations has spies everywhere. [*To the Countess*] You must allow me to search her luggage at once, before she knows that I have found her out.

THE COUNTESS. But I have missed nothing. I am sure she hasnt stolen anything. What do you want to search her luggage for?

TALLBOYS. For maroons.

THE COUNTESS.⎱ [*together*] ⎰Maroons!
AUBREY.   ⎰   ⎱Maroons!

TALLBOYS. Yes, maroons. I inspected the stores this morning; and the maroons are missing. I particularly wanted them to recall me at lunch time when I go sketching. I am rather a dab at watercolors. And there is not a single maroon left. There should be fifteen.

AUBREY. Oh, I can clear that up. It's one of your men: Meek. He goes about on a motor bicycle with a sack full of maroons and a lot of wire. He said he was surveying. He was evidently very anxious to get rid of me; so I did not press my inquiries. But that accounts for the maroons.

TALLBOYS. Not at all. This is very serious. Meek is a half witted creature who should never have been enlisted. He is like a child: this woman could do anything she pleases with him.

THE COUNTESS. But what could she possibly want with maroons?

TALLBOYS. I dont know. This expedition has been sent out without the sanction of the League of Nations. We always forget to consult it when there is anything serious in hand. The woman may be an emissary of the League. She may be working against us.

THE COUNTESS. But even so, what harm can she do us?

TALLBOYS [tapping his revolver] My dear lady, do you suppose I am carrying this for fun? Dont you realize that the hills here are full of hostile tribes who may try to raid us at any moment? Look at that electric horn there. If it starts honking, look out; for it will mean that a body of tribesmen has been spotted advancing on us.

THE COUNTESS [alarmed] If I'd known that, you wouldnt have got me here. Is that so, Popsy?

AUBREY. Well, yes; but it doesnt matter: theyre afraid of us.

TALLBOYS. Yes, because they dont know that we are a mere handful of men. But if this woman is in communication with them and has got hold of that idiot Meek, we may have them down on us like a swarm of hornets. I dont like this at all. I must get to the bottom of it at once. Ah! here she comes.

Meek appears at the entrance to the pavilion. He stands politely aside to let the patient pass him, and remains there.

MEEK. The colonel would like a word with you, Miss.

AUBREY. Go easy with her, Colonel. She can run like a deer. And she has muscles of iron. You had better turn out the guard before you tackle her.

TALLBOYS. Pooh! Here, you!

The patient comes to him past the Countess with an air of disarming innocence; falls on her knees; lifts her palms, and smites the ground with her forehead.

TALLBOYS. They tell me you can run fast. Well, a bullet can run faster. [*He taps his revolver*]. Do you understand that?

THE PATIENT [*salaaming*] Bmal elttil a dah yram wons sa etihw saw eceelf sti —

TALLBOYS [*tonitruant*] And everywhere that Mary went —

THE PATIENT [*adroitly cutting in*] That lamb was sure to go. Got me, Colonel. How clever of you! Well, what of it?

TALLBOYS. That is what I intend to find out. You are not a native.

THE PATIENT. Yes, of Somerset.

TALLBOYS. Precisely. Well, why are you disguised? Why did you try to make me believe that you dont understand English?

THE PATIENT. For a lark, Colonel.

TALLBOYS. Thats not good enough. Why have you passed yourself off on this lady as a native servant? Being a servant is no lark. Answer me. Dont stand there trying to invent a lie. Why did you pretend to be a servant?

THE PATIENT. One has so much more control of the house as a servant than as a mistress nowadays, Colonel.

TALLBOYS. Very smart, that. You will tell me next that one controls a regiment much more effectively as a private than as a colonel, eh?

The klaxon sounds stridently. The Colonel draws his revolver and makes a dash for the top of the sandhill, but is outraced by Meek, who gets there first and takes the word of command with irresistible authority, leaving him stupent. Aubrey, who has scrambled to his feet, moves towards the sand dunes to see what is happening. Sweetie clutches the patient's arm in terror and drags her towards the pavilion. She is fiercely shaken off; and Mops stands her ground defiantly and runs towards the sound of the guns when they begin.

MEEK. Stand to. Charge your magazines. Stand by the maroons. How many do you make them, sergeant? How far off?

SERGEANT FIELDING [*invisible*] Forty horse. Nine hundred yards, about, I make it.

MEEK. Rifles at the ready. Cut-offs open. Sights up to eighteen hundred, right over their heads: no hitting. Ten rounds rapid: fire. [*Fusillade of rifles*]. How is that?

SERGEANT'S VOICE. Theyre coming on, sir.

MEEK. Number one maroons: ready. Contact. [*Formidable explosions on the right*]. How is that?

SERGEANT'S VOICE. Theyve stopped.

MEEK. Number two maroons ready. Contact. [*Explosions on the left*]. How is that?

SERGEANT'S VOICE. Bolted, sir, every man of them.

Meek returns from the hill in the character of an insignificant private, followed by Aubrey, to the Colonel's left and right respectively.

MEEK. Thats all right, sir. Excuse interruption.

TALLBOYS. Oh! You call this an interruption?

MEEK. Yessir: theres nothing in it to trouble you about. Shall I draw up the report, sir? Important engagement: enemy routed: no British casualties. D.S.O. for you, perhaps, sir.

TALLBOYS. Private Meek: may I ask – if you will pardon my presumption – who is in command of this expedition, you or I?

MEEK. You, sir.

TALLBOYS [*repouching the revolver*] You flatter me. Thank you. May I ask, further, who the devil gave you leave to plant the entire regimental stock of maroons all over the hills and explode them in the face of the enemy?

MEEK. It was the duty of the intelligence orderly, sir. I'm the intelligence orderly. I had to make the enemy believe that the hills are bristling with British cannon. They think that now, sir. No more trouble from them.

TALLBOYS. Indeed! Quartermaster's clerk, interpreter, intelligence orderly. Any further rank of which I have not been informed?

MEEK. No sir.

TALLBOYS. Quite sure youre not a fieldmarshal, eh?

MEEK. Quite sure, sir. I never was anything higher than a colonel.

TALLBOYS. You a colonel? What do you mean?

MEEK. Not a real colonel, sir. Mostly a brevet, sir, to save appearances when I had to take command.

TALLBOYS. And how do you come to be a private now?

MEEK. I prefer the ranks, sir. I have a freer hand. And the conversation in the officers' mess doesnt suit me. I always resign a commission and enlist again.

TALLBOYS. Always! How many commissions have you held?

MEEK. I dont quite remember, sir. Three, I think.

TALLBOYS. Well, I am dashed!

THE PATIENT. Oh, Colonel! And you mistook this great military genius for a half wit!!!

TALLBOYS [*with aplomb*] Naturally. The symptoms are precisely the same. [*To Meek*] Dismiss.

Meek salutes and trots smartly out past the hut.

AUBREY. By Jove!!

THE COUNTESS. Well I ne – [*Correcting herself*] Tiens, tiens, tiens, tiens!

THE PATIENT. What are you going to do about him, Colonel?

TALLBOYS. Madam: the secret of command, in the army and elsewhere, is never to waste a moment doing anything that can be delegated to a subordinate. I have a passion for sketching in watercolors. Hitherto the work of commanding my regiment has interfered very seriously with its gratification. Henceforth I shall devote myself almost entirely to sketching, and leave the command of the expedition to Private Meek. And since you all seem to be on more intimate terms with him than I can claim, will you be good enough to convey to him – casually, you understand – that I already possess the D.S.O. and that what I am out for at present is a K.C.B. Or rather, to be strictly accurate, that is what my wife is out for. For myself, my sole concern for the moment is whether I should paint that sky with Prussian blue or with cobalt.

THE COUNTESS. Fancy you wasting your time on painting pictures!

TALLBOYS. Countess: I paint pictures to make me feel sane. Dealing with men and women makes me feel mad. Humanity always fails me: Nature never.

ACT III

A narrow gap leading down to the beach through masses of soft brown sandstone, pitted with natural grottoes. Sand and big stones in the foreground. Two of the grottoes are accessible from the beach by mounting from the stones, which make rough platforms in front of them. The soldiers have amused themselves by hewing them into a rude architecture and giving them fancy names. The one on your right as you descend the rough path through the gap is taller than it is broad, and has a natural pillar and a stone like an altar in it, giving a Gothic suggestion which has been assisted by knocking the top of the opening into something like a pointed arch, and surmounting it with the inscription ST PAULS. *The grotto to the left is much wider. It contains a bench long enough to accommodate two persons: its recesses are illuminated rosily by bulbs wrapped in pink paper; and some scholarly soldier has carved above it in Greek characters the word* Αγαπεμονε, *beneath which is written in red chalk* THE ABODE OF LOVE, *under which again some ribald has added in white chalk,* NO NEED TO WASTE THE ELECTRIC LIGHT.*

For the moment The Abode of Love has been taken possession of by the sergeant, a wellbuilt handsome man, getting on for forty. He is sitting on the bench, and is completely absorbed in two books, comparing them with rapt attention.

St Pauls is also occupied. A very tall gaunt elder, by his dress and bearing a well-to-do English gentleman, sits on a stone at the altar, resting his elbows on it with his chin in his hands. He is in the deepest mourning; and his attitude is one of hopeless dejection.

Sweetie, now fully and brilliantly dressed, comes slowly down the path through the gap, moody and bored. On the beach she finds nothing to interest her until the sergeant unconsciously attracts her notice by finding some remarkable confirmation or contradiction between his two books, and smiting one of them appreciatively with his fist. She instantly brightens up, climbs to the mouth of the grotto eagerly; and posts herself beside him, on his right. But he is so rapt in his books that she waits in vain to be noticed.

SWEETIE [*contemplating him ardently*] Ahem!

The Sergeant looks up. Seeing who it is, he springs to his feet and stands to attention.

SWEETIE [*giving herself no airs*] You neednt stand up for me, you know.

THE SERGEANT [*stiffly*] Beg pardon, your ladyship. I was not aware of your ladyship's presence.

SWEETIE. Can all that stuff, Sergeant. [*She sits on the bench on his right*]. Dont lets waste time. This place is as dull for me as it is for you. Dont you think we two could amuse ourselves a bit if we were friends?

THE SERGEANT [*with stern contempt*] No, my lady, I dont. I saw a lot of that in the war: pretty ladies brightening up the hospitals and losing their silly heads, let alone upsetting the men; and I dont hold with it. Keep to your class: I'll keep to mine.

SWEETIE. My class! Garn! I'm no countess; and I'm fed up with pretending to be one. Didnt you guess?

THE SERGEANT [*resuming his seat and treating her as one of his own class*] Why should I trouble to start guessing about you? Any girl can be a countess nowadays if she's goodlooking enough to pick up a count.

SWEETIE. Oh! You think I'm goodlooking, do you?

THE SERGEANT. Come! If youre not a countess what are you? Whats the game, eh?

SWEETIE. The game, darling, is that youre my fancy. I love you.

THE SERGEANT. Whats that to me? A man of my figure can have his pick.

SWEETIE. Not here, dear. Theres only one other white woman within fifty miles: and she's a real lady. She wouldnt look at you.

THE SERGEANT. Well, thats a point. Thats a point, certainly.

SWEETIE [*snuggling to him*] Yes, isnt it?

THE SERGEANT [*suffering the advance but not responding*]

This climate plays the devil with a man, no matter how serious minded he is.

SWEETIE [*slipping her arm through his*] Well, isnt it natural? Whats the use of pretending?

THE SERGEANT. Still, I'm not a man to treat a woman as a mere necessity. Many soldiers do: to them a woman is no more than a jar of marmalade, to be consumed and put away. I dont take that view. I admit that there is that side to it, and that for people incapable of anything better — mere animals as you might say — thats the beginning and the end of it. But to me thats only the smallest part of it. I like getting a woman's opinions. I like to explore her mind as well as her body. See these two little books I was deep in when you accosted me? I carry them with me wherever I go. I put the problems they raise for me to every woman I meet.

SWEETIE [*with growing misgiving*] What are they?

THE SERGEANT [*pointing to them successively*] The Bible. The Pilgrim's Progress from this world to that which is to come.

SWEETIE [*dismayed, trying to rise*] Oh, my God!

THE SERGEANT [*holding her ruthlessly in the crook of his elbow*] No you dont. Sit quiet: and dont take the name of the Lord your God in vain. If you believe in him, it's blasphemy: if you dont, it's nonsense. You must learn to exercise your mind: what is a woman without an active mind to a man but a mere convenience?

SWEETIE. I have plenty to exercise my mind looking after my own affairs. What I look to you for, my lad, is a bit of fun.

THE SERGEANT. Quite. But when men and women pick one another up just for a bit of fun, they find theyve picked up more than they bargained for, because men and women have a top storey as well as a ground floor; and you cant have the one without the other. Theyre always trying to; but it doesnt work. Youve picked up my mind as well as my body; and youve got to explore it. You thought you could have a face and a figure like mine with the limitations of a gorilla. Youre finding out your mistake: thats all.

SWEETIE. Oh, let me go: I have had enough of this. If I'd thought you were religious I'd have given you a wide berth, I tell you. Let me go, will you?

THE SERGEANT. Wait a bit. Nature may be using me as a sort of bait to draw you to take an interest in things of the mind. Nature may be using your pleasant animal warmth to stimulate my mind. I want your advice. I dont say I'll take it; but it may suggest something to me. You see, I'm in a mess.

SWEETIE. Well, of course. Youre in the sergeants' mess.

THE SERGEANT. Thats not the mess I mean. My mind's in a mess – a muddle. I used to be a religious man; but I'm not so clear about it as I was.

SWEETIE. Thank goodness for that, anyhow.

THE SERGEANT. Look at these two books. I used to believe every word of them because they seemed to have nothing to do with real life. But war brought those old stories home quite real; and then one starts asking questions. Look at this bit here [*he points to a page of The Pilgrim's Progress*]. It's on the very first page of it. 'I am for certain informed that this our city will be burned with fire from heaven, in which fearful overthrow both myself, with thee my wife, and you my sweet babes, shall miserably come to ruin, except some way of escape can be found whereby we may be delivered.' Well, London and Paris and Berlin and Rome and the rest of them will be burned with fire from heaven all right in the next war: thats certain. Theyre all Cities of Destruction. And our Government chaps are running about with a great burden of corpses and debts on their backs, crying 'What must we do to be saved?' There it is: not a story in a book as it used to be, but God's truth in the real actual world. And all the comfort they get is 'Flee from the wrath to come.' But where are they to flee to?

There they are, meeting at Geneva or hobnobbing at Chequers over the weekend, asking one another, like the man in the book, 'Whither must we flee?' And nobody can tell them. The man in the book says 'Do you see yonder shining light?' Well, today the place is blazing with shining lights: shining lights in parliament, in the papers, in the churches, and in the books that they call Outlines – Outlines of History and Science and what not – and in spite of all their ballyhoo here we are waiting in the City of Destruction like so many sheep for the wrath to come. This uneducated tinker tells me the way is straight before us and so narrow that we cant miss it. But he starts by calling the place the wilderness of this world. Well, theres no road in a wilderness: you have to make one. All the straight roads are made by soldiers; and the soldiers didnt get to heaven along them. A lot of them landed up in the other place. No, John: you could tell a story well; and they say you were a soldier; but soldiers that try to make storytelling do for service end in the clink; and thats where they put you. Twelve years in Bedford Gaol, he got. He used to read the Bible in gaol; and –

SWEETIE. Well, what else was there to read there? It's all they give you in some gaols.

THE SERGEANT. How do you know that?

SWEETIE. Never you mind how I know it. It's nothing to do with you.

THE SERGEANT. Nothing to do with me! You dont know me, my lass. Some men would just order you off; but to me the most interesting thing in the world is the experience of a woman thats been shut up in a cell for years at a time with nothing but a Bible to read.

SWEETIE. Years! What are you talking about? The longest I ever did was nine months; and if anyone says I ever did a day longer she's a liar.

THE SERGEANT [*laying his hand on the bible*] You could read that book from cover to cover in nine months.

95

SWEETIE. Some of it would drive you melancholy mad. It only got me into trouble: it did. The chaplain asked me what I was in for. Spoiling the Egyptians, I says; and heres chapter and verse for it. He went and reported me, the swine; and I lost seven days remission for it.

THE SERGEANT. Serve you right! I dont hold with spoiling the Egyptians. Before the war, spoiling the Egyptians was something holy. Now I see plainly it's nothing but thieving.

SWEETIE [*shocked*] Oh, you shouldnt say that. But what I say is, if Moses might do it why maynt I?

THE SERGEANT. If thats the effect it had on your mind, it's a bad effect. Some of this scripture is all right. Do justice; love mercy; and walk humbly before your God. That appeals to a man if only it could be set out in plain army regulations. But all this thieving, and slaughtering your enemies without giving quarter, and offering up human sacrifices, and thinking you can do what you like to other people because youre the chosen people of God, and you are in the right and everyone else is in the wrong: how does that look when you have had four years of the real thing instead of merely reading about it. No: damn it, we're civilized men; and though it may have gone down with those old Jews it isnt religion. And, if it isnt, where are we? Thats what I want to know.

SWEETIE. And is this all you care about? Sitting here and thinking of things like that?

THE SERGEANT. Well, somebody must think about them, or whats going to become of us all? The officers wont think about them. The colonel goes out sketching: the lootnants go out and kill the birds and animals, or play polo. They wont flee from the wrath to come, not they. When they wont do their military duties I have to do them. It's the same with our religious duties. It's the chaplain's job, not mine; but when you get a real religious chaplain you find he doesnt believe any of the old stuff; and if you get a

gentleman, all he cares about is to shew you that he's a real
sport and not a mealy mouthed parson. So I have to puzzle
it out for myself.

SWEETIE. Well, God help the woman that marries you:
thats all I have to say to you. I dont call you a man. [*She
rises quickly to escape from him*].

THE SERGEANT [*also rising, and seizing her in a very hearty embrace*] Not a man, eh? [*He kisses her*] How does that feel,
Judy?

SWEETIE [*struggling, but not very resolutely*] You let me go,
will you. I dont want you now.

THE SERGEANT. You will if I kiss you half a dozen times,
more than you ever wanted anything in your life before.
Thats a hard fact of human nature; and its one of the facts
that religion has to make room for.

SWEETIE. Oh, well, kiss me and have done with it. You
cant kiss and talk about religion at the same time.

THE ELDER [*springing from his cell to the platform in front of it*]
Forbear this fooling, both of you. You, sir, are not an ignorant man: you know that the universe is wrecked.

SWEETIE [*clinging to the sergeant*] He's mad.

THE ELDER. I am sane in a world of lunatics.

THE SERGEANT [*putting Sweetie away*] It's a queer thing,
isnt it, that though there is a point at which I'd rather kiss
a woman than do anything else in the world, yet I'd rather
be shot than let anyone see me doing it?

THE ELDER. Sir: women are not, as they suppose, more
interesting than the universe. When the universe is crum-
bling let women be silent; and let men rise to something
nobler than kissing them.

*The Sergeant, interested and overawed, sits down quietly and
makes Sweetie sit beside him as before. The Elder continues to
declaim with fanatical intensity.*

THE ELDER. Yes, sir: the universe of Isaac Newton, which
has been an impregnable citadel of modern civilization for
three hundred years, has crumbled like the walls of Jericho

97

before the criticism of Einstein. Newton's universe was the
stronghold of rational Determinism: the stars in their orbits
obeyed immutably fixed laws; and when we turned from
surveying their vastness to study the infinite littleness of the
atoms, there too we found the electrons in their orbits obeying the same universal laws, Every moment of time dictated
and determined the following moment, and was itself dictated and determined by the moment that came before it.
Everything was calculable: everything happened
because it must: the commandments were erased from the
tables of the law: and in their place came the cosmic
algebra: the equations of the mathematicians. Here was my
faith: here I found my dogma of infallibility: I, who scorned
alike the Catholic with his vain dream of responsible Free
Will, and the Protestant with his pretence of private judgment. And now – now – what is left of it? The orbit of the
electron obeys no law: it chooses one path and rejects
another: it is as capricious as the planet Mercury, who
wanders from his road to warm his hands at the sun. All is
caprice: the calculable world has become incalculable:
Purpose and Design, the pretexts for all the vilest superstitions, have risen from the dead to cast down the mighty
from their seats and put paper crowns on presumptuous
fools. Formerly, when differences with my wife, or business
worries, tried me too hard, I sought consolation and
reassurance in our natural history museums, where I could
forget all common cares in wondering at the diversity of
forms and colors in the birds and fishes and animals, all
produced without the agency of any designer by the operation of Natural Selection. Today I dare not enter an
aquarium, because I can see nothing in those grotesque
monsters of the deep but the caricatures of some freakish
demon artist: some Zeus-Mephistopheles with paintbox
and plasticine, trying to surpass himself in the production
of fantastic and laughable creatures to people a Noah's ark
for his baby. I have to rush from the building lest I go mad,

crying, like the man in your book, 'What must I do to be saved?' Nothing can save us from a perpetual headlong fall into a bottomless abyss but a solid footing of dogma; and we no sooner agree to that than we find that the only trustworthy dogma is that there is no dogma. As I stand here I am falling into that abyss, down, down, down. We are all falling into it; and our dizzy brains can utter nothing but madness. My wife has died cursing me. I do not know how to live without her: we were unhappy together for forty years. My son, whom I brought up to be an incorruptible Godfearing atheist, has become a thief and a scoundrel; and I can say nothing to him but 'Go, boy: perish in your villainy; for neither your father nor anyone else can now give you a good reason for being a man of honor.'

He turns from them and is rushing distractedly away when Aubrey, in white tropicals, comes strolling along the beach from the St Pauls side, and hails him nonchalantly.

AUBREY. Hullo, father, is it really you? I thought I heard the old trombone: I couldnt mistake it. How the dickens did you turn up here?

THE ELDER [*to the sergeant*] This is my prodigal son.

AUBREY. I am not a prodigal son. The prodigal son was a spendthrift and neer-do-weel who was reduced to eating the husks that the swine did eat. I am not ruined: I am rolling in money. I have never owed a farthing to any man. I am a model son; but I regret to say that you are' very far from being a model father.

THE ELDER. What right have you to say that, sir? In what way have I fallen short?

AUBREY. You tried to thwart my manifest destiny. Nature meant me for the Church. I had to get ordained secretly.

THE ELDER. Ordained! You dared to get ordained without my knowledge!

AUBREY. Of course. You objected. How could I have done it with your knowledge? You would have stopped my allowance.

THE ELDER [*sitting down on the nearest stone, overwhelmed*] My son a clergyman! This will kill me.

AUBREY [*coolly taking another stone, on his father's right*] Not a bit of it: fathers are not so easily killed. It was at the university that I became what was then called a sky pilot. When the war took me it seemed natural that I should pursue that avocation as a member of the air force. As a flying ace I won a very poorly designed silver medal for committing atrocities which were irreconcilable with the profession of a Christian clergyman. When I was wounded and lost my nerve for flying, I became an army chaplain. I then found myself obliged to tell mortally wounded men that they were dying in a state of grace and were going straight to heaven when as a matter of fact they were dying in mortal sin and going elsewhere. To expiate this blasphemy I kept as much under fire as possible; but my nerve failed again: I had to take three months leave and go into a nursing home. In that home I met my doom.

THE ELDER. What do you mean by your doom? You are alive and well, to my sorrow and shame.

AUBREY. To be precise, I met Sweetie. Thats Sweetie.

SWEETIE. Very pleased to meet Popsy's father, I'm sure.

THE ELDER. My son was called Popsy in his infancy, I put a stop to it, on principle, when he entered on his sixth year. It is strange to hear the name from your lips after so long an interval.

SWEETIE. I always ask a man what his mother called him, and call him that. It takes the starch out of him, somehow.

AUBREY [*resuming his narrative*] Sweetie was quite the rottenest nurse that ever raised the mortality of a hospital by ten per cent. But –

SWEETIE. Oh, what a lie! It was the other nurses that killed the men: waking them up at six in the morning and washing them! Half of them died of chills.

AUBREY. Well, you will not deny that you were the prettiest woman in the place.

SWEETIE. You thought so, anyhow.

THE ELDER. Oh, cease – cease this trifling. I cannot endure this unending sex appeal.

AUBREY. During the war it was found that sex appeal was as necessary for wounded or shellshocked soldiers as skilled nursing; so pretty girls were allowed to pose as nurses because they could sit about on beds and prevent the men from going mad. Sweetie did not prevent me going mad: on the contrary, she drove me mad. I saw in Sweetie not only every charm, but every virtue. And she returned my love. When I left that nursing home, she left it too. I was discharged as cured on the third of the month: she had been kicked out on the first. The trained staff could stand a good deal; but they could not stand Sweetie.

SWEETIE. They were jealous; and you know it.

AUBREY. I daresay they were. Anyhow, Sweetie and I took the same lodgings; and she was faithful to me for ten days. It was a record for her.

SWEETIE. Popsy: are you going to give the whole show away, or only part of it? The Countess Valbrioni would like to know.

AUBREY. We may as well be frank up to the point at which we should lose money by it. But perhaps I am boring the company.

THE ELDER. Complete your confession, sir. You have just said that you and this lady took the same lodging. Am I to understand that you are husband and wife.

SWEETIE. We might have been if we could have depended on you for a good time. But how could I marry an army chaplain with nothing but his pay and an atheist for his father?

AUBREY. So that was the calculation, Sweetie, was it? I never dreamt that the idea of marriage had occurred to either of us. It certainly never occurred to me. I went to live with you quite simply because I felt I could not live without you. The improbability of that statement is the measure of my infatuation.

SWEETIE. Dont you be so spiteful. Did I give you a good time or did I not?

AUBREY. Heavenly. That also seems improbable; but it is gospel truth.

THE ELDER. Wretched boy: do not dare to trifle with me. You said just now that you owe no man anything, and that you are rolling in money. Where did you get that money?

AUBREY. I stole a very valuable pearl necklace and restored it to the owner. She rewarded me munificently. Hence my present opulence. Honesty is the best policy – sometimes.

THE ELDER. Worse even than a clergyman! A thief!

AUBREY. Why make such a fuss about nothing?

THE ELDER. Do you call the theft of a pearl necklace nothing?

AUBREY. Less than nothing, compared to the things I have done with your approval. I was hardly more than a boy when I first dropped a bomb on a sleeping village. I cried all night after doing that. Later on I swooped into a street and sent machine gun bullets into a crowd of civilians: women, children, and all. I was past crying by that time. And now you preach to me about stealing a pearl necklace! Doesnt that seem a little ridiculous?

THE SERGEANT. That was war, sir.

AUBREY. It was me, sergeant: ME. You cannot divide my conscience into a war department and a peace department. Do you suppose that a man who will commit murder for political ends will hesitate to commit theft for personal ends? Do you suppose you can make a man the mortal enemy of sixty millions of his fellow creatures without making him a little less scrupulous about his next door neighbor?

THE ELDER. I did not approve. Had I been of military age I should have been a conscientious objector.

AUBREY. Oh, you were a conscientious objector to everything, even to God. But my mother was an enthusiast for everything: that was why you never could get on with her. She would have shoved me into the war if I had needed any shoving. She shoved my brother into it, though he did not believe a word of all the lies we were stuffed with, and didnt want to go. He was killed, and when it came out afterwards that he was right, and that we were all a parcel of fools killing one another for nothing, she lost the courage to face life, and died of it.

THE SERGEANT. Well, sir, I'd never let a son of mine talk to me like that. Let him have a bit of your Determinism, sir.

THE ELDER [*rising impulsively*] Determinism is gone, shattered, buried with a thousand dead religions, evaporated with the clouds of a million forgotten winters. The science I pinned my faith to is bankrupt: its tales were more foolish than all the miracles of the priests, its cruelties more horrible than all the atrocities of the Inquisition. Its spread of enlightenment has been a spread of cancer: its counsels that were to have established the millennium have led straight to European suicide. And I — I who believed in it as no religious fanatic has ever believed in his superstition! For its sake I helped to destroy the faith of millions of worshippers in the temples of a thousand creeds. And now look at me and behold the supreme tragedy of the atheist who has lost his faith — his faith in atheism, for which more martyrs have perished than for all the creeds put together. Here I stand, dumb before my scoundrel of a son; for that is what you are, boy, a common scoundrel and nothing else.

AUBREY. Well, why not? If I become an honest man I shall become a poor man; and then nobody will respect me: nobody will admire me: nobody will say thank you to me. If on the contrary I am bold, unscrupulous, acquisitive, successful and rich, everyone will respect me, admire me, court me, grovel before me. Then no doubt I shall be able to afford the luxury of honesty. I learnt that from my religious education.

THE ELDER. How dare you say that you had a religious education. I shielded you from that, at least.

AUBREY. You thought you did, old man; but you reckoned without my mother.

THE ELDER. What!

AUBREY. You forbad me to read the Bible; but my mother made me learn three verses of it every day, and whacked me if I could not repeat them without misplacing a word. She threatened to whack me still worse if I told you.

THE ELDER [*thunderstruck*] Your mother!!!

AUBREY. So I learnt my lesson. Six days on the make, and on the seventh shalt thou rest. I shall spend another six years on the make, and then I shall retire and be a saint.

THE ELDER. A saint! Say rather the ruined son of an incorrigibly superstitious mother. Retire now – from the life you have dishonored. There is the sea. Go. Drown yourself. In that graveyard there are no lying epitaphs. [*He mounts to his chapel and again gives way to utter dejection*].

AUBREY [*unconcerned*] I shall do better as a saint. A few thousands to the hospitals and the political party funds will buy me a halo as large as Sweetie's sun hat. That is my program. What have any of you to say against it?

THE SERGEANT. Not the program of a gentleman, as I understand the word, sir.

AUBREY. You cannot be a gentleman on less than fifty thousand a year nowadays, sergeant.

THE SERGEANT. You can in the army, by God.

AUBREY. Yes: because you drop bombs on sleeping villages. And even then you have to be an officer. Are you a gentleman?

THE SERGEANT. No, sir: it wouldnt pay me. I couldnt afford it.

Disturbance. A voice is heard in complaint and lamentation. It is that of the Elderly Lady, Mrs Mopply. She is pursuing Colonel Tallboys down the path through the gap, the lady distracted and insistent, the colonel almost equally distracted: she clutching him and stopping him: he breaking loose and trying to get away from her. She is dressed in black precisely as if she were in Cheltenham, except that she wears a sun helmet. He is equipped with a box of sketching materials slung over his shoulder, an easel, which he has tucked under his left arm, and a sun umbrella, a substantial affair of fawn lined with red, podgily rolled up, which he carries in his right hand.

MRS MOPPLY. I wont be patient. I wont be quiet. My child is being murdered.

TALLBOYS. I tell you she is not being murdered. Will you be good enough to excuse me whilst I attend to my business.

MRS MOPPLY. Your business is to save my child. She is starving.

TALLBOYS. Nonsense. Nobody starves in this country. There are plenty of dates. Will you be good enough –

MRS MOPPLY. Do you think my child can live on dates? She has to have a sole for breakfast, a cup of nourishing soup at eleven, a nice chop and a sweetbread for lunch, a pint of beef-tea with her ordinary afternoon tea, and a chicken and some lamb or veal –

TALLBOYS. Will you be good enough –

MRS MOPPLY. My poor delicate child with nothing to eat but dates! And she is the only one I have left: they were all delicate –

TALLBOYS. I really must – [*He breaks away and hurries off along the beach past the Abode of Love*].

MRS MOPPLY [*running after him*] Colonel, Colonel: you might have the decency to listen to a distracted mother for a moment. Colonel: my child is dying. She may be dead for all I know. And nobody is doing anything: nobody cares. Oh dear, wont you listen – [*Her voice is lost in the distance*].

Whilst they are staring mutely after the retreating pair, the patient, still in her slave girl attire, but with some brilliant variations, comes down the path.

THE PATIENT. My dream has become a nightmare. My mother has pursued me to these shores. I cannot shake her off. No woman can shake off her mother. There should be no mothers: there should be only women, strong women able to stand by themselves, not clingers. I would kill all the clingers. Mothers cling: daughters cling: we are all like drunken women clinging to lamp posts: none of us stands upright.

THE ELDER. There is great comfort in clinging, and great loneliness in standing alone.

THE PATIENT. Hallo! [*She climbs to the St Pauls platform and peers into the cell*]. A sententious anchorite! [*To Aubrey*]. Who is he?

AUBREY. The next worst thing to a mother: a father.

THE ELDER. A most unhappy father.

AUBREY. My father, in fact.

THE PATIENT. If only I had had a father to stand between me and my mother's care. Oh, that I had been an orphan!

THE SERGEANT. You will be, miss, if the old lady drives the colonel too hard. She has been at him all the morning, ever since she arrived; and I know the colonel. He has a temper; and when it gives way, it's a bit of high explosive. He'll kill her if she pushes him too far.

THE PATIENT. Let him kill her. I am young and strong: I want a world without parents: there is no room for them in my dream. I shall found a sisterhood.

AUBREY. All right, Mops. Get thee to a nunnery.

THE PATIENT. It need not be a nunnery if men will come in without spoiling everything. But all the women must be rich. There must be no chill of poverty. There are plenty of rich women like me who hate being devoured by parasites.

AUBREY. Stop. You have the most disgusting mental pictures. I really cannot stand intellectual coarseness. Sweetie's vulgarity I can forgive and even enjoy. But you say perfectly filthy things that stick in my mind, and break my spirit. I can bear no more of it. [*He rises angrily and tries to escape by the beach past the Abode of Love*].

SWEETIE. Youre dainty, arnt you? If chambermaids were

as dainty as you, youd have to empty your own slops.

AUBREY [*recoiling from her with a yell of disgust*] You need not throw them in my teeth, you beast. [*He sits in his former place, sulking*].

THE ELDER. Silence, boy. These are home truths. They are good for you. [*To the patient*] May I ask young woman, what are the relations between you and my son, whom you seem to know.

THE PATIENT. Popsy stole my necklace, and got me to run away with him by a wonderful speech he made about freedom and sunshine and lovely scenery. Sweetie made me write it all down and sell it to a tourist agency as an advertisement. And then I was devoured by parasites: by tourist agencies, steamboat companies, railways, motor car people, hotel keepers, dressmakers, servants, all trying to get my money by selling me things I dont really want; shoving me all over the globe to look at what they call new skies, though they know as well as I do that it is only the same old sky everywhere; and disabling me by doing all the things for me that I ought to do for myself to keep myself in health. They preyed on me to keep themselves alive: they pretended they were making me happy when it was only by drinking and drugging – cocktails and cocaine – that I could endure my life.

AUBREY. I regret to have to say it, Mops; but you have not the instincts of a lady. [*He sits down moodily on a stone a little way up the path*].

THE PATIENT. You fool, there is no such thing as a lady. I have the instincts of a good housekeeper: I want to clean up this filthy world and keep it clean. There must be other women who want it too. Florence Nightingale had the same instinct when she went to clean up the Crimean war. She wanted a sisterhood; but there wasnt one.

THE ELDER. There were several. But steeped in superstition, unfortunately.

THE PATIENT. Yes, all mixed up with things that I dont

believe. Women have to set themselves apart to join them. I dont want to set myself apart. I want to have every woman in my sisterhood, and to have all the others strangled.

THE ELDER. Down! down! down! Even the young, the strong, the rich, the beautiful, feel that they are plunging into a bottomless pit.

THE SERGEANT. Your set, miss, if you will excuse me saying so, is only a small bit of the world. If you dont like the officers' mess, the ranks are open to you. Look at Meek! That man could be an emperor if he laid his mind to it: but he'd rather be a private. He's happier so.

THE PATIENT. I dont belong to the poor, and dont want to. I always knew that there were thousands of poor people; and I was taught to believe that they were poor because God arranged it that way to punish them for being dirty and drunken and dishonest, and not knowing how to read and write. But I didnt know that the rich were miserable. I didnt know that I was miserable. I didnt know that our respectability was uppish snobbery and our religion gluttonous selfishness, and that my soul was starving on them. I know now. I have found myself out thoroughly – in my dream.

THE ELDER. You are young. Some good man may cure you of this for a few happy years. When you fall in love, life will seem worth living.

THE PATIENT. I did fall in love. With that thing. And though I was never a hotel chambermaid I got tired of him sooner than Sweetie did. Love gets people into difficulties, not out of them. No more lovers for me: I want a sisterhood. Since I came here I have been wanting to join the army, like Joan of Arc. It's a brotherhood, of a sort.

THE SERGEANT. Yes, miss: that is so; and there used to be a peace of mind in the army that you could find nowhere else. But the war made an end of that. You see, miss, the great principle of soldiering, I take it, is that the world is kept going by the people who want the right thing killing the people who want the wrong thing. When the soldier is doing that, he is doing the work of God, which my mother brought me up to do. But thats a very different thing from killing a man because he's a German and he killing you because youre an Englishman. We were not killing the right people in 1915. We werent even killing the wrong people. It was innocent men killing one another.

THE PATIENT. Just for the fun of it.

THE SERGEANT. No, miss: it was no fun. For the misery of it.

THE PATIENT. For the devilment of it, then.

THE SERGEANT. For the devilment of the godless rulers of this world. Those that did the killing hadnt even the devilment to comfort them: what comfort is there in screwing on a fuse or pulling a string when the devilment it makes is from three to forty miles off, and you dont know whether you have only made a harmless hole in the ground or blown up a baby in its cradle that might have been your own? That wasnt devilment: it was damnation. No, miss: the bottom has come out of soldiering. What the gentleman here said about our all falling into a bottomless pit came home to me. I feel like that too.

THE ELDER. Lost souls, all of us.

THE PATIENT. No: only lost dogs. Cheer up, old man: the lost dogs always find their way home. [*The voice of the Elderly Lady is heard returning*]. Oh! here she comes again!

Mrs Mopply is still pursuing the colonel, who is walking doggedly and steadily away from her, with closed lips and a dangerous expression on his set features.

MRS MOPPLY. You wont even speak to me. It's a disgrace. I will send a cable message home to the Government about it. You were sent out here to rescue my daughter from these dreadful brigands. Why is nothing being done? What are the relations between yourself and that disgraceful countess who ought to have her coronet stripped off her back? You are all in a conspiracy to murder my poor lost darling child. You are in league with the brigands. You are –

The Colonel turns at bay, and brings down his umbrella whack on poor Mrs Mopply's helmet.

MRS MOPPLY. Oh! Oh! Oh! Oh! [*With a series of short, dry, detached screams she totters and flutters back along the beach out of sight like a wounded bird*].

General stupefaction. All stare at the Colonel aghast. The Sergeant rises in amazement, and remains standing afterwards as a matter of military etiquette.

THE PATIENT. Oh, if only someone had done that to her twenty years ago, how different my childhood would have been! But I must see to the poor old dear. [*She runs after her mother*].

AUBREY. Colonel: you have our full, complete, unreserved sympathy. We thank you from the bottom of our hearts. But that does not alter the fact that the man who would raise his hand to a woman, save in the way of kindness, is unworthy the name of Briton.

TALLBOYS. I am perfectly aware of that, sir. I need no reminder. The lady is entitled to an apology. She shall have it.

THE ELDER. But have you considered the possibility of a serious injury –

TALLBOYS [*cutting him short*] My umbrella is quite uninjured, thank you. The subject is now closed. [*He sits down on the stone below St Pauls recently vacated by Aubrey. His manner is so decisive that nobody dares carry the matter further*].

As they sit uneasily seeking one another's eyes and avoiding them again, dumbfounded by the violence of the catastrophe, a noise like that of a machine gun in action reaches their ears from afar. It increases to shattering intensity as it approaches. They all put their fingers to their ears. It diminishes slightly, then suddenly rises to a climax of speed and uproar, and stops.

TALLBOYS. Meek.

AUBREY. Meek.

SWEETIE. Meek.

THE ELDER. What is this? Why do you all say Meek?

Meek, dusty and gritty, but very alert, comes down the path through the gap with a satchel of papers.

TALLBOYS. My dear Meek, can you not be content with a motor cycle of ordinary horse power? Must you always travel at eighty miles an hour?

MEEK. I have good news for you, Colonel; and good news should travel fast.

TALLBOYS. For me?

MEEK. Your K.C.B., sir. [*Presenting a paper*] Honors list by wireless.

TALLBOYS [*rising joyously to take the paper*] Ah! Congratulate me, my friends. My dear Sarah is Lady Tallboys at last. [*He resumes his seat and pores over the paper*].

AUBREY		Splendid!
THE SERGEANT	[*together*]	You deserve it, sir, if I may say so.
SWEETIE		Delighted, I am sure.

THE ELDER. May I crave to know the nature of the distinguished service which has won this official recognition, sir?

TALLBOYS. I have won the battle of the maroons. I have suppressed brigandage here. I have rescued a British lady from the clutches of the brigands. The Government is preparing for a general election, and has had to make the most of these modest achievements.

THE ELDER. Brigands! Are there any here?

TALLBOYS. None.

THE ELDER. But – ? The British lady? In their clutches?

TALLBOYS. She has been in my clutches, and perfectly safe, all the time.

THE ELDER [*more and more puzzled*] Oh! Then the battle of the –

TALLBOYS. Won by Private Meek. I had nothing whatever to do with it.

AUBREY. I invented the brigands and the British lady. [*To Tallboys*] By the way, Colonel, the impressive old party in the shrine is my father.

TALLBOYS. Indeed! Happy to meet you, sir, though I cannot congratulate you on your son, except in so far as you have brought into the world the most abandoned liar I have ever met.

THE ELDER. And may I ask, sir, is it your intention not only to condone my son's frauds, but to take advantage of them to accept a distinction which you have in no way earned?

TALLBOYS. I have earned it, sir, ten times over. Do you suppose, because the brigandage which I am honored for suppressing has no existence, that I have never suppressed real brigands? Do you forget that though this battle of which I am crowned victor was won by a subordinate, I, too, have won real battles, and seen all the honors go to a brigadier who did not even know what was happening? In the army these things average themselves out: merit is rewarded in the long run. Justice is none the less justice though it is always delayed, and finally done by mistake. My turn today: Private Meek's tomorrow.

THE ELDER. And meanwhile Mr Meek -- this humble and worthy soldier -- is to remain in obscurity and poverty whilst you are strutting as a K.C.B.

TALLBOYS. How I envy him! Look at me and look at him! I, loaded with responsibilities whilst my hands are tied, my body disabled, my mind crippled because a colonel must not do anything but give orders and look significant and profound when his mind is entirely vacant! he, free to turn his hand to everything and to look like an idiot when he feels like one! I have been driven to sketching in watercolors because I may not use my hands in life's daily useful business. A commanding officer must not do this, must not do that, must not do the other, must not do anything but tell other men to do it. He may not even converse with them. I see this man Meek doing everything that is natural to a complete man: carpentering, painting, digging, pulling and hauling, fetching and carrying, helping himself and everybody else, whilst I, with a bigger body to exercise and quite as much energy, must loaf and loll, allowed to do nothing but read the papers and drink brandy and water to prevent myself going mad. I should have become a drunkard had it not been for the colors.

THE SERGEANT. Ah yes, sir, the colors. The fear of disgracing them has kept me off the drink many a time.

TALLBOYS. Man: I do not mean the regimental colors, but the watercolors. How willingly would I exchange my pay, my rank, my K.C.B., for Meek's poverty, his obscurity!

MEEK. But, my dear Colonel – sorry, sir: what I mean to say is that you can become a private if you wish. Nothing easier: I have done it again and again. You resign your commission; take a new and very common name by deed poll; dye your hair and give your age to the recruiting sergeant as twenty-two; and there you are! You can select your own regiment.

TALLBOYS. Meek: you should not tantalize your commanding officer. No doubt you are an extraordinary soldier. But have you ever passed the extreme and final test of manly courage?

MEEK. Which one is that, sir?

TALLBOYS. Have you ever married?

MEEK. No, sir.

TALLBOYS. Then do not ask me why I do not resign my commission and become a free and happy private. My wife would not let me.

THE COUNTESS. Why dont you hit her on the head with your umbrella?

TALLBOYS. I dare not. There are moments when I wish some other man would. But not in my presence. I should kill him.

THE ELDER. We are all slaves. But at least your son is an honest man.

TALLBOYS. Is he? I am glad to hear it. I have not spoken

to him since he shirked military service at the beginning of the war and went into trade as a contractor. He is now so enormously rich that I cannot afford to keep up his acquaintance. Neither need you keep up that of your son. By the way, he passes here as the half step-brother of this lady, the Countess Valbrioni.

SWEETIE. Valbrioni be blowed! My name is Susan Simpkins. Being a countess isnt worth a damn. There's no variety in it: no excitement. What I want is a month's leave for the sergeant. Wont you give it to him, Colonel?

TALLBOYS. What for?

SWEETIE. Never mind what for. A fortnight might do; but I dont know for certain yet. There's something steadying about him; and I suppose I will have to settle down some day.

TALLBOYS. Nonsense! The sergeant is a pious man, not your sort. Eh, Sergeant?

THE SERGEANT. Well, sir, a man should have one woman to prevent him from thinking too much about women in general. You cannot read your Bible undisturbed if visions and wandering thoughts keep coming between you and it. And a pious man should not marry a pious woman: two of a trade never agree. Besides, it would give the children a onesided view of life. Life is very mixed, sir: it is not all piety and it is not all gaiety. This young woman has no conscience: but I have enough for two. I have no money; but she seems to have enough for two. Mind: I am not committing myself; but I will go so far as to say that I am not dead set against it. On the plane of this world and its vanities – and weve got to live in it, you know, sir – she appeals to me.

AUBREY. Take care, sergeant. Constancy is not Sweetie's strong point.

THE SERGEANT. Neither is it mine. As a single man and a wandering soldier I am fair game for every woman. But if I settle down with this girl she will keep the others off. I'm a bit tired of adventures.

SWEETIE. Well, if the truth must be told, so am I. We were made for one another, Sergeant. What do you say?

THE SERGEANT. Well, I dont mind keeping company for a while, Susan, just to see how we get along together.

The voice of Mrs Mopply is again heard. Its tone is hardy and even threatening; and its sound is approaching rapidly.

MRS MOPPLY'S VOICE. You just let me alone, will you? Nobody asked you to interfere. Get away with you.

General awe and dismay. Mrs Mopply appears striding resolutely along the beach. She walks straight up to the Colonel, and is about to address him when he rises firmly to the occasion and takes the word out of her mouth.

TALLBOYS. Mrs Mopply: I have a duty to you which I must discharge at once. At out last meeting, I struck you.

MRS MOPPLY. Struck me! You bashed me. Is that what you mean?

TALLBOYS. If you consider my expression inadequate I am willing to amend it. Let us put it that I bashed you. Well, I apologize without reserve, fully and amply. If you wish, I will give it to you in writing.

MRS MOPPLY. Very well. Since you express your regret, I suppose there is nothing more to be said.

TALLBOYS [*darkening ominously*] Pardon me. I apologized. I did not express my regret.

AUBREY. Oh, for heaven's sake, Colonel, dont start her again. Dont qualify your apology in any way.

MRS MOPPLY. You shut up, whoever you are.

TALLBOYS. I do not qualify my apology in the least. My apology is complete. The lady has a right to it. My action was inexcusable. But no lady – no human being – has a right to impose a falsehood on me. I do not regret my action. I have never done anything which gave me more thorough and hearty satisfaction. When I was a company officer I once cut down an enemy in the field. Had I not done so he would have cut me down. It gave me no satisfaction: I was half ashamed of it. I have never before spoken of it. But this time I struck with unmixed enjoyment. In fact I am grateful to Mrs Mopply. I owe her one of the very few delightfully satisfactory moments of my life.

MRS MOPPLY. Well, thats a pretty sort of apology, isnt it?

TALLBOYS [*firmly*] I have nothing to add, madam.

MRS MOPPLY. Well, I forgive you, you peppery old blighter.

> *Sensation. They catch their breaths, and stare at one another in consternation. The patient arrives.*

THE PATIENT. I am sorry to say, Colonel Tallboys, that you have unsettled my mother's reason. She wont believe that I am her daughter. She's not a bit like herself.

MRS MOPPLY. Isnt she? What do you know about myself? my real self? They told me lies; and I had to pretend to be somebody quite different.

TALLBOYS. Who told you lies, madam? It was not with my authority.

MRS MOPPLY. I wasnt thinking of you. My mother told me lies. My nurse told me lies. My governess told me lies. Everybody told me lies. The world is not a bit like what they said it was. I wasnt a bit like what they said I ought to be. I thought I had to pretend. And I neednt have pretended at all.

THE ELDER. Another victim! She, too, is falling through the bottomless abyss.

MRS MOPPLY. I dont know who you are or what you think you mean; but you have just hit it: I dont know my head from my heels. Why did they tell me that children couldnt live without medicine and three meat meals a day? Do you know that I have killed two of my children because they told me that? My own children! Murdered them, just!

THE ELDER. Medea! Medea!

MRS MOPPLY. It isnt an idea: it's the truth. I will never believe anything again as long as I live. I'd have killed the only one I had left if she hadnt run away from me. I was told to sacrifice myself – to live for others; and I did it if ever a woman did. They told me that everyone would love me for it; and I thought they would; but my daughter ran away when I had sacrificed myself to her until I found myself wishing she would die like the others and leave me a little to myself. And now I find it was not only my daughter that hated me but that all my friends, all the time they were pretending to sympathize, were just longing to bash me over the head with their umbrellas. This poor man only did what all the rest would have done if theyd dared. When I said I forgave you I meant it: I am greatly obliged to you. [*She kisses him*]. But now what am I to do? How am I to behave in a world thats just the opposite of everything I was told about it?

THE PATIENT. Steady, mother! steady! steady! Sit down. [*She picks up a heavy stone and places it near the Abode of Love for Mrs Mopply to sit on*].

MRS MOPPLY [*seating herself*] Dont you call me mother. Do you think my daughter could carry rocks about like that? she that had to call the nurse to pick up her Pekingese dog when she wanted to pet it! You think you can get round me by pretending to be my daughter; but that just shews what a fool you are; for I hate my daughter and my daughter hates me, because I sacrificed myself to her. She was a horrid selfish girl, always ill and complaining, and never satisfied, no matter how much you did for her. The only sensible thing she ever did was to steal her own necklace and sell it and run away to spend the money on herself. I expect she's in bed somewhere with a dozen nurses and six doctors all dancing attendance on her. Youre not a bit like her, thank goodness: thats why Ive taken a fancy to you. You come with me, darling. I have lots of money, and sixty years of a misspent life to make up for; so you will have a good time with me. Come with me as my companion; and lets forget that there are such miserable things in the world as mothers and daughters.

THE PATIENT. What use shall we be to one another?

MRS MOPPLY. None, thank God. We can do without one another if we dont hit it off.

THE PATIENT. Righto! I'll take you on trial until Ive had time to look about me and see what I'm going to do. But only on trial, mind.

MRS MOPPLY. Just so, darling. We'll both be on trial. So thats settled.

THE PATIENT. And now, Mr Meek, what about the little commission you promised to do for me? Have you brought back my passport?

THE COUNTESS. Your passport? Whatever for?

AUBREY. What have you been up to, Mops? Are you going to desert me?

Meek advances and empties a heap of passports from his satchel on the sand, kneeling down to sort out the patient's.

TALLBOYS. What is the meaning of this? Whose passports are these? What are you doing with them? Where did you get them?

MEEK. Everybody within fifty miles is asking me to get a passport visa'd.

TALLBOYS. Visa'd! For what country?

MEEK. For Beotia, sir.

TALLBOYS. Beotia?

MEEK. Yessir. The Union of Federated Sensible Societies, sir. The U.F.S.S. Everybody wants to go there now, sir.

THE COUNTESS. Well I never!

THE ELDER. And what is to become of our unhappy country if all its inhabitants desert it for an outlandish place in which even property is not respected?

MEEK. No fear, sir: they wont have us. They wont admit any more English, sir: they say their lunatic asylums are too full already. I couldnt get a single visa, except [*to the Colonel*] for you, sir.

TALLBOYS. For me! Damn their impudence! I never asked for one.

MEEK. No, sir; but their people have so much leisure that they are at their wits' end for some occupation to keep them out of mischief. They want to introduce the only institution of ours that they admire.

THE ELDER. And pray which one is that?

MEEK. The English school of watercolor painting, sir. Theyve seen some of the Colonel's work; and theyll make him head of their centres of repose and culture if he'll settle there.

TALLBOYS. This cannot be true, Meek. It indicates a degree of intelligence of which no Government is capable.

MEEK. It's true, sir, I assure you.

TALLBOYS. But my wife –

MEEK. Yessir: I told them. [*He repacks his satchel*].

TALLBOYS. Well, well: there is nothing for it but to return to our own country.

THE ELDER. Can our own country return to its senses, sir? that is the question.

TALLBOYS. Ask Meek.

MEEK. No use, sir: all the English privates want to be colonels: there's no salvation for snobs. [*To Tallboys*] Shall I see about getting the expedition back to England, sir?

TALLBOYS. Yes. And get me two tubes of rose madder and a big one of Chinese White, will you?

MEEK [*about to go*] Yessir.

THE ELDER. Stop. There are police in England. What is to become of my son there?

SWEETIE [*rising*] Make Popsy a preacher, old man. But dont start him until weve gone.

THE ELDER. Preach, my son, preach to your heart's content. Do anything rather than steal and make your military crimes an excuse for your civil ones. Let men call you the reverend. Let them call you anything rather than thief.

AUBREY [*rising*] If I may be allowed to improve the occasion for a moment –

119

General consternation. All who are seated rise in alarm, except the patient, who jumps up and claps her hands in mischievous encouragement to the orator.

MRS MOPPLY		You hold your tongue, young man.
SWEETIE		Oh Lord! we're in for it now.
THE ELDER	*[together]*	Shame and silence would better become you, sir.
THE PATIENT		Go on, Pops. It's the only thing you do well.

AUBREY *[continuing]* – it is clear to me that though we seem to be dispersing quietly to do very ordinary things: Sweetie and the Sergeant to get married [*the Sergeant hastily steals down from his grotto, beckoning to Sweetie to follow him. They both escape along the beach*] the colonel to his wife, his watercolors, and his K.C.B. [*the colonel hurries away noiselessly in the opposite direction*] Napoleon Alexander Trotsky Meek to his job of repatriating the expedition [*Meek takes to flight up the path through the gap*] Mops, like Saint Teresa, to found an unladylike sisterhood with her mother as cook-housekeeper [*Mrs Mopply hastily follows the sergeant, dragging with her the patient, who is listening to Aubrey with signs of becoming rapt in his discourse*] yet they are all, like my father here, falling, falling, falling endlessly and hopelessly through a void in which they can find no footing. [*The Elder vanishes into the recesses of St Pauls, leaving his son to preach in solitude*]. There is something fantastic about them, something unreal and perverse, something profoundly unsatisfactory. They are too absurd to be believed in: yet they are not fictions: the newspapers are full of them: what storyteller, however reckless a liar, would dare to invent figures so improbable as men and women with their minds stripped naked? Naked bodies no longer shock us: our sunbathers, grinning at us from every illustrated summer number of our magazines, are nuder than shorn lambs. But the horror of the naked mind is still more than we can bear. Throw off the last rag of your bathing costume; and I shall not blench nor expect you to blush. You may even throw away the outer garments of your souls: the manners, the morals, the decencies. Swear; use dirty words; drink cocktails; kiss and caress and cuddle until girls who are like roses at eighteen are like battered demireps at twenty-two: in all these ways the bright young things of the victory have scandalized their dull old prewar elders and left nobody but their bright young selves a penny the worse. But how are we to bear this dreadful new nakedness: the nakedness of the souls who until now have always disguised themselves from one another in beautiful impossible idealisms to enable them to bear one another's company. The iron lightning of war has burnt great rents in these angelic veils, just as it has smashed great holes in our cathedral roofs and torn great gashes in our hillsides. Our souls go in rags now; and the young are spying through the holes and getting glimpses of the reality that was hidden. And they are not horrified: they exult in having found us out: they expose their own souls: and when we their elders desperately try to patch our torn clothes with scraps of the old material, the young lay violent hands on us and tear from us even the rags that were left to us. But when they have stripped themselves and us utterly naked, will they be able to bear the spectacle? You have seen me try to strip my soul before my father; but when these two young women stripped themselves more boldly than I – when the old woman had the mask struck from her soul and revelled in it instead of dying of it – I shrank from the revelation as from a wind bringing from the unknown regions of the future a breath which may be a breath of life, but of a life too keen for me to bear, and therefore for me a blast of death. I stand midway between youth and age like a man who has missed his train: too late for the last and too early for the next. What am I to do? What am I? A soldier who has lost his nerve, a thief who at his first great theft has found honesty the best policy and restored his booty to its

owner. Nature never intended me for soldiering or thieving: I am by nature and destiny a preacher. I am the new
Ecclesiastes. But I have no Bible, no creed: the war has shot
both out of my hands. The war has been a fiery forcing
house in which we have grown with a rush like flowers in
a late spring following a terrible winter. And with what
result? This: that we have outgrown our religion, outgrown
our political system, outgrown our own strength of mind
and character. The fatal word NOT has been miraculously
inserted into all our creeds: in the desecrated temples where
we knelt murmuring 'I believe' we stand with stiff knees
and stiffer necks shouting 'Up, all! the erect posture is the
mark of the man: let lesser creatures kneel and crawl: we
will not kneel and we do not believe.' But what next? Is NO
enough? For a boy, yes: for a man, never. Are we any the
less obsessed with a belief when we are denying it than
when we were affirming it? No: I must have affirmations to
preach. Without them the young will not listen to me; for
even the young grow tired of denials. The negativemonger
falls before the soldiers, the men of action, the fighters,
strong in the old uncompromising affirmations which give
them status, duties, certainty of consequences; so that the
pugnacious spirit of man in them can reach out and strike
deathblows with steadfastly closed minds. Their way is
straight and sure: but it is the way of death; and the
preacher must preach the way of life. Oh, if I could only
find it! [*A white sea fog swirls up from the beach to his feet, rising
and thickening round him*]. I am ignorant: I have lost my nerve
and am intimidated: all I know is that I must find the way
of life, for myself and all of us, or we shall surely perish. And
meanwhile my gift has possession of me: I must preach and
preach and preach no matter how late the hour and how
short the day, no matter whether I have nothing to say –

*The fog has enveloped him; the gap with its grottoes is lost to
sight; the ponderous stones are wisps of shifting white cloud; there
is left only fog: impenetrable fog; but the incorrigible preacher will*

not be denied his peroration, which, could we only hear it distinctly, would probably run —

— or whether in some pentecostal flame of revelation the Spirit will descend on me and inspire me with a message the sound whereof shall go out unto all lands and realize for us at last the Kingdom and the Power and the Glory for ever and ever. Amen.

The audience disperses (or the reader puts down the book) impressed in the English manner with the Pentecostal flame and the echo from the Lord's Prayer. But fine words butter no parsnips. A few of the choicer spirits will know that the Pentecostal flame is always alight at the service of those strong enough to bear its terrible intensity. They will not forget that it is accompanied by a rushing mighty wind, and that any rascal who happens to be also a windbag can get a prodigious volume of talk out of it without ever going near enough to be shrivelled up. The author, though himself a professional talk maker, does not believe that the world can be saved by talk alone. He has given the rascal the last word; but his own favorite is the woman of action, who begins by knocking the wind out of the rascal, and ends with a cheerful conviction that the lost dogs always find their own way home. So they will, perhaps, if the women go out and look for them.

THE SIMPLETON
OF THE UNEXPECTED ISLES:

A VISION OF JUDGMENT

with

Preface on Days of Judgment

First presented by the Theatre Guild at the Guild
Theatre, New York, on 18 February 1935.

EMIGRATION OFFICER (HUGO HYERING)	Rex O'Malley
WILKS	Lionel Pape
YOUNG WOMAN (MRS HYERING)	Patricia Calvert
STATION MASTER	Reginald Malcolm
PRA, A PRIEST	McKay Morris
PROLA, A PRIESTESS	Alla Nazimova
LADY FARWATERS	Viola Roache
SIR CHARLES FARWATERS	Lawrence Grossmith
REVEREND PHOSPHOR HAMMINGTAP	Romney Brent
JANGA	Leon Janney
KANCHIN	Franklin Gray
MAYA	Alma Lloyd
VASHTI	Rita Vale
THE ANGEL	Louis Hector

Period – Approaching Judgment Day

PROLOGUE:
  Scene 1 *The Emigration Office at a Tropical Port in the British Empire*
  Scene 2 *A Grassy Cliff-top overhanging the Sea*
  Scene 3 *A Shelf of Rock halfway down the Cliff*
ACT I: *The Lawn of a Stately House on the North Coast of a Tropical Island in the Pacific. About 20 years later*
ACT II: *The Same. A Fine Forenoon Some Years Later. (During this act the lights are dimmed to denote the passage of time)*

Preface on Days of Judgment

THE increasing bewilderment of my journalist critics as to why I should write such plays as The Simpleton culminated in New York in February 1935, when I was described as a dignified old monkey throwing coco-nuts at the public in pure senile devilment. This is an amusing and graphic description of the effect I produce on the newspapers; but as a scientific criticism it is open to the matter-of-fact objection that a play is not a coco-nut nor I a monkey. Yet there is an analogy. A coco-nut is impossible without a suitable climate; and a play is impossible without a suitable civilization. If author and journalist are both placid Panglossians, convinced that their civilization is the best of all possible civilizations, and their countrymen the greatest race on earth: in short, if they have had a university education, there is no trouble: the press notices are laudatory if the play is entertaining. Even if the two are pessimists who agree with Jeremiah that the heart of man is deceitful above all things and desperately wicked, and with Shakespear that political authority only transforms its wielders into angry apes, there is still no misunderstanding; for that dismal view, or a familiar acquaintance with it, is quite common.

Such perfect understanding covers much more than nine hundred and ninety cases out of every thousand new plays. But it does not cover the cases in which the author and the journalist are not writing against the same background. The simplest are those in which the journalist is ignorant and uncultivated, and the author is assuming a high degree of knowledge and culture in his audience. This occurs oftener than it should; for some newspaper editors think that any reporter who has become stage struck by seeing half a dozen crude melodramas is thereby qualified to deal with Sophocles and Euripides, Shakespear and Goethe, Ibsen and Strindberg, Tolstoy and Tchekov, to say nothing of myself. But the case with which I am concerned here is one in which a reasonably well equipped critic shoots wide because he cannot see the target nor even conceive its existence. The two parties have not the same vision of the world. This sort of vision varies enormously from individual to individual. Between the super-statesman whose vision embraces the whole politically organized world, or the astronomer whose vision of the universe transcends the range of our utmost telescopes, and the peasant who fiercely resists a main drainage scheme for his village because others as well as he will benefit by it, there are many degrees. The Abyssinian Danakil kills a stranger at sight and is continually seeking for an excuse to kill a friend to acquire trophies enough to attract a wife. Livingstone risked his life in Africa every day to save a black man's soul. Livingstone did not say to the sun colored tribesman 'There is between me and thee a gulf that nothing can fill': he proposed to fill it by instructing the tribesman on the assumption that the tribesman was as capable mentally as himself, but ignorant. That is my attitude when I write prefaces. My newspaper critics may seem incapable of anything better than the trash they write; but I believe they are capable enough and only lack instruction.

I wonder how many of them have given serious thought to the curious changes that take place in the operation of human credulity and incredulity. I have pointed out on a former occasion that there is just as much evidence for a law of the Conservation of Credulity as of the Conservation of Energy. When we refuse to believe in the miracles of religion for no better reason fundamentally than that we are no longer in the humor for them we refill our minds with the miracles of science, most of which the authors of the Bible would have refused to believe. The humans who have lost their simple childish faith in a flat earth and in Joshua's feat of stopping the sun until he had finished his battle with the Amalekites, find no difficulty in swallowing an expanding boomerang universe.

They will refuse to have their children baptized or circumcized, and insist on their being vaccinated, in the teeth of overwhelming evidence that vaccination has killed thousands of children in quite a horrible way whereas no child has ever been a penny the worse for baptism since John the Baptist recommended it. Religion is the mother of scepticism: Science is the mother of credulity. There is nothing that people will not believe nowadays if only it be presented to them as Science, and nothing they will not disbelieve if it be presented to them as religion. I myself began like that; and I am ending by receiving every scientific statement with dour suspicion whilst giving very respectful consideration to the inspiration and revelations of the prophets and poets. For the shift of credulity from religious divination to scientific invention is very often a relapse from comparatively harmless romance to mischievous and even murderous quackery.

Some credulities have their social uses. They have been invented and imposed on us to secure certain lines of behavior as either desirable for the general good or at least convenient to our rulers. I learned this early in life. My nurse induced me to abstain from certain troublesome activities by threatening that if I indulged in them the cock would come down the chimney. This event seemed to me so apocalyptic that I never dared to provoke it nor even to ask myself in what way I should be the worse for it. Without this device my nurse could not have ruled me when her back was turned. It was the first step towards making me rule myself.

Mahomet, one of the greatest of the prophets of God, found himself in the predicament of my nurse in respect of having to rule a body of Arab chieftains whose vision was not co-extensive with his own, and who therefore could not be trusted, when his back was turned, to behave as he himself would have behaved spontaneously. He did not tell them that if they did such and such things the cock would come down the chimney. They did not know what a chimney was. But he threatened them with the most disgusting penances in a future life if they did not live according to his word, and promised them very pleasant times if they did. And as they could not understand his inspiration otherwise than as a spoken communication by a personal messenger he allowed them to believe that the angel Gabriel acted as a celestial postman between him and Allah, the fountain of all inspiration. Except in this way he could not have made them believe in anything but sacred stones and the seven deadly sins.

The Christian churches and the Christian Kings were driven to the same device; and when I evolved beyond the cock and chimney stage I found myself possessed with a firm belief that all my Roman Catholic fellow children would inevitably burn in blazing brimstone to all eternity, and even that I myself, in spite of my Protestant advantages, might come to the same endless end if I were not careful. The whole civilized world seemed to be governed that way in those days. It is so to a considerable extent still. A friend of mine lately asked a leading Irish statesman why he did not resort to a rather soulless stroke of diplomacy. Because, replied the statesman, I happen to believe that there is such a place as hell.

Anywhere else than in Ireland the obsolescence of this explanation would have been startling. For somehow there has been a shift of credulity from hell to perishing suns and the like. I am not thinking of the humanitarian revolt against everlasting brimstone voiced by the late Mrs Bradlaugh Bonner, nor of Tolstoy's insistence on the damnation on earth of the undetected, unpunished, materially prosperous criminal. I am leaving out of the question also the thoughtful, sentimental, honorable, conscientious people who need no hell to intimidate them into considerate social behavior, and who have naturally outgrown the devil with his barbed tail and horns just as I outgrew the cock in the chimney.

But what of the people who are capable of no restraint except that of intimidation? Must they not be either restrained or, as the Russians gently put it, liquidated? No State can afford the expense of providing policemen enough to watch them all continually; consequently the restraint must, like the fear of hell, operate when nobody is looking. Well, a shift of credulity has destroyed the old belief in hell. How then is the social work previously done by that belief to be taken up and carried on? It is easy to shirk the problem by pointing out that the belief in hell did not prevent even the most superstitious people from committing the most damnable crimes. But though we know of these failures of infernal terrorism we have no record of its successes. We know that naïve attempts to bribe divine justice led to a trade in absolutions, pardons, and indulgences which proved by the hardness of the cash the sinners put down and the cost of the cathedrals they put up that there was a continual overdrawing of salvation accounts by firm believers in the brimstone; but we do not know, and never shall know, how many crimes were refrained from that would have been committed but for the dread of damnation. All we can do is to observe and grapple with the effect of the shift of credulity which has robbed hell of its terrors.

No community, however devout, has ever trusted wholly to damnation and excommunication as deterrents. They have been supplemented by criminal codes of the most hideous barbarity (I have been contemporary with Europeans whose amusements included seeing criminals broken on the wheel). Therefore their effect on conduct must be looked for in that very extensive part of it which has not been touched by the criminal codes, or in which the codes actually encourage anti-social action and penalize its opposite, as when the citizen is forced by taxation or compulsory military service to become an accomplice in some act of vulgar pugnacity and greed disguised as patriotism.

Unless and until we get a new column in the census papers on the point we can only guess how far the shift of credulity has actually taken place in countries like our own in which children, far from being protected against the inculcation of the belief in brimstone, are exposed to it in every possible way, and are actually, when they have been confirmed, legally subject to ruinous penalties for questioning it. It happens, however, that in one of the largest States in the world, Russia, the children are protected from proselytizing (otherwise than by the State itself). not only by the negative method called Secular Education, but by positive instruction that there is no personal life after death for the individual, the teaching being that of Ecclesiastes in our own canon 'Whatsoever thy hand findeth to do, do it with thy might; for there is no work, nor device, nor knowledge, nor wisdom, in the grave whither thou goest.' We may take it that no civilized Russian born within the last twenty years has any apprehension of having to suffer after death for sins committed before it. At the same time the list of activities blacklisted by the Russian State as felonious has been startlingly extended; for the Russian Government has turned the country's economic morals down-side. up by breaking away from our Capitalist Utopia and adopting instead the views of the Bolshevist prophets whose invectives and warnings fill the last books of the Old Testament, and the Communist principles of Jesus, Peter, and Paul. Not that the Soviet Republic allows the smallest authority to Jesus or Peter, Jeremiah or Micah the Morasthite. They call their economic system, not Bolshevik Christianity, but Scientific Socialism. But as their conclusions are the same, they have placed every Russian under a legal obligation to earn his own living, and made it a capital crime on his part to compel anyone else to do it for him. Now outside Russia the height of honor and success is to be a gentleman or lady, which means that your living is earned for you by other people (mostly untouchables), and that, far from being under an obligation to work, you are so disgraced by the mere suggestion of it that you dare not be seen carrying a parcel along a fashionable thoroughfare. Nobody has ever seen a lady or gentleman carrying a jug of milk down Bond Street or the *rue de la Paix*. A white person doing such a thing in Capetown would be socially ruined. The physical activities called Sport, which are needed to keep the gentry in health, must be unpaid and unproductive: if payment is accepted for such activities the payee loses caste and is no longer called Mister. Labor is held to be a cross and a disgrace; and the lowest rank known is that of laborer. The object of everyone's ambition is an unearned income; and hundreds of millions of the country's income are lavished annually on ladies and gentlemen whilst laborers are underfed, ill clothed, and sleeping two or three in a bed and ten in a room.

Eighteen years ago this anti-labor creed of ours was the established religion of the whole civilized world. Then suddenly, in one seventh of that world, it was declared a damnable heresy, and had to be rooted out like any other damnable heresy. But as the heretics were carefully taught at the same time that there is no such thing as damnation, how were they to be dealt with? The well-to-do British Liberal, clamoring for freedom of conscience, objects to heretics being restrained in any way: his panacea for that sort of difficulty is Toleration. He thinks that Quakers and Ritualists should tolerate one another; and this solution works quite well because it does not now matter a penny to the State or the individual whether a citizen belongs to one persuasion or the other. But it was not always so. George Fox, the heroic founder of the Quakers, could not hear a church bell without dashing into the church and upsetting the service by denouncing the whole business of ritual religion as idolatrous. The bell, he said, 'struck on his heart.' Consequently it was not possible for the Churches to tolerate George Fox, though both Cromwell and Charles II liked the man and admired him.

Now the heretic in Russia is like Fox. He is not content with a quiet abstract dissent from the State religion of Soviet Russia: he is an active, violent, venomous saboteur. He plans and carries out breakages of machinery, falsifies books and accounts to produce insolvencies, leaves the fields unsown or the harvests to rot unreaped, and slaughters farm stock in millions even at the cost of being half starved (sometimes wholly starved) by the resultant 'famine' in his fanatical hatred of a system which makes it impossible for him to become a gentleman. Toleration is impossible: the heretic-saboteur will not tolerate the State religion; consequently the State could not tolerate him even if it wanted to.

This situation, though new to our generation of Liberal plutocrats, is not new historically. The change from paganism and Judaism to Christianity, from the worship of consecrated stones to an exalted monotheism under Mahomet, and from world catholicism to national individualism at the Reformation, all led to the persecution and virtual outlawry of the heretics who would not accept the change. The original official Roman Catholic Church, which had perhaps the toughest job, was compelled to develop a new judicial organ, called the Inquisition or Holy Office, to deal with heresy; and though in all the countries in which the Reformation triumphed the Inquisition became so unpopular that its name was carefully avoided when similar organs were developed by the Protestant and later on by the Secularist governments, yet the Holy Office cropped up again under all sorts of disguises. Protestant England would never have tolerated the Star Chamber if it had called itself an Inquisition and given Laud the official title borne by Torquemada. In the end all the specific Inquisitions petered out, not in the least through a growth of real tolerance, but because, as the world settled down into the new faiths, and the heretics stopped sabotaging and slaughtering, it was found that the ordinary courts could do all the necessary persecution, such as transporting laborers for reading the works of Thomas Paine, or imprisoning poor men for making sceptical jokes about the parthenogenesis of Jesus.

Thus the Inquisition came to be remembered in England only as an obsolete abomination which classed respectable Protestants with Jews, and burned both. Conceive, then, our horror when the Inquisition suddenly rose up again in Russia. It began as the Tcheka; then it became the Gay-pay-oo

(Ogpu); now it has settled down as part of the ordinary police force. The worst of its work is over: the heretics are either liquidated, converted, or intimidated. But it was indispensable in its prime. The Bolsheviks, infected as they were with English Liberal and Agnostic notions, at first tried to do without it; but the result was that the unfortunate Commissars who had to make the Russian industries and transport services work, found themselves obliged to carry pistols and execute saboteurs and lazy drunkards with their own hands. Such a Commissar was Djerjinsky, now, like Lenin, entombed in the Red Square. He was not a homicidally disposed person; but when it fell to his lot to make the Russian trains run at all costs, he had to force himself to shoot a station master who found it easier to drop telegrams into the waste paper basket than to attend to them. And it was this gentle Djerjinsky who, unable to endure the duties of an executioner (even had he had time for them), organized the Tcheka.

Now the Tcheka, being an Inquisition and not an ordinary police court dealing under written statutes and established precedents with defined offences, and sentencing the offenders to prescribed penalties, had to determine whether certain people were public spirited enough to live in a Communist society, and, if not, to blow their brains out as public nuisances. If you would not work and pull your weight in the Russian boat, then the Tcheka had to make you do it by convincing you that you would be shot if you persisted in your determination to be a gentleman. For the national emergencies were then desperate; and the compulsion to overcome them had to be fiercely in earnest.

I, an old Irishman, am too used to Coercion Acts, suspension of the Habeas Corpus Act, and the like, to have any virtuous indignation left to spare for the blunders and excesses into which the original Tcheka, as a body of well intentioned amateurs, no doubt fell before it had learnt the limits of its business by experience. My object in citing it is to draw attention to the legal novelty and importance of its criterion of human worth. I am careful to say legal novelty because of course the criterion must have been used in the world long before St Paul commanded that 'if any would not work, neither should he eat.' But our courts have never taken that Communist view: they have always upheld unconditional property, private property, real property, do-what-you-like-with-your-own property, which, when it is insanely extended to the common earth of the country, means the power to make landless people earn the proprietors' livings for them. Such property places the social value of the proprietor beyond question. The propertyless man may be challenged as a rogue and a vagabond to justify himself by doing some honest work; but if he earns a gentleman's living for him he is at once vindicated and patted on the back. Under such conditions we have lost the power of conceiving ourselves as responsible to society for producing a full equivalent of what we consume, and indeed more. On the contrary, every inducement to shirk that primary duty is continually before us. We are taught to think of an Inquisition as a tribunal which has to decide whether we accept the divinity of Christ or are Jews, whether we believe in transubstantiation or merely in the Supper, whether we are prelatists or Presbyterians, whether we accept the authority of the Church or the conclusions of our private judgments as the interpreters of God's will, whether we believe in a triune godhead or a single one, whether we accept the 39 Articles or the Westminster Confession, and so on. Such were the tests of fitness to live accepted by the old Inquisitions. The public never dreams of an economic test except in the form of a Means Test to baffle the attempts of the very poor to become sinecurists like ladies and gentlemen.

My own acquaintance with such a possibility began early in life and shocked me somewhat. My maternal grandfather, a country gentleman who was an accomplished sportsman, was out shooting one day. His dog, growing old, made a mistake: its first. He instantly shot it. I learnt that he always shot his sporting dogs when they were past their work. Later on I heard of African tribes doing the same with their grand-parents. When I took seriously to economic studies before electric traction had begun I found that tramway companies had found that the most profitable way of exploiting horses was to work them to death in four years. Planters in certain districts had found the like profitable term for slaves to be eight years. In fully civilized life there was no provision except a savagely penal Poor Law for workers thrown out of our industrial establishments as 'too old at forty.'

As I happen to be one of those troublesome people who are not convinced that whatever is is right these things set me thinking. My thoughts would now be attributed to Bolshevik propaganda; and pains would be taken by our rulers to stop propaganda under the impression that this would stop the thoughts; but there was no Bolshevik propaganda in those days; and I can assure the Foreign Office that the landed gentry in the person of my grandfather, the tramway com-panies, and the capitalist planters, made the question of whether individual dogs and men are worth their salt familiar to me a whole generation before the Tcheka ever existed.

It still seems to me a very pertinent question, as I have to pay away about half my earnings in tribute to the lady-and-gentleman business in order to get permission to live on this earth; and I consider it money very ill spent. For if the people who live on my earnings were changed by some Arabian Nights magician into dogs, and handed over to the sporting successors of my grandfather, they would be shot; and if they were changed into horses or slaves they would be worn out by overwork before their natural time. They are now worn out by underwork.

Nevertheless I do not plead a personal grievance, because though I still amuse myself with professional pursuits and make money by them, I also have acquired the position of a gentleman, and live very comfortably on other people's earn-ings to an extent which more than compensates me for the depredations of which I am myself the victim. Now my grandfather's dog had no such satisfaction. Neither had the tram-way horses nor the slaves, nor have the discarded 'too old at forty.' In their case there was no proper account keeping. In the nature of things a human creature must incur a consider-able debt for its nurture and education (if it gets any) before it becomes productive. And as it can produce under modern conditions much more than it need consume it ought to be possible for it to pay off its debt and provide for its old age in addition to supporting itself during its active period. Of course if you assume that it is no use to itself and is there solely to support ladies and gentlemen, you need not bother about this: you can just leave it to starve when it ceases to be useful to its superiors. But if, discarding this view, you assume that a human creature is created for its own use and should have matters arranged so that it shall live as long as it can, then you will have to go into people's accounts and make them all pay their way. We need no Bolshevik propaganda to lead us to this obvious conclusion; but it makes the special inquisitionary work of the Tcheka intelligible. For the Tcheka was simply carrying out the executive work of a constitution which had abolished the lady and gentleman exactly as the Inquisition carried out the executive work of a catholic constitution which had abolished Jupiter and Diana and Venus and Apollo.

Simple enough; and yet so hard to get into our genteel heads that in making a play about it I have had to detach it altogether from the great Russian change, or any of the actual political changes which threaten to raise it in the National-Socialist and Fascist countries, and to go back to the old vision of a day of reckoning by divine justice for all mankind.

Now the ordinary vision of this event is almost pure bugaboo; we see it as a colossal Old Bailey trial, with the good people helped up into heaven and the bad ones cast headlong into hell; but as to what code of law will govern the judgment and classify the judged as sheep or goats as the case may be we have not troubled to ask. We are clear about Judas Iscariot going to hell and Florence Nightingale to heaven; but we are not so sure about Brutus and Cromwell. Our general knowledge of mankind, if we dare bring it into play, would tell us that an immense majority of the prisoners at the bar will be neither saints nor scoundrels, but borderland cases of extreme psychological complexity. It is easy to say that to divine justice nothing is impossible; but the more divine the justice the more difficult it is to conceive how it could deal with every case as one for heaven or hell. But we think we need not bother about it; for the whole affair is thought of as a grand finish to the human race and all its problems, leaving the survivors in a condition of changeless unprogressive bliss or torment for the rest of eternity.

To me this vision is childish; but I must take people's minds as I find them and build on them as best I can. It is no use my telling them that their vision of judgment is a silly superstition, and that there never will be anything of the kind. The only conclusion the pious will draw is that I, at all events, will go to hell. As to the indifferent and the sceptical, I may do them the mischief against which Jesus vainly warned our missionaries. I may root out of their minds the very desirable conception that they are all responsible to divine justice for the use they make of their lives, and put nothing in its place except a noxious conceit in their emancipation and an exultant impulse to abuse it. The substitution of irresponsibility for responsibility may present itself as an advance; but it is in fact a retreat which may leave its victim much less eligible as a member of a civilized community than the crudest Fundamentalist. A prudent banker would lend money on personal security to Bunyan rather than to Casanova. Certainly I should if I were a banker.

Who shall say, then, that an up-to-date Vision of Judgment is not an interesting subject for a play, especially as events in Russia and elsewhere are making it urgently desirable that believers in the Apocalypse should think out their belief a little? In a living society every day is a day of judgment; and its recognition as such is not the end of all things but the beginning of a real civilization. Hence the fable of The Simpleton of the Unexpected Isles. In it I still retain the ancient fancy that the race will be brought to judgment by a supernatural being, coming literally out of the blue; but this inquiry is not whether you believe in Tweedledum or Tweedledee but whether you are a social asset or a social nuisance. And the penalty is liquidation. He has appeared on the stage before in the person of Ibsen's button moulder. And as history always follows the stage, the button moulder came to life as Djerjinsky. My Angel comes a day after the fair; but time enough for our people, who know nothing of the button moulder and have been assured by our gentleman-ladylike newspapers that Djerjinsky was a Thug.

The button moulder is a fiction; and my Angel is a fiction. But the pressing need for bringing us to the bar for an investigation of our personal social values is not a fiction. And Djerjinsky is not a fiction. He found that as there are no button moulders and no angels and no heavenly tribunals available, we must set up earthly ones, not to ascertain whether Mr Everyman in the dock has committed this or that act or holds this or that belief, but whether he or she is a creator of social values or a parasitical consumer and destroyer of them.

Unfortunately the word tribunal immediately calls up visions not only of judgment but of punishment and cruelty. Now there need be no more question of either of these abominations than there was in the case of my grandfather's dog. My grandfather would have been horribly ashamed of himself if the dog's death had not been instantaneous and unanticipated. And the idea of punishment never entered either his mind or the dog's. (Djerjinsky, by the way, is believed to have devised a similar method of painless liquidation.) It may be expedient that one man should die for the people; but it does not follow in the least that he should be tortured or terrified. Public savagery may demand that the law shall torment a criminal who does something very provoking; for the Sermon on The Mount is still a dead letter in spite of all the compliments we pay it. But to blow a man's brains out because he cannot for the life of him see why he should not employ labor at a profit, or buy things solely to sell them again for more than he gave for them, or speculate in currency values: all of them activities which have for centuries enjoyed the highest respectability, is an innovation which should be carried out with the utmost possible delicacy if public opinion is to be quite reconciled to it. We have also to reckon with the instinctive shrinking from outright killing which makes so many people sign petitions for the reprieve of even the worst murderers, and take no further interest if a reprieve decrees that their lives shall be taken by the slow torture of imprisonment. Then we have a mass of people who think that murderers should be judicially killed, but that the lives of the most mischievous criminals should be held sacred provided they do not commit murder. To overcome these prejudices we need a greatly increased intolerance of socially injurious conduct and an uncompromising abandonment of punishment and its cruelties, together with a sufficient school inculcation of social responsibility to make every citizen conscious that if his life costs more than it is worth to the community the community may painlessly extinguish it.

The result of this, however, will finally be a demand for codification. The citizen will say 'I really must know what I may do and what I may not do without having my head shot off.' The reply 'You must keep a credit balance always at the national bank' is sufficiently definite if the national accountancy is trustworthy and compulsory unemployment made impossible. In fact it is so definite that it finally takes the matter out of the hands of the Inquisition and makes an overdraft an ordinary offence to be dealt with by the police. But police measures are not enough. Any intelligent and experienced administrator of the criminal law will tell you that there are people who come up for punishment again and again for the same offence, and that punishing them is a cruel waste of time. There should be an Inquisition always available to consider whether these human nuisances should not be put out of their pain, or out of their joy as the case may be. The community must drive a much harder bargain for the privilege of citizenship than it now does; but it must also make the bargain not only practicable but in effect much easier than the present very imperfect bargain. This involves a new social creed. A new social creed involves a new heresy. A new heresy involves an Inquisition. The precedents established by the Inquisition furnish the material for a new legal code. Codification enables the work of the Inquisition to be done by an ordinary court of law. Thereupon the Inquisition, as such, disappears, precisely as the Tcheka has disappeared. Thus it has always been; and thus it ever shall be.

The moral of the dramatic fable of The Simpleton is now clear enough. With amateur Inquisitions under one name or another or no name at work in all directions, from Fascist *autos-da-fé* to American Vigilance Committees with lynching mobs as torturers and executioners, it is time for us to reconsider our Visions of Judgment, and see whether we cannot change them from old stories in which we no longer believe and new stories which are only too horribly true to serious and responsible public tribunals.

By the way, I had better guard myself against the assumption that because I have introduced into my fable a eugenic experiment in group marriage I am advocating the immediate adoption of that method of peopling the world for immediate practice by my readers. Group marriage is a form of marriage like any other; and it is just as well to remind our western and very insular Imperialists that marriage in the British Empire is startlingly different in the east from marriage in the British Isles; but I have introduced it only to bring into the story the four lovely phantasms who embody all the artistic, romantic, and military ideals of our cultured suburbs. On the Day of Judgment not merely do they cease to exist like the useless and predatory people: it becomes apparent that they never did exist. And, enchanting as they may be to our perfumers, who give us the concentrated odor of the flower without the roots or the clay or even the leaves, let us hope they never will.

On the Indian Ocean, April 1935

PROLOGUE

The emigration office at a tropical port in the British Empire. The office is an annex of the harbor and customs sheds on one side and of the railway station on the other. Placards direct passengers TO THE CUSTOMS *and* TO THE TRAINS *through the open doors right and left respectively. The emigration officer, an unsatisfactory young man of unhealthy habits, is sitting writing at his table in the middle of the room. His clerk is at a standing desk against the wall on the customs side. The officer wears tropical clothes, neither too tidy nor too clean. The clerk is in a shabby dark lounge suit.*

THE E. O. [*finishing his writing*] Is that the lot?

CLERK. It's the lot from the French ship; but there is that case standing over from the Liverpool one.

THE E. O. [*exasperated*] Now look here, Wilks. Are you the emigration officer here or am I? Did I tell you that the girl was to be sent back or did I not?

WILKS. Well I thought –

THE E. O. What business had you to think? I told you she was to go back. I suppose she tipped you to let her come here and make a scene on the chance of getting round me.

WILKS [*hotly*] Youll either take that back or prove it.

THE E. O. I will neither take it back nor prove it until you explain why you are letting this girl bother me again, though she has no papers, no passports, and is in excess of the quota without any excuse for it.

WILKS. Who's letting her bother you again? She told the High Commissioner that you turned her down; and he told her she had better see you again.

THE E. O. And why the devil didnt you tell me that at first, instead of blithering about her as if she was a common case?

WILKS. The High Commissioner's daughter was on the ship coming back from school. He came down to meet her. This girl had made friends with her or taken care of her or something.

THE E. O. Thats no good. We cant let her through on that.

WILKS. Well, will you see her?

THE E. O. Is she waiting to see me?

WILKS. She says she's waiting to see what will happen to her.

THE E. O. Same thing, isnt it?

WILKS. I suppose so. But she put it as if there was a difference. I think she's a bit mad. But the Medical Officer says she passes all his tests of sanity, though I could see that he has his doubts.

THE E. O. Oh, shut up. You need a medical test yourself, I think. Fetch her in.

Wilks goes out sulkily through the customs door and returns with a young woman. He leads her to the table and then goes back to his desk.

THE Y. W. Good morning, sir. You dont look as well as you did yesterday. Did you stay up too late?

THE E. O. [*nonplussed for the moment*] I – er – [*Collecting himself*] Look here, young lady. You have to answer questions here, not to ask them.

THE Y. W. You have been drinking.

THE E. O. [*springing up*] What the hell do you mean?

THE Y. W. You have. I smell it.

THE E. O. Very well. Back you go by the next boat, my lady.

THE Y. W. [*unmoved*] At this hour of the morning too! Dont you know you shouldnt?

THE E. O. [*to Wilks*] Take her away, you. [*To the young woman*] Out you go.

THE Y. W. I ought to speak to somebody about it. And look at the state the office is in! Whose business is it to see that it's properly dusted? Let me talk to them for you.

THE E. O. What concern is it of yours?

THE Y. W. I hate to see dust lying about. Look! You could write your name in it. And it's just awful to see a young man drinking before eleven in the morning.

WILKS [*propitiatory*] Dont say anything about it, Miss: I will see to the dust. Everybody starts the day with a drink here. Dont go talking, Miss, will you?

THE E. O. [*suddenly breaking down in tears*] You can go and tell who you damn well please. For two pins I'd chuck myself into the harbor and have done with it. This climate is hell: you cant stand it unless you drink til you see blue monkeys.

WILKS. Never mind him, Miss: he has nerves. We all have them here sooner or later, off and on. Here! I'll give you a landing ticket; and you just clear off and say nothing. [*He takes a ticket from the table and gives it to her*].

THE E. O. [*weeping*] A man's a slave here worse than a nigger. Spied on, reported on, checked and told off til he's afraid to have a pound note in his pocket or take a glass in his hand for fear of being had up for bribery or drinking. I'm fed up with it. Go and report me and be damned to you: what do I care? [*He sniffs and blows his nose, relieved by his outburst*].

WILKS. Would you have the kindness to clear out, Miss. We're busy. Youre passed all right: nothing to do but shew the ticket. You wont have to go back: we was only joking.

THE Y. W. But I want to go back. If this place is what he says, it is no place for me. And I did so enjoy the voyage out: I ask nothing better than to begin it all over again.

THE E. O. [*with the calm of despair*] Let her have her own way, Wilks. Shew her the way to the ship and shew her the way to the dock gate. She can take which she pleases. But get her out of this or I shall commit suicide.

THE Y. W. Why? Arnt you happy? It's not natural not to be happy. I'd be ashamed not to be happy.

THE E. O. What is there to make a man happy here?

THE Y. W. But you dont need to be made happy.

THE E. O. My inside! Oh Lord!

THE Y. W. Well, you can make your inside all right if you

eat properly and stop drinking and keep the office dusted and your nice white clothes clean and tidy. You two are a disgrace.

THE E. O. [*roaring with rage*] Chuck that woman out.

WILKS. Chuck her yourself. What can *I* do? [*Imploringly to her*] If youd only have the goodness to go, Miss. We're so busy this morning.

THE Y. W. But I am a stranger here: I have nobody else to talk to. And you have nothing to do until the next boat comes in.

THE E. O. The next boat is due the day after tomorrow at five in the afternoon. Do you expect us to sit here talking to you until then?

THE Y. W. Well, it's I who have to do most of the talking, isnt it? Couldnt you shew me round the town? I'll pay for the taxi.

THE E. O. [*feebly rebellious*] Look here: you cant go on like this, you know.

THE Y. W. What were you going to do with yourself this morning if I hadnt come?

THE E. O. I – I – Whats that to you?

THE Y. W. I see you hadnt made up your mind. Let me make it up for you. Put on your hat and come along and shew me round. I seem to spend my life making up other people's minds for them.

THE E. O. [*helplessly*] All right, all right, all right. You neednt make a ballyhoo about it. But I ask myself –

THE Y. W. Dont ask yourself anything, my child. Let life come to you. March.

THE E. O. [*at the railway door, to Wilks, in a last effort to assert himself*] Carry on, you. [*He goes*].

THE Y. W. Wouldnt you like to come too?

WILKS. Yes, Miss: but somebody must stay in the office; and it had better be me than him. I am indispensable.

THE Y. W. What a word! Dispensables and indispensables: there you have the whole world. I wonder am I a dispensable or an indispensable. [*She goes out through the railway door*].

WILKS [*alone*] Let life come to you. Sounds all right, that. Let life come to you. Aye; but suppose life doesnt come to you! Look at me! What am I? An empire builder: thats what I am by nature. Cecil Rhodes: thats me. Why am I a clerk with only two shirts to my back, with that young waster wiping his dirty boots on me for doing the work he cant do himself, though he gets all the praise and all the pudding? Because life never came to me like it came to Rhodes. Found his backyard full of diamonds, he did; and nothing to do but wash the clay off them and be a millionaire. I had Rhodes's idea all right. Let the whole earth be England, I said to the school teacher; and let Englishmen govern it. Nobody put that into my head: it came of itself. But what did I find in my backyard? Next door's dead cat. Could I make myself head of a Chartered Company with a dead cat? And when I threw it back over the wall my mother said 'You have thrown away your luck, my boy' she says 'you shouldnt have thrown it back: you should have passed it on, like a chain letter. Now you will never have no more luck in this world.' And no more I have. I says to her 'I'll be in the papers yet some day' I says 'like Cecil Rhodes: you see if I'm not.' 'Not you, my lad' she says. 'Everything what comes to you you throw it back.' Well, so I do. Look at this girl here. 'Come with me' she says. And I threw the cat back again. 'Somebody must be left in the office' I says. 'I am indispensable' I says. And all the time I knew that nobody neednt be in the office, and that any Jew boy could do all I do here and do it better. But I promised my mother I'd get into the papers; and I will. I have that much of the Rhodes touch in me. [*He sits at the table and writes on a luggage label; then reads what he has written*] 'Here lies a man who might have been Cecil Rhodes if he had had Rhodes's luck. Mother, farewell: your son has kept his word.' [*He ties the label to the lapel of his coat*] Wheres that fool's gun? [*He opens a drawer and takes out a brandy flask and an automatic pistol, which he throws on the table*]. I'll damned well shew em whether I'm an empire builder or not. That lassie shant say that I didnt leave the place tidy either, though she can write in the dust of it with her finger. [*He shuts the drawer, and places the chair trimly at the table. Then he goes to his desk and takes out a duster, with which he wipes first the desk and then the table. He replaces the duster in the desk, and takes out a comb and a hand mirror. He tidies his hair; replaces the comb and glass in the desk; closes it and sets the stool in its place before it. He then returns to the table, and empties the flask at a draught*]. Now for it. The back of the head: thats the Russian touch. [*He takes the pistol and presents it over his shoulder to his occiput*]. Let the whole earth be England; and let Englishmen rule it. [*Singing*] Rule Britannia: Britannia rules the wa –

He blows his brains out and falls dead. The Station Master enters.

THE STATION MASTER. Here! Who's been shooting here? [*He sees the body*] Wilks!! Dear! dear! dear! What a climate! The fifth this month. [*He goes to the door*]. Hallo there, Jo. Bring along the stretcher and two or three with you. Mr Wilks has shot himself.

JO [*without, cheerfully*] Right you are, sir.

THE STATION MASTER. What a climate! Poor old Wilks!

SCENE II

A grassy cliff top overhanging the sea. A seat for promenaders. The young woman and the emigration officer stand on the brink.

THE Y. W. Pity theres no beach. We could bathe.

THE E. O. Not us. Not likely. Theres sharks there. And killer whales, worse than any sharks.

THE Y.. W. It looks pretty deep.

THE E. O. I should think it is. The biggest liners can get close up. Like Plymouth. Like Lulworth Cove. Dont stand so close. Theres a sort of fascination in it; and you might get giddy.

They come away from the edge and sit on the seat together: she on his left, he nearest the sea.

THE Y. W. It's lovely here. Better than the town.

THE E. O. Dont deceive yourself. It's a horrible place. The climate is something terrible. Do you know that if you hadnt come in this morning I'd have done myself in.

THE Y. W. Dont talk nonsense. Why should you do yourself in?

THE E. O. Yes I should. I had the gun ready in the drawer of that table. I'd have shot Wilks and then shot myself.

THE Y. W. Why should you shoot poor Wilks? What has he done?

THE E. O. I hate him. He hates me. Everybody here hates everybody else. And the fellow is so confoundedly smug and happy and satisfied: it drives me mad when I can hardly bear my own life. No fear of him shooting himself: not much. So I thought I'd save him the trouble.

THE Y. W. But that would be murder.

THE E. O. Not if I shot myself after. That would make us quits.

THE Y. W. Well, I am surprised to hear a young man like you, in the prime of life as you might say, talking like that. Why dont you get married?

THE E. O. My salary's too small for a white woman. Theyre all snobs; and they want a husband only to take them home out of this.

THE Y. W. Why, it's an earthly paradise.

THE E. O. Tell them so; and see what theyll say to you.

THE Y. W. Well, why not marry a colored woman?

THE E. O. You dont know what youre talking about. Ive tried. But now theyre all educated they wont look at a white man. They tell me I'm ignorant and that I smell bad.

THE Y. W. Well, so you do. You smell of drink and indigestion and sweaty clothes. You were quite disgusting when you tried to make up to me in the taxi. Thats why I got out, and made for the sea air.

THE E. O. [*rising hurriedly*] I cant stand any more of this. [*He takes a wallet of papers from his breast pocket and throws them on the seat*]. Hand them in at the office, will you: theyll be wanted there. I am going over.

He makes for the edge of the cliff. But there is a path down the cliff face, invisible from the seat. A native priest, a handsome man in the prime of life, beautifully dressed, rises into view by this path and bars his way.

PRIEST. Pardon, son of empire. This cliff contains the temple of the goddess who is beyond naming, the eternal mother, the seed and the sun, the resurrection and the life. You must not die here. I will send an acolyte to guide you to the cliff of death, which contains the temple of the goddess's brother, the weeder of the garden, the sacred scavenger, the last friend on earth, the prolonger of sleep and the giver of rest. It is not far off: life and death dwell close together: you need prolong your unhappiness only a bare five minutes. The priest there will attend to your remains and see they are disposed of with all becoming rites.

THE E. O. [*to the young woman*] Is he real; or is it the drink?

THE Y. W. He's real. And, my word! isnt he jolly good looking? [*To the priest*] Youll excuse this young man, sir, wont you? He's been drinking pretty hard.

THE PRIEST [*advancing between them*] Blame him not, sweet one. He comes from a strange mad country where the young are taught languages that are dead and histories that are lies, but are never told how to eat and drink and clothe themselves and reproduce their species. They worship strange ancient gods; and they play games with balls marvellously well; but of the great game of life they are ignorant. Here, where they are in the midst of life and loveliness, they die by their own hands to escape what they call the horrors. We do not encourage them to live. The empire is for those who can live in it, not for those who can only die in it. Take your friend to the cliff of death; and bid him farewell tenderly; for he is very unhappy.

THE E. O. Look here: I am an Englishman; and I shall commit suicide where I please. No nigger alive shall dictate to me.

THE PRIEST. It is forbidden.

THE E. O. Who's to stop me? Will you?

The priest shakes his head and makes way for him.

THE Y. W. Oh, you are not going to let him do it, are you?

THE PRIEST [*holding her back*] We never offer violence to the unhappy. Do not interfere with his destiny.

THE E. O. [*planting himself on the edge and facing the abyss*] I am going to do it: see? Nobody shall say that I lived a dog's life because I was afraid to make an end of it. [*He bends his knees to spring, but cannot*]. I WILL. [*He makes another effort, bending almost to his haunches, but again fails to make the spring-up a spring-over*].

THE PRIEST. Poor fellow! Let me assist you. [*He shoots his foot against the E. O.'s posterior and sends him off the cliff*].

THE E. O. [*in a tone of the strongest remonstrance as he is catapulted into the void*] Oh! [*A prodigious splash*].

THE Y. W. Murderer!

THE PRIEST. Not quite. There are nets below, and a palisade to keep out the sharks. The shock will do him good.

THE Y. W. Well, I never!

THE PRIEST. Come, young rose blossom, and feast with us in the temple.

THE Y. W. Not so much rose blossom, young man. Are there any priestesses down there?

THE PRIEST. Of course. How can men feast without women?

THE Y. W. Well, let life come to you I always say; and dont cry out until youre hurt. After you, sir.

They descend.

SCENE III

A shelf of rock half way down the cliff forms an esplanade between the sea and a series of gigantic images of oriental deities in shallow alcoves cut in the face of the wall of rock. A feast of fruit and bread and soft drinks is spread on the ground. The young woman is sitting at it between the priest on her right nearest the sea and a very handsome young native priestess in robes of dusky yellow silk on her left nearest the images.

THE Y. W. You know, to me this is a funny sort of lunch. You begin with the dessert. We begin with the entrées. I suppose it's all right; but I have eaten so much fruit and stuff that I dont feel I want any meat.

THE PRIEST. We shall not offer you any. We dont eat it.

THE Y. W. Then how do you keep up your strength?

THE PRIEST. It keeps itself up.

THE Y. W. Oh, how could that be? [*To the priestess*] You wouldnt like a husband that didnt eat plenty of meat, would you? But then youre a priestess; so I suppose it doesnt matter to you, as you cant marry.

THE PRIESTESS. I am married.

THE Y. W. Oh! And you a priestess!

THE PRIESTESS. I could not be a priestess if I were not married. How could I presume to teach others without a completed human experience? How could I deal with children if I were not a mother?

THE Y. W. But that isnt right. My sister was a teacher; but when she married they took her job away from her and wouldnt let her teach any more.

THE PRIESTESS. The rulers of your country must be mad.

THE Y. W. Oh no. Theyre all right: just like other people. [*To the priest*] I say, reverend. What about the poor lad you kicked over the cliff? Is he really safe? I dont feel easy about him.

THE PRIEST. His clothes are drying in the sun. They will

lend him some clothes and send him up here as soon as he has recovered from his ducking.

An English lady tourist, Baedeker in hand, has wandered in, trying to identify the images with the aid of her book. She now comes behind the seated group and accosts the priest.

THE L. T. Excuse me; but can you tell me which of these figures is the principal god?

THE PRIEST [*rising courteously*] The principal one? I do not understand.

THE L. T. I get lost among all these different gods: it is so difficult to know which is which.

THE PRIEST. They are not different gods. They are all god.

THE L. T. But how can that be? The figures are different.

THE PRIEST. God has many aspects.

THE L. T. But all these names in the guide book?

THE PRIEST. God has many names.

THE L. T. Not with us, you know.

THE PRIEST. Yes: even with you. The Father, the Son, the Spirit, the Immaculate Mother

THE L. T. Excuse me. We are not Catholics.

THE PRIESTESS [*sharply*] Are your temples then labelled 'For men only'?

THE L. T. [*shocked*] Oh, really! So sorry to have troubled you. [*She hurries away*].

THE PRIEST [*resuming his seat*] You should not be rude to the poor lady. She is English, and doesnt understand.

THE PRIESTESS. I find these heathen idolaters very trying. Is it really kind to treat them according to their folly instead of to our wisdom?

THE Y. W. Here! Steady on, you. Who are you calling heathen idolaters? Look at all those images. I should say, if you ask me, that the boot is on the other leg.

THE PRIEST. Those images are not idols: they are personifications of the forces of nature by which we all live. But of course to an idolater they are idols.

THE Y. W. You talk a lot about religion here. Cant you think of something livelier? I always say let life come to you; and dont bother about religion.

THE PRIESTESS. An excellent rule. But the more you let life come to you, the more you will find yourself bothering about religion.

The Emigration Officer rises into view in a spotless white robe. He is clean and rather pale, but looks regenerated.

THE Y. W. Oh boy, you do look the better for your dip. Why, he's an angel, a lamb. What have you done to him?

THE E. O. [*seating himself at the end of the table with his back to the sea*] Well, if you want to know, this blighter kicked me into the sea; and when I'd swallowed a ton or two of your best salt water they fished me out in a net and emptied me out. I brought up my immortal soul. They gave me what I thought was a nice cup of their tea to settle my stomach; but it made me ten times as sick as I was before. Theres nothing of the man you met this morning left except his skin and bones. You may regard me as to all intents and purposes born again.

THE PRIEST. Do you still wish to kill yourself?

THE E. O. When you have been through what I have been through since they fished me out of the water you wont worry about trifles as I used to, old man.

THE Y. W. Thats right. Let life come to you, I always say.

THE E. O. Yes, let life come. The premises are quite empty.

THE LADY TOURIST [*returning and addressing the priest*] Excuse me; but I have been thinking so much about you since you spoke to me. Would you mind accepting and reading this little tract?

THE PRIEST [*rising and coming forward to her, meanwhile reading the title with a polite show of interest*] 'Where will you spend eternity?'

THE L. T. [*strangely moved*] I have been haunted by your face. I could not bear to think of your spending eternity in torment. I feel sure it is a Christian face.

THE PRIEST. It is very kind of you. I will read the tract with the greatest attention. Thank you.

The lady, having no excuse for staying, moves away reluctantly towards the images.

THE PRIESTESS [*calling after her imperiously*] Where have you spent eternity so far, may I ask? That which has no end can have no beginning?

THE L. T. Excuse me: I have no desire to speak to you.

THE Y. W. [*indicating the priest*] Fallen in love with him, have you? Well, let yourself rip. Let life come to you.

THE L. T. Oh! How dare you? Really! Really!! [*She goes out indignantly*].

THE PRIESTESS. Another conquest, Pra?

THE Y. W. Is his name Pra?

THE PRIESTESS. He has many names; but he answers to Pra when you call him.

THE Y. W. Oh, what a way to put it! The man isnt a dog, is he?

THE PRIESTESS. He inspires a doglike devotion in women. He once did in me; so I know.

THE PRIEST. Dont be vindictive, Prola. I dont do it on purpose. [*He sits down again, this time next to her on her left*].

THE PRIESTESS. No: you do it by instinct. That, also, is rather doglike.

THE PRIEST. No matter: I shall soon get the poor lady beyond the doglike stage.

THE E. O. [*who has been unable to take his eyes off the priestess*] Is your name Prola?

THE PRIEST. She has many names: some of them terrible ones; but she answers to Prola when you call her.

THE PRIESTESS. Young man: are my eyes like the fishpools of Heshbon?

THE E. O. Well, I have never seen the fishpools of Heshbon; but your eyes make me feel like that.

THE Y. W. Seems to me theres some sort of magic about this old cave thats dangerous. If you dont mind, I'll bid you all good morning. I always say let life come to you;

but here it's coming a bit too thick for me. [*She rises*].

THE PRIESTESS. Wait. We can share him.

THE Y. W. Well I never! [*She flops back into her seat, flabbergasted*].

THE PRIESTESS. Hush. Look.

The Lady Tourist returns and again goes to the priest.

THE L. T. Excuse me; but could I have a word with you alone?

THE PRIEST [*rising*] Certainly. Come with me.

They go into the caves together.

THE E. O. What about a word with me alone, Prola?

THE Y. W. [*with redoubled emphasis*] Well I NEVER!!

THE PRIESTESS [*to the Officer*] You are not yet sufficiently regenerated. But you may hope.

THE Y. W. You take care, boy. I think youve got a touch of the sun. You cant be too careful in the tropics.

An English male tourist enters from among the images. He is on the young side of middle age, with pleasant aristocratic appearance and manners.

THE M. T. Excuse me: I have mislaid my wife. English lady with a guide book. Wears glasses. Bi-focals.

THE Y. W. Her husband! Oh, I say!

THE E. O. [*rising deferentially*] Just left us, Sir Charles.

THE M. T. Hallo! Weve met before, I think, havnt we?

THE E. O. When you landed, Sir Charles. I am the emigration officer.

SIR CHARLES. Ah, of course: yes. You know Lady Farwaters by sight. Which way did she go?

THE E. O. I am sorry: I didnt notice.

SIR CHARLES [*worried*] I wonder what she can be doing.

THE Y. W. So do I.

SIR CHARLES. I beg your pardon?

THE Y. W. Granted.

THE PRIESTESS [*rising and coming to him*] May I shew you round the temple, Sir Charles? We shall probably find her there.

SIR CHARLES [*who has not yet hitherto looked particularly at her*] No thank you, no, no.

THE PRIESTESS. It is interesting. I am not a professional guide: I am a priestess; and I will see that you are not asked for anything. You had better come with me.

SIR CHARLES. No: I — [*he looks at her. His tone changes instantly*]. Well, yes, if you will be so good. Certainly. Thank you.

They go into the alcoves together.

THE Y. W. [*leaving the table*] Oh boy, what do you think of this abode of love? Lady Farwaters, as white as Canterbury veal, has fallen for a brown bishop; and her husband, the whitest English west-end white, has been carried off to her den by an amber colored snake charmer. Lets get out of it while we're safe.

THE E. O. I feel quite safe, thank you. I have been cleaned up. You havnt.

THE Y. W. What do you mean, I havnt?

THE E. O. I mean that you were quite right to object to me half an hour ago. Your offensive personal remarks were fully justified. But now the tables are turned. I havnt gone through the fire; but Ive gone through the water. And the water has gone through me. It is for me now to object and to make personal remarks.

THE Y. W. Make as much as one; and you will get your face smacked.

THE E. O. [*seizing her by the wrist and the back of her collar*] Go and get cleaned up, you disgusting little devil. [*He rushes her to the edge*].

THE Y. W. [*screaming*] No.

THE E. O. Yes. [*He hurls her over*].

A scream cut short by a splash. The E. O. sits down at the table and attacks the remains of the feast ravenously.

THE PROLOGUE ENDS

ACT I

The lawn of a stately house on the north coast of a tropical island in the Pacific commands a fine view of the ocean and of a breakwater enclosing a harbor, large enough to accommodate a fleet, but at present shipless. The western face of the house is reached by a terrace and a flight of steps. The steps lead down to a crescent formed by two curved stone seats separated by a patch of sward surrounding a circular well with a low marble parapet. This parapet, like the stone seats, has silk cushions scattered about it.

Behind the crescent the lawn is banked to a higher level and becomes a flower garden, sheltered from the wind by shrubberies. To the west of the flower garden the lawn falls away to the sea, but not to sea level, all that is visible of the port being the top of the lighthouse. There are trees enough in all directions to provide shade everywhere.

However, the raised flower garden is the centre of interest; for in it are four shrines marking the corners of a square. In the two foremost shrines two girl-goddesses sit crosslegged. In the two further ones two youthful gods are sitting in the same fashion. The ages of the four appear to be between 17 and 20. They are magically beautiful in their Indian dresses, softly brilliant, making the tropical flowers of the garden seem almost crude beside them. Their expressions are intent, grave, and inscrutable. They face south with their backs to the sea. The goddess to the east has raven black hair, a swarthy skin, and robes of a thousand shades of deep carnation, in contrast to the younger one on her right, who is a ravishing blonde in a diaphanous white and gold sari. There is a parallel contrast between the two youths, the one on the west being the younger and more delicate, and the one on his left older and more powerfully framed.

The four figures give the garden a hieratic aspect which has its effect on a young English clergyman, who wanders into the grounds at the north west corner, looking curiously and apprehensively about him with the air of a stranger who is trespassing. When he catches sight of the four figures he starts nervously and whips off his hat; then approaches them on tiptoe. He has a baby complexion, and a childish expression, credulous and disarmingly propitiatory. His age is at most 24.

Down the steps at this moment comes Pra, about twenty years older than when we saw him last, but splendidly preserved. His approach is dignified and even courteous, though not warmly so. He evidently wants to know what the stranger is doing in his garden.

THE CLERGYMAN [*nervously, hat in hand*] I beg your pardon. I fear I am trespassing. I am a stranger here; and I could not find a road up from the beach. I thought I might cut across through your grounds. [*Indicating the figures*] But I assure you I had no idea I was intruding on consecrated ground.

PRA. You are not on consecrated ground, except in so far as all ground is consecrated.

THE CLERGYMAN. Oh, excuse me. I thought -- those idols --

PRA. Idols!

THE CLERGYMAN. No, of course not idols. I meant those gods and goddesses --

PRA. They are very beautiful, are they not? [*He speaks without awe or enthusiasm, with a touch of pity for the parson and weariness on his own part*].

THE CLERGYMAN. They are most beautiful. Quite marvelous even to me, an English clergyman. I can hardly wonder at your worshipping them, though of course you shouldnt.

PRA. Beauty is worshipful, within limits. When you have worshipped your fill may I shew you the shortest way out? It is through the house. Where do you wish to go, by the way?

THE CLERGYMAN. I dont know. I am lost.

PRA. Lost?

THE CLERGYMAN. Yes, quite lost. I dont know where I am. I mean I dont even know what country I am in.

PRA. You are in the Unexpected Isles, a Crown Colony of the British Empire.

THE CLERGYMAN. Do you mean the isles that came up out of the sea when I was a baby.

PRA. Yes. [*Pointing to the breakwater*] That is the harbor of the port of Good Adventure.

THE CLERGYMAN. They put me on shore there.

PRA. Who put you on shore?

THE CLERGYMAN. The pirates.

PRA. Pirates!

THE CLERGYMAN. Yes. I was their chaplain.

PRA. You were their – ! [*He turns to the house and calls*] Prola. Prola.

PROLA'S VOICE. Yes. What is it?

PRA. Come out here.

> *Prola comes down the steps. She, like Pra, is twenty years older; but the years have only made her beauty more impressive.*

THE CLERGYMAN [*gaping at her in undisguised awe and admiration*] Oh dear! Is this the lady of the house?

PROLA [*coming past Pra to the Clergyman*] Who is this gentleman?

PRA. He does not seem to know. I think he has escaped from the asylum.

THE CLERGYMAN [*distressed*] Oh, dear beautiful lady, I am not mad. Everybody thinks I am. Nobody believes what I say, though it is the simple truth. I know it is very hard to believe.

PROLA. In the Unexpected Isles nothing is unbelievable. How did you get in here?

THE CLERGYMAN. I lost my way trying to find a short cut up from the beach. I climbed the fence. I am so sorry.

PROLA. Really sorry?

THE CLERGYMAN. I did not mean to intrude. I apologize most sincerely.

PROLA. I did not ask you to apologize: you are quite welcome. I asked were you really sorry. Do you regret finding yourself in this garden?

THE CLERGYMAN. Oh no. It's like the Garden of Eden: I

should like to stay here forever. [*Suddenly breaking down to the verge of tears*] I have nowhere to go.

PROLA. Perhaps he is weak with hunger.

THE CLERGYMAN. No: it's not that. I have been under a great strain for a long time; and now that I have escaped – and the beauty of those four – and your lovely awfulness – and – oh [*collapsing on the stone seat*] I am making a fool of myself. I always make a fool of myself. Dont mind me.

PRA. He thinks he has been chaplain in a pirate ship.

THE CLERGYMAN [*rising in desperate protest*] But I have. I have. They kidnapped me at Weston Super Mare where I was doing locum tenens for the Rector of Saint Biddulphs. It was on a Sunday afternoon: I had my clerical clothes on after taking the afternoon service. 'You look so innocent and respectable' they said. 'Just what we want!' They took me all over the world, where I couldnt speak the language and couldnt explain.

PRA. And they wanted you to minister to them spiritually?

THE CLERGYMAN. No no: that was what was so dreadful. They were crooks, racketeers, smugglers, pirates, anything that paid them. They used me to make people believe that they were respectable. They were often so bored that they made me hold a service and preach; but it was only to make themselves ill laughing at me. Though perhaps I shouldnt say that. Some of them were such dear nice fellows: they assured me it did them no end of good. But they got tired of me and put me ashore here. [*He again resorts to the stone seat, clasping his temples distractedly*] Oh dear! oh dear! nothing ever happens to me that happens to other people. And all because I was not a natural baby. I was a nitrogen baby.

PROLA. A nitrogen baby!

PRA [*to Prola*] Steady. There may be something in this. [*He goes to the clergyman and sits down beside him*] What do you mean by a nitrogen baby?

THE CLERGYMAN. You see, my father is a famous biological chemist.

PROLA. I do not see. Your father may be a biological chemist; but biological chemists' children are like other people's children.

THE CLERGYMAN. No. No, I assure you. Not my father's children. You dont know my father. Even my Christian name is Phosphor.

PRA. Is what?

THE CLERGYMAN. Phosphor. [*He spells it*] P.H.O.S.P.H. O.R. The name of the morning star. Phosphorus, you know. The stuff they make matches with. Such a name to baptize a boy by! Please dont call me by it.

PRA. Come come! Neither your father nor your godfathers and godmothers could change your human nature by giving you an unusual name in baptism.

THE CLERGYMAN. But it wasnt only the name. My father fed our cow on nitrogen grass.

PRA. Nitrogen gas, you mean.

THE CLERGYMAN. No: nitrogen grass. Some sort of grass that came up when he sprinkled our fields with chemicals. The cows ate it; and their butter was very yellow and awfully rich. So was the milk. I was fed on that sort of milk and butter. And the wheat in my bread was grown from special nitrates that my father made.

PRA [*to Prola*] I believe he is not mad after all.

THE CLERGYMAN. I assure you I am not. I am weak minded; but I am not mad.

PRA. I have read some very interesting articles about this by an English chemist named Hammingtap.

THE CLERGYMAN. Thats my father. My name is Hammingtap. The old family name is Hummingtop; but my grandfather changed it when he was at Oxford.

PRA. Prola: our young friend here may really be a new sort of man. Shall we go in and tell the others about him? We might take him into the family for a while, as an experiment.

THE CLERGYMAN [*alarmed*] Oh please, no. Why does everyone want to make an experiment of me?

PROLA. All men and women are experiments. What is your religion?

THE CLERGYMAN. The Christian religion, of course. I am a clergyman.

PROLA. What is the Christian religion?

THE CLERGYMAN. Well, it is — well, I suppose it is the Christian religion. I thought everybody knew. But then of course you are a heathen.

PROLA. What does the Christian religion mean to you?

THE CLERGYMAN. Oh, to me it means everything that is good and lovely and kind and holy. I dont profess to go any further than that.

PROLA. You need not. You had better not. Wait here until we return. We may find some use for you. Come, Pra.

She goes up the steps into the house, followed by Pra. The Clergyman, left with the four figures, looks at them, looks round to make sure that nobody is watching. Then he steals up to the fair goddess.

THE CLERGYMAN. Oh, how lovely you are! How I wish you were alive and I could kiss your living lips instead of the paint on a hard wooden image. I wonder is it idolatry to adore you? St Peter in Rome is only a bronze image; but his feet have been worn away by the kisses of Christian pilgrims. You make me feel as I have never felt before. I must kiss you. [*He does so and finds that she is alive. She smiles as her eyes turn bewitchingly towards him*]. Oh!!! [*He stands gasping, palpitating*].

THE ELDER YOUTH. Beware.

THE YOUNGER. On guard.

THE FAIR GIRL. Let him worship. His lips are sweet and pure.

THE DARK ONE. 'For he on honey dew hath fed' —

THE FAIR ONE. — 'and drunk the milk of paradise.'

THE DARK ONE. I, Vashti, can see his aura. It is violet.

THE FAIR ONE. I, Maya, can see his halo. It is silvery.

VASHTI. Blessed are the shining ones!

MAYA. Blessed are the simple ones!

THE ELDER YOUTH. Beware. I, Janga, warn thee.

THE YOUNGER YOUTH. On guard. I, Kanchin, shew thee the red light.

JANGA. Their eyebrows are drawn bows.

KANCHIN. Their arrows feel sweet in the heart –

JANGA. – but are deadly.

KANCHIN. The ground within reach of their arms is enchanted.

JANGA. Vashti is lovely even to her brothers.

KANCHIN. Little children would die for Maya.

JANGA. Beware.

KANCHIN. On guard.

JANGA. Trust them not.

KANCHIN. They will break thy spear.

JANGA. They will pierce thy shield.

VASHTI. Fear not, beginner: I will strengthen thee.

MAYA. Strive not, beloved: I will keep thy soul for thee.

THE 2 YOUTHS [*together, fortissimo*] Beware.

> *The two girl-goddesses suddenly and simultaneously spring from their shrines and march down upon him, Vashti to his left, Maya to his right.*

VASHTI. Dare you tread the plains of heaven with us, young pilgrim?

MAYA. We are waves of life in a sea of bliss. Dare you breast them, young swimmer?

THE CLERGYMAN. Oh, I dont know whether you are gods and goddesses or real people. I only know that you fill my heart with inexpressible longings.

MAYA. We are the awakening.

VASHTI. We are the way.

MAYA. We are the life.

VASHTI. I am the light. Look at me. [*She throws her arm round him and turns his face to hers*].

MAYA. I am the fire. Feel how it glows [*She also throws her arm round him*].

Lady Farwaters comes from the house, and pauses at the top of the steps to take in what is going on.

THE CLERGYMAN. Oh, one at a time, please.

VASHTI. Perfect love casteth out choice.

MAYA. In love there is neither division nor measure.

LADY FARWATERS [*rushing to him and dragging him away from them*] Stop it, children: you are driving the man mad. Go away, all of you.

The two youths spring from their pedestals and whirl the girls away through the shrubberies.

VASHTI [*invisible, calling*] I will return in dreams.

MAYA [*similarly*] I leave my arrow in your heart.

LADY FARWATERS. You mustnt mind them.

Prola and Pra come down the steps, followed by Sir Charles Farwaters and by Hugo Hyering C.B. and Mrs Hyering. Hyering is the former emigration officer, now an elderly and very different man, disciplined, responsible and well groomed. His wife is the emigrant girl twenty years older and better drilled socially, but still very much her old self. Lady Farwaters, once a gaunt and affected tourist visiting cave temples and distributing tracts to the heathen, is now a bland and attractive matron.

PRA. Mr Hammingtap: let me introduce you to the Governor of the Unexpected Isles, Sir Charles Farwaters.

SIR CHARLES [*offering his hand*] How do you do, Mr Hammingtap?

THE CLERGYMAN [*jerkily nervous*] Very pleased. [*They shake hands*].

Sir Charles sits down in the middle of the stone seat nearest the steps.

PRA. Lady Farwaters.

LADY FARWATERS [*smiles and proffers her hand*]!

THE CLERGYMAN. Most kind – er. [*He shakes*].

Lady Farwaters sits down in the middle of the other stone seat.

PRA. This is Mr Hugo Hyering, political secretary to the Isles.

THE CLERGYMAN. How do you do, Sir Hugo?

HYERING [*shaking hands*] Not Sir Hugo. [*Introducing*] Mrs. Hyering.

MRS HYERING [*shaking hands*] C.B., in case you are addressing a letter. [*She sits down on Sir Charles's left*].

THE CLERGYMAN. Oh, I am so sorry.

HYERING. Not at all. [*He sits on Lady Farwaters' right*].

PRA [*indicating the parapet of the well*] You had better sit here.

THE CLERGYMAN [*sitting down as directed*] Thank you.
   Prola sits down on Sir Charles's left, and Pra on Lady Farwaters' left.

LADY FARWATERS. You have made the acquaintance of our four children, Mr Hammingtap?

THE CLERGYMAN. I couldnt help it. I mean –

PROLA. We know what you mean. You need not explain.

THE CLERGYMAN. But I assure you I – that is –

MRS HYERING. Dont apologize, Mr Hammingtap. We know quite well what our daughters are capable of when they are attracted by a young stranger.

THE CLERGYMAN. I did not understand. They are so sunburnt, and their dresses are so eastern: I thought they were orientals.

SIR CHARLES. They are half orientals. You see, the family is a mixed one. This lady, whom you may address as Prola, and this gentleman, known as Pra, are both entirely oriental, and very dominant personalities at that; so that naturally our children would have a strong oriental strain, would they not?

THE CLERGYMAN [*hastily*] Oh, of course. Quite. Certainly. [*He looks piteously at their gracious unconcerned faces, which tell him nothing*]. I beg your pardon. I am frightfully sorry; but my nerves are in rags; and I cannot follow what you are saying.

HYERING. Oh yes you can. It's all right: you have understood perfectly.

MRS HYERING. Buck up, Mr Hammingtap. Let life come to you.

LADY FARWATERS. Our family arrangements are not those usual in England. We are making a little domestic experiment –

THE CLERGYMAN. Oh, not an experiment, I hope. Chemical experiments are bad enough: I am one myself; but they are scientific. I dont think I could countenance a domestic experiment. And in spite of what you say I am not sure that I am not going mad.

SIR CHARLES. We are distracting you. Let us change the subject. Would you like to be a bishop?

THE CLERGYMAN. Oh dear! Can you make me one?

SIR CHARLES. Well, my recommendation would probably be decisive. A bishop is needed here: a bishop in partibus infidelium. Providence seems to have thrown you on this shore for the purpose, like Jonah. Will you undertake it?

THE CLERGYMAN. I should like to have a bishop's salary, certainly. But unfortunately I am weakminded.

SIR CHARLES. Many bishops are; and they are the best sort. A strongminded bishop is a horror.

THE CLERGYMAN. I am too young.

SIR CHARLES. You will not remain so. Most bishops are too old.

THE CLERGYMAN [tempted] It would be rather a lark, wouldnt it?

MRS HYERING. Thats right, Mr Hammingtap: let life come to you.

PRA. What objection have you to be a bishop?

THE CLERGYMAN. Oh, none, I assure you. Of course no clergyman could object to be a bishop. But why do you want to make me one?

SIR CHARLES. I will be quite frank with you, Mr Hammingtap. Twenty years ago my wife and I, with Mr and Mrs Hyering, joined this eastern gentleman and his colleague in a eugenic experiment. Its object was to try out the result of a biological blend of the flesh and spirit of the west with the flesh and spirit of the east. We formed a family of six parents.

THE CLERGYMAN. Six?

SIR CHARLES. Yes, six. The result has been a little disappointing from the point of view of numbers; but we have produced four children, two of each sex, and educated them in the most enlightened manner we were capable of. They have now grown up; consequently the time has arrived when the family group must be extended by young persons of their own age, so that the group may produce a second generation. Now sooner or later this extension of the family group will set people talking.

THE CLERGYMAN. It would strike my people dumb, if I grasp your meaning rightly.

SIR CHARLES. You do. I mean exactly what I say. There will be a struggle with public opinion in the empire. We shall not shirk it: it is part of our plan to open people's minds on the subject of eugenics and the need for mixing not only western and eastern culture but eastern and western blood. Still, we do not want to be stopped, as the Mormons were, or as the Oneida Community would have been if it had not voluntarily broken up. We want to set the intelligent people talking, and to strike the stupid people dumb. And we think we could do both by adding a bishop to the family.

MRS HYERING. And that is where you come in, young man.

PRA. There is another consideration that weighs with us: at least with me. I am convinced that there is something lacking in the constitution of the children. It may be a deficiency of nitrogen. It certainly is a deficiency of something that is essential to a complete social human being.

THE CLERGYMAN. Oh, I cannot believe that. They seemed to me to be quite perfect. I cannot imagine anyone more perfect than Maya.

PRA. Well, what did you think of Maya's conscience, for example?

THE CLERGYMAN [*bewildered*] Her conscience? I suppose –
I dont know – I –

PRA. Precisely. You dont know. Well, we do know. Our four wonderful children have all sorts of talents, all sorts of accomplishments, all sorts of charms. And we are heartily tired of all their attractions because, though they have artistic consciences, and would die rather than do anything ugly or vulgar or common, they have not between the whole four of them a scrap of moral conscience. They have been very carefully fed: all the vitamins that the biological chemists have discovered are provided in their diet. All their glands are scientifically nourished. Their physical health is perfect. Unfortunately the biological chemists have not yet discovered either the gland that produces and regulates the moral conscience or the vitamins that nourish it. Have you a conscience, Mr Hammingtap?

THE CLERGYMAN. Oh yes: I wish I hadnt. It tortures me. You know, I should have enjoyed being a pirate's chaplain sometimes if it hadnt been for my terrible conscience. It has made my life one long remorse; for I have never had the strength of mind to act up to it.

PRA. That suggests very strongly that the conscientious man is, chemically speaking, the nitrogenic man. Here, then, we have four young adults, insufficiently nitrogenized, and therefore deficient in conscience. Here also we have a young adult saturated with nitrogen from his cradle, and suffering from a morbid excess of conscience. A union between him and our girls is clearly indicated.

THE CLERGYMAN. You mean that I ought to marry one of them?

PRA. Not at all. They would regard that as an invidious proceeding.

THE CLERGYMAN. Invidious! I dont understand.

LADY FARWATERS [*goodnaturedly*] Let me try to break it to

you, Mr Hammingtap. The two girls attract you very much, dont they?

THE CLERGYMAN. How can one help being attracted, Lady Farwaters? Theyre quite beautiful.

LADY FARWATERS. Both of them?

THE CLERGYMAN. Oh, as a clergyman I could not be attracted by more than one at a time. Still, somehow, I seem to love them all in an inexpressible sort of way. Only, if there were any question of marriage, I should have to choose.

PROLA. And which would you choose?

THE CLERGYMAN. Oh, I should choose Maya.

PROLA. Maya would at once reject you.

THE CLERGYMAN [*much dejected*] I suppose so. I know I am no catch for Maya. Still, she was very kind to me. In fact – but perhaps I oughtnt to tell you this – she kissed me.

SIR CHARLES. Indeed? That shews that she contemplates a union with you.

LADY FARWATERS. You must not think she would reject you on the ground of any personal unworthiness on your part.

THE CLERGYMAN. Then on what ground? Oh, I shouldnt have kissed her.

MRS HYERING. Oho! You said it was she who kissed you.

THE CLERGYMAN. Yes: I know I should have explained that. But she let me kiss her.

MRS HYERING. That must have been a thrill, Mr Hammingtap. Life came to you that time, didnt it?

THE CLERGYMAN. Oh please, I cant speak of it. But why should she reject me if I make her an honorable proposal?

LADY FARWATERS. Because she will consider your honorable proposal dishonorable, Mr Hammingtap, unless it includes all the ladies of the family. You will not be allowed to pick and choose and make distinctions. You marry all or none.

THE CLERGYMAN. Oh dear! My poor little brain is giving

way. I cant make sense of what you are saying. I know that your meaning must be perfectly right and respectable, Lady Farwaters; but it sounds like a dreadful sort of wickedness.

LADY FARWATERS. May I try to explain?

THE CLERGYMAN. Please do, Lady Farwaters. But I wish you wouldnt call me Mr Hammingtap. I am accustomed to be called Iddy among friends.

MRS HYERING. What does Iddy stand for?

THE CLERGYMAN. Well, in our home I was known as the idiot.

MRS HYERING. Oh! I am sorry: I didnt know.

THE CLERGYMAN. Not at all. My sister was the Kiddy; so I became the Iddy. Do please call me that. And be kind to me: I am weakminded and lose my head very easily; and I can see that you are all wonderfully clever and strong-minded. That is why I could be so happy here. I can take in anything if you will only tell it to me in a gentle hushabyebaby sort of way and call me Iddy. Now go on, Lady Farwaters. Excuse me for interrupting you so long.

LADY FARWATERS. You see, Iddy –

IDDY. Oh thanks!

LADY FARWATERS [continuing] – our four children are not like European children and not like Asiatic children. They have the east in their brains and the west in their blood. And at the same time they have the east in their blood and the west in their brains. Well, from the time when as tiny tots they could speak, they invented fairy stories. I thought it silly and dangerous, and wanted to stop them; but Prola would not let me: she taught them a game called the heavenly parliament in which all of them told tales and added them to the general stock until a fairyland was built up, with laws and religious rituals, and finally a great institution which they called the Superfamily. It began by my telling them in my old conventional English way to love oneanother; but they would not have that at all: they said it was vulgar nonsense and made them interfere with oneanother and hate oneanother. Then they hit out for themselves the idea that they were not to love oneanother, but that they were to be oneanother.

IDDY. To be oneanother! I dont understand.

SIR CHARLES. Neither do I. Pra and Prola think they understand it; but Lady Farwaters and I dont; and we dont pretend to. We are too English. But the practical side of it – the side that concerns you – is that Vashti and Maya are now grown up. They must have children. The boys will need a young wife.

IDDY. You means two wives.

LADY FARWATERS. Oh, a dozen, if so many of the right sort can be found.

IDDY. But – but – but that would be polygamy.

PROLA. You are in the east, Mr Iddy. The east is polygamous. Try to remember that polygamists form an enormous majority of the subjects of the British Empire, and that you are not now in Clapham.

IDDY. How dreadful! I never thought of that.

LADY FARWATERS. And the girls will need a young husband.

IDDY [imploringly] Two young husbands, Lady Farwaters. Oh please, two.

LADY FARWATERS. I think not, at first.

IDDY. Oh! But I am not an oriental. I am a clergyman of the Church of England.

HYERING. That means nothing to Vashti.

PRA. And still less to Maya.

IDDY. But – but – oh dear! dont you understand? I want to marry Maya. And if I marry Maya I cannot marry Vashti. An English clergyman could not marry two women.

LADY FARWATERS. From their point of view they are not two women: they are one. Vashti is Maya; and Maya is Vashti.

IDDY. But even if such a thing were possible how could I

be faithful to Vashti without being unfaithful to Maya? I couldnt bear to be unfaithful to Maya.

LADY FARWATERS. Maya would regard the slightest unfaithfulness to Vashti as a betrayal of herself and a breach of your marriage vow.

IDDY. But thats nonsense: utter nonsense. Please dont put such things into my head. I am trying so hard to keep sane; but you are terrifying me. If only I could bring myself never to see Maya again I should rush out of this garden and make for home. But it would be like rushing out of heaven. I am most unhappy; and yet I am dreadfully happy. I think I am under some sort of enchantment.

MRS HYERING. Well, stick to the enchantment while it lasts. Let life come to you.

PRA. May I remind you that not only Vashti and Maya, but all the ladies here, are included in the superfamily compact.

IDDY. Oh, how nice and comfortable that would be! They would be mothers to me.

PROLA [rebuking Pra] Let him alone, Pra. There is such a thing as calf love. Vashti and Maya are quite enough for him to begin with. Maya has already driven him half mad. There is no need for us old people to drive him quite out of his senses. [She rises] This has gone far enough. Wait here alone, Mr Hammingtap, to collect your thoughts. Look at the flowers; breathe the air; open your soul to the infinite space of the sky. Nature always helps.

IDDY [rising] Thank you, Lady Prola. Yes: that will be a great help.

PROLA. Come. [She goes up the steps and into the house].

They all rise and follow her, each bestowing a word of counsel or comfort on the distracted clergyman.

PRA. Relax. Take a full breath and then relax. Do not strangle yourself with useless anxieties. [He goes].

LADY FARWATERS. Cast out fear, Iddy. Warm heart. Clear mind. Think of having a thousand friends, a thousand wives, a thousand mothers. [*She pats him on the shoulder and goes*].

SIR CHARLES. Stand up to it, my boy. The world is changing. Stand up to it. [*He goes*].

MRS HYERING. Dont let that conscience of yours worry you. Let life come to you. [*She goes*].

HYERING. Try to sleep a little. The morning has been too much for you. [*He goes*].

IDDY. Sleep! I will not sleep. They want me to disgrace my cloth; but I wont. I wont relax: I wont disobey my conscience: I wont smell those flowers: I wont look at the sky. Nature is not good for me here. Nature is eastern here: it's poison to an Englishman. I will think of England and tighten myself up and pull myself together. England! The Malverns! the Severn plain! the Welsh border! the three cathedrals! England that is me: I that am England! Damn and blast all these tropical paradises: I am an English clergyman; and my place is in England. Floreat Etona! Back to England and all that England means to an Englishman! In this sign I shall conquer. [*He turns resolutely to go out as he came in, and finds himself face to face with Maya, who has stolen in and listened gravely and intently to his exhortation*].

IDDY [*collapsing in despair on the parapet of the well*] Oh, Maya, let me go, let me go.

MAYA [*sinking beside him with her arm round his neck*] Speak to me from your soul, and not with words that you have picked up in the street.

IDDY. Respect my cloth, Miss Farwaters.

MAYA. Maya. Maya is my name. I am the veil of the temple. Rend me in twain.

IDDY. I wont. I will go home and marry some honest English girl named Polly Perkins. [*Shuddering in her embrace*] Oh, Maya, darling: speak to me like a human being.

MAYA. That is how I speak to you; but you do not recognize human speech when you hear it: you crave for slang and small talk, and for readymade phrases that mean nothing. Speak from your soul; and tell me: do you love Vashti? Would you die for Vashti?

IDDY. No.

MAYA [*with a flash of rage, springing up*] Wretch! [*Calmly and conclusively*] You are free. Farewell [*She points his way through the house*].

IDDY [*clutching at her robe*] No, no. Do not leave me. I love you – you. I would die for you. That sounds like a word picked up in the street; but it is true. I would die for you ten times over.

MAYA. It is not true. Words, words, words out of the gutter. Vashti and Maya are one: you cannot love me if you do not love Vashti: you cannot die for me without dying for Vashti.

IDDY. Oh, I assure you I can.

MAYA. Lies, lies. If you can feel one heart throb for me that is not a throb for Vashti: if for even an instant there are two women in your thoughts instead of one, then you do not know what love can be.

IDDY. But it's just the contrary. I –

VASHTI [*who has entered silently, sits beside him and throws an arm round his shoulders*] Do you not love me? Would you not die for me?

IDDY [*mesmerized by her eyes*] Oh DEAR!!! Yes: your eyes make my heart melt: your voice opens heaven to me: I love you. I would die a thousand times for you.

VASHTI. And Maya? You love Maya. You would die a million times for Maya?

IDDY. Yes, yes. I would die for either, for both: for one, for the other –

MAYA. For Vashti Maya?

IDDY. For Vashti Maya, for Maya Vashti.

VASHTI. Your lives and ours are one life.

MAYA [*sitting down beside him*] And this is the Kingdom of love.

The three embrace with interlaced arms and vanish in black darkness.

ACT II

A fine forenoon some years later. The garden is unchanged; but inside the distant breakwater the harbor is crowded with cruisers; and on the lawn near the steps is a writing table littered with papers and furnished with a wireless telephone. Sir Charles is sitting at the end of it with his back to the house. Seated near him is Pra. Both are busy writing. Hyering enters.

SIR CHARLES. Morning, Hyering.

HYERING. Morning. [*He sits at the other end of the table after waving an acknowledgment of Pra's indication of a salaam*]. Anything fresh?

SIR CHARLES [*pointing to the roadstead*] Look! Five more cruisers in last night. The papers say it is the first time the fleets of the British Empire have ever assembled in one place.

HYERING. I hope it will never happen again. If we dont get rid of them quickly there will be the biggest naval battle on record. They are quarrelling already like Kilkenny cats.

SIR CHARLES. What about?

HYERING. Oh, about everything. About moorings, about firing salutes: which has the right to fire first? about flags, about shore parties, about nothing. We shall never be able to keep the peace between them. The Quebec has got alongside the Belfast. The Quebec has announced Mass at eleven on All Saints Day; and the Belfast has announced firing practice at the same hour. Do you see that sloop that came in last night?

SIR CHARLES. What is it?

HYERING. The Pitcairn Island fleet. They are Seventh Day Adventists, and are quite sure the Judgment Day is fixed for five o'clock this afternoon. They propose to do nothing until then but sing hymns. The Irish Free State admiral threatens to sink them if they dont stop. How am I to keep them quiet?

PRA. Dont keep them quiet. Their squabbles will make them forget what they were sent here for.

HYERING. Forget! not they. I have six ultimatums from their admirals, all expiring at noon today. Look. [*He takes a batch of letters from his pocket and throws them on the table*].

SIR CHARLES [*pointing to the letters on the table*] Look at these!

PRA. All about Iddy.

SIR CHARLES. Iddy has got into the headlines at home. The cables are humming with Iddy. Iddy has convulsed the Empire, confound him!

HYERING. Anything fresh from London or Delhi?

SIR CHARLES. The same old songs. The Church of England wont tolerate polygamy on any terms, and insists on our prosecuting Iddy if we cannot whitewash him. Delhi declares that any attempt to persecute polygamy would be an insult to the religions of India.

PRA. The Cultural Minister at Delhi adds a postscript to say that as he has been married two hundred and thirtyfour times, and could not have lived on his salary without the dowries, the protest of the Church of England shews a great want of consideration for his position. He has a hundred and seventeen children surviving.

SIR CHARLES. Then there's a chap I never heard of, calling himself the Caliph of British Islam. He demands that Iddy shall put away all his wives except four.

HYERING. What does the Foreign Office say to that?

PRA. The Foreign Office hails it as a happy solution of a difficulty that threatened to be very serious.

HYERING. What do you think about it all yourself, Pra?

PRA. Think! Thought has no place in such discussions. Each of them must learn that its ideas are not everybody's ideas. Here is a cablegram from the League of British Imperial Womanhood, Vancouver and Pretoria. 'Burn him alive and his hussies with him.' Do you expect me to think about such people?

HYERING. Nobody has made any practical suggestion, I suppose?

PRA. The United States intervene with a friendly suggestion that the parties should be divorced. But the Irish Free State will not hear of divorce, and points out that if the parties become Catholics their marriages can be annulled with the greatest ease.

HYERING. Oh, the west! the west! the west!

PRA. Oh, the east! the east! the east! I tried to reconcile them; and I had only two successes: you and Lady Farwaters.

HYERING. You kicked me into the sea.

SIR CHARLES. You made love to Lady Farwaters.

PRA. I had to use that method with very crude novices; and Lady Farwaters, with her English ladylike bringing-up, was so crude that she really could not understand any purely intellectual appeal. Your own mind, thanks to your public school and university, was in an even worse condition; and Prola had to convert you by the same elementary method. Well, it has worked, up to a point. The insight you obtained into eastern modes of thought has enabled you to govern the eastern crown colonies with extraordinary success. Downing Street hated you; but Delhi supported you; and since India won Dominion status Delhi has been the centre of the British Empire. You, Hyering, have had the same diplomatic success in the east for the same reason. But beyond this we have been unable to advance a step. Our dream of founding a millennial world culture; the dream which united Prola and Pra as you first knew them, and then united us all six, has ended in a single little household with four children, wonderful and beautiful, but sterile. When we had to find a husband for the blossoming girls, only one man was found capable of merging himself in the unity of the family: a man fed on air from his childhood. And how has this paragon turned out? An impotent simpleton. It would be impossible to conceive a human being of less consequence in the world. And yet, look! There is the Imperial Armada, in which every petty province insists on its separate fleet, every trumpery islet its battleship, its cruiser, or at least its sloop or gunboat! Why are they here, armed to the teeth, threatening what they call their sanctions? a word that once meant the approval of the gods, and now means bombs full of poison gas. Solely on account of the simpleton. To reform his morals, half of them want to rain destruction on this little household of ours, and the other half is determined to sink them if they attempt it.

HYERING. They darent use their bombs, you know.

PRA. True; but what is to prevent them from taking to their fists and coming ashore to fight it out on the beach with sticks and bottles and stones, or with their fists? What do the ultimatums say, Hyering?

HYERING [*reading them*] Number one from the English admiral. 'If the polygamist-adulterer Hammingtap is not handed over by noon tomorrow' that is today 'I shall be obliged to open fire on Government House.' Number two, from the commander of the Bombay Squadron. 'Unless an unequivocal guarantee of the safety and liberty of Mr Hammingtap be in my hands by noon today' that came this morning 'I shall land a shore party equipped with machine guns and tear gas bombs to assist the local police in the protection of his person.' Number three: 'I have repeatedly informed you that the imperial province of Holy Island demands the immediate and exemplary combustion of the abominable libertine and damnable apostate known as Phosphor Hammingtap. The patience of the Holy Island fleet will be exhausted at noon on the 13th' today 'and the capital of the Unexpected Islands must take the consequences.' Number four —

SIR CHARLES. Oh, bother number four! They are all the same: not one of them has originality enough to fix half-past-eleven or a quarter-to-one.

HYERING. By the way, Pra, have you taken any steps? I havnt.

PRA. Yes I have. Dont worry. I have sent a message.

SIR CHARLES. What message?

PRA. The Mayor of the Port earnestly begs the commanders of the imperial fleet to suspend action for another day, as his attention is urgently occupied by a serious outbreak of smallpox in the harbor district.

SIR CHARLES. Good. [*The boom of a cannon interrupts him*] There goes the noonday cannon!

HYERING. I hope they got the message in time.

The garden and its occupants vanish. When they reappear, the harbor is empty: not a ship is visible. The writing table, with its chairs and papers, has been removed and replaced by a small tea-table. Tea is ready. The wireless telephone is still there.

Vashti and Maya are in their shrines. Lady Farwaters is sitting on the western stone seat, with Mrs Hyering beside her on her right. Prola is sitting on the eastern seat. All five ladies are taking tea.

Pra comes from the house with Sir Charles and Hyering. They help themselves to tea. Pra abstains.

SIR CHARLES. Not a blessed ship left in the harbor! Your message certainly did the trick, Pra. [*He sits down beside Prola, on her left*].

PRA [*sitting down between the two British ladies*] They may come back.

HYERING [*sitting beside Prola, on her right*] Not a bit of it. By the time the fleet realizes that it has been humbugged the Empire will be tired of Iddy.

VASHTI. The world is tired of Iddy.

MAYA. *I* am tired of Iddy.

VASHTI. Iddy is a pestilence.

MAYA. Iddy is a bore.

VASHTI. Let us throw ourselves into the sea to escape from Iddy.

MAYA. Let us throw Iddy into the sea that he may escape from himself.

VASHTI. You are wise, Prola. Tell us how to get rid of Iddy.

MAYA. We cannot endure Iddy for ever, Prola.

PROLA. You two chose him, not I.

MAYA. We were young: we did not know.

VASHTI. Help us, Pra. You have lost faith in us; but your wits are still keen.

MAYA. Pra: we beseech thee. Abolish the incubus.

VASHTI. Give him peace that we may have rest.

MAYA. Give him rest that we may have peace.

VASHTI. Let him be as he was before we knew him.

MAYA. When we were happy.

VASHTI. When he was innocent.

PRA. You raised this strange spirit. I cannot exorcise him.

VASHTI. Rather than endure him I will empty the heavens of their rain and dew.

MAYA. Silence him, O ye stars.

Iddy comes from the house in a condition of lazy self-complacence. He is received in dead silence. Nobody looks at him. He pours himself out a cup of tea. The silence becomes grim. He sits down on the grass at Prola's feet, and sips his tea. The silence continues.

IDDY [*at last*] I am a futile creature.

They all turn as if stung and look at him. Then they resume their attitudes of deadly endurance.

IDDY. It is a terrible thing to be loved. I dont suppose any man has ever been loved as I have been loved, or loved as I have loved. But there's not so much in it as people say. I am writing a sermon about it. It is a sermon on Eternity.

They look at him as before.

IDDY. The line I am going to take is this. We have never been able to imagine eternity properly. St John of Patmos started the notion of playing harps and singing praises for ever and ever. But the organist tells me that composers have to use the harp very sparingly because, though it makes a very pretty effect at first, you get tired of it so soon. You couldnt go on playing the harp for ever; and if you sang

'Worthy is the Lamb' for ever you would drive the Lamb mad. The notion is that you cant have too much of a good thing; but you can: you can bear hardship much longer than you could bear heaven. Love is like music. Music is very nice: the organist says that when the wickedness of mankind tempts him to despair he comforts himself by remembering that the human race produced Mozart; but a woman who plays the piano all day is a curse. A woman who makes love to you all day is much worse; and yet nothing is lovelier than love, up to a point. We all love one another here in a wonderful way: I love Vashti, I love Maya, I love Prola; and they all love me so wonderfully that their three loves are only one love. But it is my belief that some day we'll have to try something else. If we dont we'll come to hate one another.

VASHTI. If it is any consolation to you, Iddy, I can assure you that I already hate you so intensely that if it were in my nature to kill anything I should kill you.

IDDY. There now! I ought to be wounded and horrified; but I'm not: I feel as if youd given me a strawberry ice. Thank you, dear Vashti, thank you. You give me hope that even Maya will get tired of me someday.

MAYA. I have been on the point of beating you to a jelly for ever so long past; but just as my fists were clenched to do it you always managed to come out with some stroke of idiocy that was either so funny or so piteous that I have kissed you instead.

IDDY. You make me happier than I have been for months. But, you know, that does not settle my difficulties. I dont know whether other people are like me or not –

LADY FARWATERS. No, Iddy: you are unique.

IDDY. Anyhow, I have made a discovery as regards myself.

VASHTI. Enough is known already.

MAYA. Seek no further: there is nothing there.

VASHTI. There never has been anything.

IDDY. Shut up, you two. This is something really interesting. I am writing a second sermon.

ALL THE REST [*gasp*] !!!!!!!

PRA. Was eternity not long enough for one sermon?

IDDY. This one is on love.

VASHTI [*springing up*] I will cast myself down from a precipice.

MAYA [*springing up*] I will gas myself.

IDDY. Oh, not until you have heard my sermon, please.

PROLA. Listen to him, children. Respect the wisdom of the fool.

VASHTI [*resuming her goddess-in-a-shrine attitude*] The oracles of the wise are unheeded. Silence for the King of Idiots.

MAYA [*also enshrining herself*] Speak, Solomon.

IDDY. Well, the discovery I have made is that we were commanded to love our enemies because loving is good for us and dreadfully bad for them. I love you all here intensely; and I enjoy loving you. I love Vashti; I love Maya; and I adore Prola with a passion that grows and deepens from year to year.

PROLA. Dolt! I am too old.

IDDY. You were never young and you will never be old. You are the way and the light for me. But you have never loved me and never will love me. You have never loved anything human: why should you? Nothing human is good enough to be loved. But every decent human creature has some capacity for loving. Look at me! What a little worm I am! My sermons are wretched stuff, except these last two, which I think really have something in them. I cannot bear being loved, because I know that I am a worm, and that nobody could love me unless they were completely deluded as to my merits. But I can love, and delight in loving. I love Vashti for hating me, because she is quite right to hate me: her hatred is a proof of her beautiful clear judgment. I love Maya for being out of all patience with me, because I know that I am enough to drive anybody mad, and she is wise enough to know how worthless I am. I love Prola

187

because she is far above loving or hating me; and there is something about her dark beauty that —

PROLA [*kicking him*] Silence, simpleton. Let the unspeakable remain unspoken.

IDDY. I dont mind your kicking me, Prola: you understand; and that is enough for me. And now you see what a jolly fine sermon it will be, and why I shall be so happy here with you from this day on. For I have the joy of loving you all without the burden of being loved in return, or the falsehood of being idolized.

MAYA. Solomon has spoken.

VASHTI. Stupendous.

LADY FARWATERS. Do not mock, darlings. There is something in what he says.

MAYA [*desperately*] But how are we to get rid of him? He is settling down with us for life.

VASHTI. We have brought him on ourselves.

MAYA. We cannot make him hate us.

VASHTI. He will go with us to heaven.

MAYA. In the depths of hell he will find us.

Kanchin and Janga enter processionally, reading newspapers.

KANCHIN. News!

JANGA. News!

They sit enshrined, foursquare with their sisters.

KANCHIN. By wireless.

JANGA. Tomorrow's three o'clock edition.

KANCHIN. The land that brought forth Iddy begins the Apocalypse.

HYERING. What do you mean? Has anything happened in England?

KANCHIN. England has broken loose.

SIR CHARLES. What do you mean? broken loose. Read the news, man. Out with it.

KANCHIN [*reading the headlines*] Dissolution of the British Empire.

JANGA [*reading*] Withdrawal of England from the Empire.

KANCHIN. England strikes for independence.

JANGA. Downing Street declares for a right little tight little island.

KANCHIN. The British Prime Minister cuts the cable and gives the new slogan.

JANGA. Back to Elizabeth's England; and to hell with the empire!

KANCHIN. Ireland to the rescue!

JANGA. Free State President declares Ireland cannot permit England to break the unity of the Empire. Ireland will lead the attack on treason and disruption.

KANCHIN. The Prime Minister's reply to the President suppressed as unprintable.

JANGA. Canada claims position of premier Dominion left vacant by the secession of England.

KANCHIN. Australia counterclaims as metropolitan dominion.

JANGA. New Zealand proclaims a butter blockade until its claim to precedence is recognized by Australia.

KANCHIN. South Africa renames Capetown Empire City, and gives notice to all Britishers to clear out of Africa within ten days.

JANGA. His Holiness the Pope calls on all Christendom to celebrate the passing away of the last vain dream of earthly empire, and the unity of all living souls in the Catholic Kingdom of God and his Church.

LADY FARWATERS. That sounds like the voice of a grown-up man through the whooping of a pack of school-boys.

JANGA [*prosaically*] So far, there have been no disturbances and little popular interest.

KANCHIN. The various international Boards are carrying on as usual.

JANGA. Today's football –

PROLA. No, Janga: certainly not.

SIR CHARLES. But what becomes of our jobs as Governor and political secretary, Hyering? Will this affect our salaries?

HYERING. They will stop: that is all. We had better proclaim the Unexpected Isles an independent republic and secure the new jobs for ourselves.

VASHTI. The world is tired of republics and their jobberies. Proclaim a kingdom.

MAYA. Or a queendom.

IDDY. Oh yes: let us make Prola queen. And I shall be her chaplain.

PRA. By all means, as far as I am concerned. Prola has always been the real ruler here.

VASHTI. Prola is she who decides.

MAYA. Prola is she who unites.

VASHTI. Prola is she who knows.

MAYA. No one can withstand Prola.

PROLA. Be quiet, you two. You shall not make an idol of me.

KANCHIN. We shall make you Empress of the Isles.

JANGA. Prola the First.

VASHTI. Homage, Prola.

MAYA. Love, Prola.

KANCHIN. Obedience, Prola.

JANGA. Absolute rule, Prola.

PROLA. All your burdens on me. Lazy idle children.

KANCHIN. Hurrah! All burdens on Prola.

JANGA. The burden of thought.

VASHTI. The burden of knowledge.

MAYA. The burden of righteousness.

VASHTI. The burden of justice.

MAYA. The burden of mercy.

PROLA. Cease, cease: these are not burdens to me: they are the air I breathe. I shall rule you as I have always done because you are too lazy to rule yourselves.

HYERING. You can rule us, Prola. But will the public ever understand you?

PRA. They will obey her. They would not do that if they understood.

IDDY. I have just been thinking –

MAYA. Solomon has been thinking.

VASHTI. Thoughts without brains.

IDDY. Will the Antiphonal Quartet, if it wants to give another concert, kindly remove itself out of hearing.·

KANCHIN. Silence for the Prophet.

JANGA. Mum!

VASHTI. Dumb.

MAYA. Tiddy iddy um. Carry on, darling.

IDDY. Prola can rule this house because she knows what is happening in it. But how is she to be an Empress if she doesnt know what is happening everywhere?

MRS HYERING. She can read the newspapers, cant she, silly?

IDDY. Yes; but fifteen years later, when the statesmen write their memoirs and autobiographies and publish them, we shall find that it never happened at all and what really happened was quite different. We dont know the truth about any of our statesmen until they are dead and cant take libel actions. Nobody knows the sort of people we really are. The papers have been full of us for weeks past; and not a single word they say about us is true. They think I am a sort of Mahdi or Mad Mullah, and that Prola and Vashti and Maya are a troop of immoral dancing girls, and that Sir Charles is a voluptuous sultan and Hyering a co-respondent. They dont live in a world of truth: they live in a world of their own ideas, which have nothing to do with our ideas. Consequently – Therefore – er – er – What was I going to say, Pra? My brain is not strong enough to keep the thread of my remarks. I ought to have written it down.

PRA. What you have arrived at is that we cannot live in a world of political facts, because we shall not know the political facts for years to come. We must therefore live in a world of original ideas, created by ourselves out of our own nature.

IDDY. Yes. We mustnt pretend to be omniscient. Even God

would not be omniscient if He read the newspapers. We must have an ideal of a beautiful and good world. We must believe that to establish that beautiful and good world on earth is the best thing we can do, and the only sort of religion and politics that is worth bothering about.

PROLA. What about the people who have no original ideas, Iddy?

PRA. The great majority of mankind?

IDDY. Theyll be only too glad to do what you tell them, Prola, if you can make them feel that it's right.

PROLA. And if they are incapable of feeling it?

JANGA. Kill.

KANCHIN. Kill.

VASHTI. Kill.

MAYA. Kill.

PROLA. They can do that as easily as I. Any fool can. And there are more of them.

JANGA. Set them to kill one another; and rule.

KANCHIN. Divide and govern.

VASHTI. Feed them on splendid words.

MAYA. Dazzle them with our beauty.

MRS HYERING. Well I never!

IDDY [rising] Excuse me. I'm going into the house to get the field glass. [He goes up the steps].

MRS HYERING. Whatever do you want the field glass for?

IDDY [pointing to the sky] There's a strange bird flying about there. I think it's an albatross. [He goes into the house].

VASHTI, MAYA, KANCHIN, JANGA [hissing after him] Liar. Baby. Dastard. Hypocrite.

SIR CHARLES [laughing] An albatross! Now would anybody in the world, over the age of six, except Iddy, invent such a ridiculous excuse for going to his room to indulge in his poor little secret vice of cigaret smoking?

MAYA. Faugh! The unkissable.

VASHTI. The air poisoner.

KANCHIN. The albatrocity.

MAYA. VASHTI. JANGA [*shocked by the pun*] Oh!!

LADY FARWATERS. Cant you four darlings do something useful instead of sitting there deafening us with your slogans?

KANCHIN [*springing erect*] Yes, action. Action!

JANGA [*rising similarly*] No more of this endless talk! talk! talk!

VASHTI. Yes, action! daring! Let us rob.

MAYA. Let us shoot.

KANCHIN. Let us die for something.

JANGA. For our flag and for our Empress.

VASHTI. For our country, right or wrong.

MAYA. Let there be sex appeal. Let the women make the men brave.

KANCHIN. We must defend our homes.

JANGA. Our women.

VASHTI. Our native soil.

MAYA. It is sweet to die for one's country.

VASHTI. It is glorious to outface death.

ALL FOUR. Yes. Death! death! Glory! glory!

PROLA. Hold your tongues, you young whelps. Is this what we have brought you up for?

PRA. Stop screaming about nothing, will you. Use your minds.

MAYA. We have no minds.

VASHTI. We have imaginations.

KANCHIN. We have made this house a temple.

JANGA. We have made Prola a goddess.

MAYA. We have made it a palace.

VASHTI. A palace for Queen Prola.

KANCHIN. She shall reign.

JANGA. For ever and ever.

VASHTI AND MAYA [*in unison*] Hail, Prola, our goddess!

KANCHIN AND JANGA [*in unison*] Hail, Prola, our empress!

ALL FOUR [*rushing down to the lawn and throwing themselves on their knees before her*] Hail!

PROLA. Will you provoke me to box your ears, you abominable idolaters. Get up this instant. Go and scrub the floors. Do anything that is dirty and grubby and smelly enough to shew that you live in a real world and not in a fool's paradise. If I catch you grovelling to me, a creature of the same clay as yourselves, but fortunately for you with a little more common sense, I will beat the slavishness out of your bones.

MAYA. Oh, what ecstasy to be beaten by Prola!

VASHTI. To feel her rule in the last extremity of pain!

KANCHIN. To suffer for her!

JANGA. To die for her!

PROLA. Get out, all four. My empire is not of such as you. Begone.

MAYA. How lovely is obedience! [*She makes an obeisance and runs away through the garden*].

VASHTI. Obedience is freedom from the intolerable fatigue of thought. [*She makes her obeisance and sails away, disappearing between the garden and the house*].

KANCHIN. You speak as an empress should speak. [*He salaams and bounds off after Maya*].

JANGA. The voice of authority gives us strength and unity. Command us always thus: it is what we need and love. [*He strides away in Vashti's footsteps*].

PROLA. An excuse for leaving everything to me. Lazy, lazy, lazy! Someday Heaven will get tired of lazy people; and the Pitcairn Islanders will see their Day of Judgment at last.

A distant fusillade of shotguns answers her.

SIR CHARLES. Shooting! What can the matter be?

They all rise and listen anxiously.

A trumpet call rings out from the sky.

HYERING. Where on earth did that come from? There is not such a thing as a trumpet in the island.

The four come rushing back into the garden, wildly excited.

KANCHIN. Look, look, quick! The albatross.

PRA [*rising*] The albatross!!

MAYA. Yes: Iddy's albatross. Look!

JANGA. Flying over the town.

VASHTI [*pointing*] There it goes. See.

A second fusillade of shotguns, much nearer.

MAYA. Oh, theyre all trying to shoot it. Brutes!

KANCHIN. They havnt hit it. Here it comes.

MAYA. It's flying this way.

VASHTI. It's swooping down.

Iddy comes from the house and trots down the steps with a field glass in his hand.

IDDY. Ive been looking at it through the window for the last five minutes. It isnt an albatross. Look at it through this. [*He hands the glass to Pra*].

KANCHIN. Then what is it?

IDDY. I think it's an angel.

JANGA. Oh get out, you silly idiot.

PRA [*looking through the glass*] That is no bird.

An angel flies down into the middle of the garden. General stupefaction. He shakes himself. Quantities of bullets and small shot fall from his wings and clothes.

THE ANGEL. Really, your people ought to know better than to shoot at an angel.

MAYA. Are you an angel?

THE ANGEL. Well, what do you suppose I am?

VASHTI. Of course he is an angel. Look at his wings.

THE ANGEL. Attention, please! Have you not heard the trumpet? This is the Judgment Day.

ALL THE REST. The what???!!!

THE ANGEL. The Judgment Day. The Day of Judgment.

SIR CHARLES. Well I'll be damned!

THE ANGEL. Very possibly.

HYERING. Do you mean that the Pitcairn Islanders were right after all?!

THE ANGEL. Yes. You are all now under judgment, in common with the rest of the English speaking peoples. Dont gape at me as if you had never seen an angel before.

PROLA. But we never have.

THE ANGEL [*relaxing*] True. Ha ha ha! Well, you thoroughly understand, dont you, that your records are now being looked into with a view to deciding whether you are worth your salt or not.

PRA. And suppose it is decided that we are not worth our salt?

THE ANGEL [*reassuring them in a pleasantly off-handed manner*] Then you will simply disappear: that is all. You will no longer exist. Dont let me keep you all standing. Sit down if you like. Never mind me: sitting and standing are all alike to an angel. However – [*he sits down on the parapet of the well*].

They sit as before, the four superchildren enshrining themselves as usual.

The telephone rings. Hyering rises and takes it.

HYERING [*to the angel*] Excuse me. [*To the telephone*] Yes? Hyering speaking ... Somebody what? ... Oh! somebody fooling on the wireless. Well, theyre not fooling: an angel has just landed here to tell us the same thing.... An angel. A for arrowroot, N for nitrogen, G for – thats it: an angel.... Well, after all, the Judgment Day had to come some day, hadnt it? Why not this day as well as another? ... I'll ask the angel about it and ring you later. Goodbye. [*He rings off*]. Look here, angel. The wireless has been on all over Europe. London reports the Judgment Day in full swing; but Paris knows nothing about it; Hilversum knows nothing about it; Berlin, Rome, Madrid, and Geneva know nothing about it; and Moscow says the British bourgeoisie has been driven mad by its superstitions. How do you account for that? If it is the Judgment Day in England it must be the Judgment Day everywhere.

THE ANGEL. Why?

HYERING [*sitting down*] Well, it stands to reason.

THE ANGEL. Does it? Would it be reasonable to try cases in hundreds of different lands and languages and creeds and colors on the same day in the same place? Of course not. The whole business will last longer than what you call a year. We gave the English speaking folk the first turn in compliment to one of your big guns – a dean – name of Inge, I think. I announced it to him last night in a dream, and asked him whether the English would appreciate the compliment. He said he thought they would prefer to put it off as long as possible, but that they needed it badly and he was ready. The other languages will follow. The United States of America will be tried tomorrow, Australasia next day, Scotland next, then Ireland –

LADY FARWATERS. But excuse me: they do not speak different languages.

THE ANGEL. They sound different to us.

SIR CHARLES. I wonder how they are taking it in England.

THE ANGEL. I am afraid most of them are incapable of understanding the ways of heaven. They go motoring or golfing on Sundays instead of going to church; and they never open a Bible. When you mention Adam and Eve, or Cain and Abel, to say nothing of the Day of Judgment, they dont know what you are talking about. The others – the pious ones – think we have come to dig up all the skeletons and put them through one of their shocking criminal trials. They actually expect us to make angels of them for ever and ever.

MRS HYERING. See here, angel. This isnt a proper sort of Judgment Day. It's a fine day. It's like Bank Holiday.

THE ANGEL. And pray why should the Day of Judgment not be a fine day?

MRS HYERING. Well, it's hardly what we were led to expect, you know.

JANGA. 'The heavens shall pass away with a great noise.'

KANCHIN. 'The elements shall melt with fervent heat.'

JANGA. 'The earth also and the works that are therein shall be burnt up.'

VASHTI. The stars are fixed in their courses. They have not fallen to the earth.

MAYA. The heavens are silent. Where are the seven thunders?

VASHTI. The seven vials full of the wrath of God?

JANGA. The four horses?

KANCHIN. The two witnesses?

THE ANGEL. My good people, if you want these things you must provide them for yourselves. If you want a great noise, you have your cannons. If you want a fervent heat to burn up the earth you have your high explosives. If you want vials of wrath to rain down on you, they are ready in your arsenals, full of poison gases. Some years ago you had them all in full play, burning up the earth and spreading death, famine, and pestilence. But the spring came and created life faster than you could destroy it. The birds sang over your trenches; and their promise of summer was fulfilled. The sun that shone undisturbed on your pitiful Day of Wrath shines today over Heaven's Day of Judgment. It will continue to light us and warm us; and there will be no noise nor wrath nor fire nor thunder nor destruction nor plagues nor terrors of any sort. I am afraid you will find it very dull.

LADY FARWATERS [*politely*] Not at all. Pray dont think that.

MRS HYERING. Well, a little good manners never does any harm; but I tell you straight, Mister Angel, I cant feel as if there was anything particular happening, in spite of you and your wings. Ive only just had my tea; and I cant feel a bit serious without any preparation or even an organ playing.

THE ANGEL. You will feel serious enough presently when things begin to happen.

MRS HYERING. Yes; but what things?

THE ANGEL. What was foretold to you. 'His angels shall gather together his elect. Then shall two be in the field: the one shall be taken and the other left. Two women shall be grinding at the mill. The one shall be taken and the other left.'

MRS HYERING. But which? Thats what I want to know.

PROLA. There is nothing new in this taking of the one and leaving the other: natural death has always been doing it.

THE ANGEL. Natural death does it senselessly, like a blind child throwing stones. We angels are executing a judgment. The lives which have no use, no meaning, no purpose, will fade out. You will have to justify your existence or perish. Only the elect shall survive.

MRS HYERING. But where does the end of the world come in?

THE ANGEL. The Day of Judgment is not the end of the world, but the end of its childhood and the beginning of its responsible maturity. So now you know; and my business with you is ended. [*He rises*]. Is there any way of getting out on the roof of this house?

SIR CHARLES [*rising*] Certainly: it is a flat roof where we often sit. [*He leads the way to the house*].

KANCHIN. In theory.

JANGA. In fact we never sit there.

THE ANGEL. That does not matter. All I want is a parapet to take off from. Like the albatross, I cannot rise from the ground without great difficulty. An angel is far from being the perfect organism you imagine. There is always something better.

VASHTI. Excelsior.

ALL FOUR [*rising and singing vociferously*] Eck-cel-see-orr! Eck-cel-see-or!

THE ANGEL [*putting his fingers in his ears*] Please, no. In heaven we are tired of singing. It is not done now. [*He follows Sir Charles out*].

KANCHIN. Lets see him take off.

The four rush up the garden and look up at the roof. The others rise and watch.

JANGA [*calling up*] Start into the wind, old man. Spring off hard, from the ball of the foot. Dont fall on us.

KANCHIN. Oopsh! Off he goes.

The beating of the angel's wings is heard.

VASHTI. He makes a noise like a vacuum cleaner.

MAYA [*wafting kisses*] Goodbye, silly old Excelsior.

The noise stops.

JANGA. His wings have stopped beating. He is soaring up the wind.

KANCHIN. He is getting smaller and smaller. His speed must be terrific.

MAYA. He is too small for an albatross.

VASHTI. He is smaller than a canary.

KANCHIN. He is out of sight.

MAYA. There! One last glint of the sun on his wings. He is gone.

The four troop back and resume their seats. The others sit as before, except that Iddy deserts Prola and sits on the well parapet. Sir Charles returns from the house with a batch of wireless messages in his hand.

SIR CHARLES [*sitting in his former place*] Well, my dears: the Judgment Day is over, it seems.

IDDY. I cant believe it was really the Judgment Day.

PRA. Why?

IDDY. Well, I thought some special notice would have been taken of the clergy. Reserved seats or something like that. But he treated me as if I were only the organ blower.

SIR CHARLES. There are such a lot of priests in the world, Iddy. It would be impossible to reserve seats for them all.

IDDY. Oh, I meant only the clergy of the Church of England, of course.

MRS HYERING. What I cant get over is their sending along just one angel to judge us, as if we didnt matter.

LADY FARWATERS. He actually went away and forgot to judge us.

PRA. I am not so sure of that.

IDDY. Well, are we sheep or goats? tell me that.

MAYA. You are a sheep, Iddy, my sweet: there can be no doubt about that.

IDDY [*bursting into tears*] I love you, Maya; and you always say unkind things to me. [*He rushes away through the garden, sobbing*].

MAYA. Oh, poor Iddy! I'll go and soothe him with a thousand kisses. [*She runs after him*].

HYERING [*to Sir Charles*] What have you got there? Any news from London?

SIR CHARLES. Yes: Exchange Telegraph and Reuters. Copyright reserved.

HYERING. Lets have it.

SIR CHARLES [*reading*] 'Judgment Day. Widespread incredulity as to anything having really happened. Reported appearance of angels in several quarters generally disbelieved. Several witnesses are qualifying or withdrawing their statements in deference to the prevailing scepticism.'

HYERING. We shall have to be careful too, Charles. Who will believe us if we tell this yarn of an angel flying down into the garden?

SIR CHARLES. I suppose so. I never thought of it in that way. Still, listen to this. [*Reading*] 'Policeman who attempted to arrest angel in Leicester Square removed to mental hospital. Church Assembly at Lambeth Palace decides by a large majority that there has been a Visitation. Dissenting minority, led by the Bishop of Edgbaston, denounces the reports as nonsense that would not impose even on the Society for Psychical Research. His Holiness the Pope warns Christendom that supernatural communications reaching the earth otherwise than through the Church are contrary to the Catholic faith, and, if authentic, must be regarded as demoniacal. Cabinet hastily summoned to discuss the situation. Prime Minister, speaking in emergency meeting at the Mansion House, declares that reports of utterances by angels are hopelessly contradictory, and that alleged verbatim reports by shorthand writers contain vulgar expressions. The Government could not in any case allow the British Empire to be placed in the position of being judged by a commission of a few angels instead of by direct divine authority. Such a slight to the flag would never be tolerated by Englishmen; and the Cabinet was unanimous in refusing to believe that such an outrage had occurred. The Prime Minister's speech was received with thunderous applause, the audience rising spontaneously to sing the National Anthem.'

PRA. They would.

SIR CHARLES [*looking at another paper*] Hallo! Whats this? [*Reading*] 'Later. During the singing of the second verse of the National Anthem at the Mansion House the proceedings were interrupted by the appearance of an angel with a flaming sword who demanded truculently what they meant by ordering God about to do their dirty political work. He was accompanied by unruly cherubim who floated about tweaking the Lord Mayor's nose, pouring ink into the Prime Minister's hat, and singing derisively Con-Found their Poll-It-Ticks. Part of the audience fell to their knees, repeating the Confession. Others rushed frantically to the doors. Two Salvation lasses stemmed the rush, at great personal danger to themselves, by standing in the doorway and singing Let Angels Prostrate Fall. Order was restored by the Prime Minister, who offered the angel an unreserved apology and an undertaking that the offending verse should not be sung again. A new one is to be provided by the Poet Laureate. The Premier's last words were lost through the misconduct of a cherub who butted him violently in the solar plexus. A wave of the angel's sword and a terrible thunderclap then threw the entire audience prone to the floor. When they rose to their feet the angel and the cherubs had disappeared.'

HYERING. Oh, an invention. We cant swallow those cherubs, really.

SIR CHARLES [*taking up a third paper*] This sounds a little more plausible. 'A representative of the Fascist Press has called at the War Office to ask whether any steps were being taken to defend the right of public meeting, and to deal with the angelic peril. The Commander-in-Chief, whilst denying that there is any such thing as a right of public meeting by undisciplined and irresponsible persons, declared that the Mansion House incident was quite incomprehensible to him, as he could not conceive how the only really practical part of the National Anthem could give any offence. Any suggestion that it was not the plain duty of the Ruler of the Universe to confound England's enemies could only lead to widespread atheism. The First Lord of the Admiralty, interviewed last night, said that he could not make head or tail of the reports, but that he could assure the public that whatever had really happened, the British Navy would not take it lying down. Later. A Hyde Park orator was thrown into the Serpentine for saying that the British Empire was not the only pebble on the beach. He has been fined thirty shillings for being in unlawful possession of a life buoy, the property of the Royal Humane Society. There can be no doubt that the disparaging remarks and assumed superiority of the angels has started a wave of patriotism throughout the country which is bound to lead to action of some sort.'

PRA. Which means, if it means anything, that England's next war will be a war with heaven.

PROLA. Nothing new in that. England has been at war with heaven for many a long year.

VASHTI [*inspired*] The most splendid of all her wars!

KANCHIN. The last conquest left to her to achieve!

VASHTI. To overcome the angels!

JANGA. To plant the flag of England on the ramparts of heaven itself! that is the final glory.

PROLA. Oh go away, children: go away. Now that Maya has gone to kiss somebody, there is nothing left for you to glorify but suicide.

VASHTI [*rising*] I rebel.

JANGA [*rising*] We rebel against Prola, the goddess empress.

KANCHIN [*rising*] Prola has turned back from the forlorn hope.

VASHTI. Prola is a coward. She fears defeat and death.

KANCHIN. Without death there can be no heroism.

JANGA. Without faith unto death there can be no faith.

VASHTI. Prola has failed us in the great Day of Judgment.

KANCHIN. Our souls have been called to their final account.

ALL THREE [*marching away through the garden*] Guilty, Prola: guilty. Adieu, Prola!

PROLA. Oh, adieu until you want your tea.

PRA. We have taught them everything except common sense.

LADY FARWATERS. We have taught them everything except how to work for their daily bread instead of praying for it.

PROLA. It is dangerous to educate fools.

PRA. It is still more dangerous to leave them uneducated.

MRS HYERING. There just shouldnt be any fools. They wernt born fools: we made fools of them.

PRA. We must stop making fools.

Iddy returns alone. Something strange has happened to him. He stares at them and tries to speak; but no sound comes from his lips.

LADY FARWATERS. What on earth is the matter with you, Iddy? Have you been drinking?

IDDY [*in a ghastly voice*] Maya.

PROLA. What has happened to Maya?

IDDY. Heaven and earth shall pass away; but I shall not pass away. That is what she said. And then there was nothing in my arms. Nothing. Nothing in my arms. Heaven and earth would pass away; but the love of Maya would never pass away. And there was nothing. [*He collapses on the well parapet, overcome, not in tears but in a profound awe*].

PRA. Do you mean that she died in your arms?

IDDY. Died? No. I tell you there was nothing. Dont you understand? Where she had just been there was nothing. There never had been anything.

PROLA. And the others? Quick, Pra: go and find the others.

PRA. What others?

PROLA. The other three: our children. I forget their names.

IDDY. They said 'Our names shall live forever.' What were their names?

HYERING. They have gone clean out of my head.

SIR CHARLES. Most extraordinary. I cant for the life of me remember. How many of them did you say there were, Prola?

PROLA. Four. Or was it four hundred?

IDDY. There were four. Their names were Love, Pride, Heroism and Empire. Love's pet name was Maya. I loved Maya. I loved them all; but it was through love of Maya that I loved them. I held Maya in my arms. She promised to endure for ever; and suddenly there was nothing in my arms. I have searched for the others; but she and they were one: I found nothing. It is the Judgment.

PROLA. Has she left a great void in your heart, Iddy, that girl who turned to nothing in your arms?

IDDY. No. This is a beautiful climate; and you are beautiful people; but you are not real to me; and the sun is not what it is in the valley of the Severn. I am glad I am an English clergyman. A village and a cottage: a garden and a church: these things will not turn to nothing. I shall be content with my little black coat and my little white collar and my little treasure of words spoken by my Lord Jesus. Blessed be the name of the Lord: I shall not forget it as I shall forget Maya's. [*He goes out seaward like a man in a trance*].

LADY FARWATERS [*troubled, half rising*] But, Iddy, –

PROLA. Let him go. The pigeon knows its way home.

Lady Farwaters sinks back into her seat. There is a moment of rather solemn silence. Then the telephone rings.

PRA [*taking up the receiver*] Yes? ... What? ... Yes: amazing news: we know all about that. What is the latest? ... Yes: 'plot to destroy our most valuable citizens': I got that; but what was the first word? What plot? ... Oh, Russian plot. Rubbish! havnt you some sensible reports? ... Special news broadcast just coming in? ... Good: put me on to it. [*To the others*] I'm through to London Regional. Listen: I'll repeat it as it comes. [*He echoes the news*] Extraordinary disappearances. Indescribable panic. Stock Exchange closes: only two members left. House of Commons decimated: only fourteen members to be found: none of Cabinet rank. House of Lords still musters fifty members; but not one of them has ever attended a meeting of the Chamber. Mayfair a desert: six hotels left without a single guest. Fresh disappearances. Crowded intercession service at Westminster Abbey brought to a close by disappearance of the congregation at such a rate that the rest fled leaving the dean preaching to the choir. At the Royal Institution Sir Ruthless Bonehead, Egregious Professor of Mechanistic Biology to the Rockefeller Foundation, drew a crowded audience to hear his address on 'Whither have they gone?' He disappeared as he opened his mouth to speak. Noted Cambridge professor suggests that what is happening is a weeding-out of nonentities. He has been deprived of his Chair; and The Times, in a leading article, points out that not only is it our most important people who are vanishing, but that it is the most unquestionably useful and popular professions that are most heavily attacked, the medical profession having disappeared almost en bloc, whilst the lawyers and clergy are comparatively immune. A situation of terrible suspense has been created everywhere. Happy husbands and fathers disappear from the family dinner with the soup. Several popular leaders of fashion and famous beauties, after ringing their bells for their maids, have been found non-existent when the bells were answered. More than a million persons have disappeared in the act of reading novels. The Morning Post contains an eloquent protest by Lady Gushing, president of the Titled Ladies' League of Social Service, on the inequality of sacrifice as between the west end and the east, where casualties have been comparatively few. Lady Gushing has since disappeared. There is general agreement that our losses are irreparable, though their bad effects are as yet unfelt. But before long –

HYERING. Whats the use of going on, Pra? The angels are weeding the garden. The useless people, the mischievous people, the selfish somebodies and the noisy nobodies, are dissolving into space, which is the simplest form of matter. We here are awaiting our own doom.

MRS HYERING. What was it the angel said?

PROLA. The lives which have no use, no meaning, no purpose, will fade out. We shall have to justify our existences or perish. We shall live under a constant sense of that responsibility. If the angels fail us we shall set up tribunals of our own from which worthless people will not come out alive. When men no longer fear the judgment of God, they must learn to judge themselves.

SIR CHARLES. I seem to remember somebody saying 'Judge not, that ye be not judged.'

PROLA. That means 'Punish not, that ye be not punished.' This is not punishment, but judgment.

HYERING. What is judgment?

PRA. Judgment is valuation. Civilizations live by their valuations. If the valuations are false, the civilization perishes as all the ancient ones we know of did. We are not being punished today: we are being valued. That is the Newest Dispensation.

LADY FARWATERS. I feel an absolute conviction that I

shall not disappear and that Charles will not disappear. We have done some queer things here in the east perhaps; but at bottom we are comfortable commonsense probable English people; and we shall not do anything so improbable as disappear.

SIR CHARLES [to his wife] Do not tempt the angels, my dear. Remember: you used to distribute tracts before you met Pra.

LADY FARWATERS. Ssh-sh-sh! Dont remind the angels of those tracts.

HYERING [rising] Look here. I have an uneasy feeling that we'd better go back to our work. I feel pretty sure that we shant disappear as long as we're doing something useful; but if we only sit here talking, either we shall disappear or the people who are listening to us will. What we have learnt here today is that the day of judgment is not the end of the world but the beginning of real human responsibility. Charles and I have still our duties: the Unexpected Isles have to be governed today just as they had to be yesterday. Sally: if you have given your orders for the housework today, go and cook something or sew something or tidy up the books. Come on, Charles. Lets get to work. [He goes into the house].

SIR CHARLES [to his wife, rising] You might take a turn in the garden, dear: gardening is the only unquestionably useful job. [He follows Hyering into the house].

LADY FARWATERS [rising] Prola: shall I bring you some knitting to occupy you?

PROLA. No, thank you. I have some thinking to do.

LADY FARWATERS. Well, dear: I hope that will count as work. I shall feel safer with my gardening basket. [She goes into the house].

MRS HYERING. J'you think itll be all right if I go and do some crossword puzzles? It cultivates the mind so, dont you think?

PROLA. Does it? Well, do the puzzles and see what will happen. Let life come to you. Goodbye.

MRS HYERING [*alarmed*] Why do you say goodbye? Do you think I am going to disappear?

PROLA. Possibly. Or possibly *I* may.

MRS HYERING. Oh then for heaven's sake dont do it in my presence. Wait til Ive gone.

She scuttles up the steps into the house, leaving Prola and Pra alone together.

PRA. Tell me the truth, Prola. Are you waiting for me to disappear? Do you feel that you can do better without me? Have you always felt that you could do better without me?

PROLA. That is a murderer's thought. Have you ever let yourself think it? How often have you said to yourself 'I could do better alone, or with another woman'?

PRA. Fairly often, my dear, when we were younger. But I did not murder you. Thats the answer. And you?

PROLA. All that stuff belongs to the past: to the childhood of our marriage. We have now grown together until we are each of us a part of the other. I no longer think of you as a separate possibility.

PRA. I know. I am part of the furniture of your house. I am a matter of course. But was I always that? Was I that in the childhood of our marriage?

PROLA. You are still young enough and manlike enough to ask mischievous questions.

PRA. No matter: we shall both disappear presently; and I have still some curiosity left. Did you ever really care for me? I know I began as a passion and have ended as a habit, like all husbands; but outside that routine there is a life of the intellect that is quite independent of it. What have I been to you in that life? A help or a hindrance?

PROLA. Pra: I always knew from the very beginning that you were an extraordinarily clever fool.

PRA. Good. That is exactly what I am.

PROLA. But I knew also that nobody but a fool would be frivolous enough to join me in doing all the mad things I wanted to do. And no ordinary fool would have been subtle enough to understand me, nor clever enough to keep off the

rocks of social ruin. Ive grown fond enough of you for all
practical purposes; —

PRA. Thank you.

PROLA. — but Ive never allowed you or any other man to
cut me off my own stem and make me a parasite on his.
That sort of love and sacrifice is not the consummation of
a capable woman's existence: it is the temptation she must
resist at all costs.

PRA. That temptation lies in the man's path too. The worst
sacrifices I have seen have been those of men's highest
careers to women's vulgarities and follies.

PROLA. Well, we two have no reproaches and no regrets
on that score.

PRA. No. We are awaiting judgment here quite simply as a
union of a mad woman with a fool.

PROLA. Who thought they had created four wonderful
children. And who are now brought to judgment and con-
victed of having created nothing. We have only repeated
the story of Helen and Faust and their beautiful child
Euphorion. Euphorion also vanished, in his highest flight.

PRA. Yes; but Helen was a dream. You are not a dream.
The children did not vanish like Euphorion in their infancy. They grew up to bore me more intensely than I have
ever been bored by any other set of human creatures.
Come, confess: did they not bore you?

PROLA. Have I denied it? Of course they bored me. They
must have bored one another terribly in spite of all their
dressing up and pretending that their fairyland was real.
How they must have envied the gardener's boy his high
spirits!

PRA. The coming race will not be like them. Meanwhile
we are face to face with the fact that we two have made a
precious mess of our job of producing the coming race by
a mixture of east and west. We are failures. We shall disappear.

PROLA. I do not feel like that. I feel like the leader of a

cavalry charge whose horse has been shot through the head and dropped dead under him. Well, a dead hobby horse is not the end of the world. Remember: we are in the Unexpected Isles; and in the Unexpected Isles all plans fail. So much the better: plans are only jigsaw puzzles: one gets tired of them long before one can piece them together. There are still a million lives beyond all the Utopias and the Millenniums and the rest of the jigsaw puzzles: I am a woman and I know it. Let men despair and become cynics and pessimists because in the Unexpected Isles all their little plans fail: women will never let go their hold on life. We are not here to fulfil prophecies and fit ourselves into puzzles, but to wrestle with life as it comes. And it never comes as we expect it to come.

PRA. It comes like a thief in the night.

PROLA. Or like a lover. Never will Prola go back to the Country of the Expected.

PRA. There is no Country of the Expected. The Unexpected Isles are the whole world.

PROLA. Yes, if our fools only had vision enough to see that. I tell you this is a world of miracles, not of jigsaw puzzles. For me every day must have its miracle, and no child be born like any child that ever was born before. And to witness this miracle of the children I will abide the uttermost evil and carry through it the seed of the uttermost good.

PRA. Then I, Pra, must continue to strive for more knowledge and more power, though the new knowledge always contradicts the old, and the new power is the destruction of the fools who misuse it.

PROLA. We shall plan commonwealths when our empires have brought us to the brink of destruction; but our plans will still lead us to the Unexpected Isles. We shall make wars because only under the strain of war are we capable of changing the world; but the changes our wars will make will never be the changes we intended them to make. We shall clamor for security like frightened children; but in the

Unexpected Isles there is no security; and the future is to those who prefer surprise and wonder to security. I, Prola, shall live and grow because surprise and wonder are the very breath of my being, and routine is death to me. Let every day be a day of wonder for me and I shall not fear the Day of Judgment. [*She is interrupted by a roll of thunder*]. Be silent: you cannot frighten Prola with stage thunder. The fountain of life is within me.

PRA. But you have given the key of it to me, the Man.

PROLA. Yes: I need you and you need me. Life needs us both.

PRA. All hail, then, the life to come!

PROLA. All Hail. Let it come.

They pat hands eastern fashion.

THE MILLIONAIRESS

with

Preface on Bosses

First presented in England by the Matthew Forsyth Repertory Company at the De La Warr Pavilion, Bexhill-on-Sea, on 17 November 1936. First professional West End production at the New Theatre, London, on 27 June 1952.

JULIUS SAGAMORE	Campbell Cotts
EPIFANIA OGNISANTI DI PARERGA FITZFASSENDEN	Katharine Hepburn
ALASTAIR FITZFASSENDEN	Peter Dynley
PATRICIA SMITH	Meriel Forbes
ADRIAN BLENDERBLAND	Cyril Ritchard
THE DOCTOR	Robert Helpmann
THE MAN (JOE)	Bertram Shuttleworth
THE WOMAN (HIS WIFE)	Nora Nicholson
HOTEL MANAGER	Vernon Greeves

Period – The Present

ACT I: *Mr Julius Sagamore's Office in Lincoln's Inn Fields. A Spring Morning*

ACT II: *The Coffee-room of the Pig and Whistle, a Riverside Inn. That Evening*

ACT III: *A Basement Sweatshop in the Commercial Road. The Following Morning*

ACT IV: *The Pig and Whistle (now the Cardinal's Hat). Five Months Later*

Preface on Bosses

THOUGH this play of The Millionairess does not pretend to be anything more than a comedy of humorous and curious contemporary characters such as Ben Jonson might write were he alive now, yet it raises a question that has troubled human life and moulded human society since the creation.

The law is equal before all of us; but we are not all equal before the law. Virtually there is one law for the rich and another for the poor, one law for the cunning and another for the simple, one law for the forceful and another for the feeble, one law for the ignorant and another for the learned, one law for the brave and another for the timid, and within family limits one law for the parent and no law at all for the child.

In the humblest cabin that contains a family you may find a *maîtresse femmè* who rules in the household by a sort of divine right. She may rule amiably by being able to think more quickly and see further than the others, or she may be a tyrant ruling violently by intensity of will and ruthless egotism. She may be a grandmother and she may be a girl. But the others find they are unable to resist her. Often of course the domestic tyrant is a man; but the phenomenon is not so remarkable in this case, as he is by convention the master and lawgiver of the hearthstone.

In every business street you will find a shopkeeper who is always in difficulties and ends his business adventures in the bankruptcy court. Hard by you will find another shopkeeper, with no greater advantages to start with, or possibly less, who makes larger and larger profits, and inspires more and more confidence in his banker, until he ends as the millionaire head of a giant multiple shop

How does the captain of a pirate ship obtain his position and maintain his authority over a crew of scoundrels who are all, like himself, outside the law? How does an obscure village priest, the son of humble fisherfolk, come to wear the triple crown and sit in the papal chair? How do common soldiers become Kings, Shahs, and Dictators? Why does a hereditary peer find that he is a nonentity in a grand house organized and ruled by his butler?

Questions like these force themselves on us so continually and ruthlessly that many turn in despair from Socialism and political reform on the ground that to abolish all the institutional tyrannies would only deliver the country helplessly into the hands of the born bosses. A king, a prelate, a squire, a capitalist, a justice of the peace may be a good kind Christian soul, owing his position, as most of us do, to being the son of his father; but a born boss is one who rides roughshod over us by some mysterious power that separates him from our species and makes us fear him: that is, hate him.

What is to be done with that section of the possessors of specific talents whose talent is for moneymaking? History and daily experience teach us that if the world does not devise some plan of ruling them, they will rule the world. Now it is not desirable that they should rule the world; for the secret of moneymaking is to care for nothing else and to work at nothing else; and as the world's welfare depends on operations by which no individual can make money, whilst its ruin by war and drink and disease and drugs and debauchery is enormously profitable to moneymakers, the supremacy of the moneymaker is the destruction of the State. A society which depends on the incentive of private profit is doomed.

And what about ambitious people who possess commanding business ability or military genius or both? They are irresistible unless they are restrained by law; for ordinary individuals are helpless in their hands. Are they to be the masters of society or its servants?

What should the nineteenth century have done in its youth with Rothschild and Napoleon? What is the United States to do with its money kings and bosses? What are we to do with ours? How is the mediocre private citizen to hold his own with the able bullies and masterful women who establish family despotisms, school despotisms, office despotisms, religious despotisms in their little circles all over the country? Our boasted political liberties are a mockery to the subjects of such despotisms. They may work well when the despot is benevolent; but they are worse than any political tyranny in the selfish cases.

It is much more difficult to attack a personal despotism than an institutional one. Monarchs can be abolished: they have been abolished in all directions during the last century and a half, with the result, however, of sometimes replacing a personally amiable and harmless monarch, reigning under strict constitutional and traditional restraints, by energetic dictators and presidents who, having made hay of constitutions and traditions, are under no restraints at all. A hereditary monarch, on the throne because he is the son of his father, may be a normal person, amenable to reasonable advice from his councils, and exercising no authority except that conferred on him (or her) by the Constitution. Behead him, as we beheaded our Charles, or the French their Louis, and the born despot Cromwell or Napoleon (I purposely avoid glaring contemporary examples because I am not quite sure where they will be by the time this book is published) takes his place. The same mysterious personal force that makes the household tyrant, the school tyrant, the office tyrant, the brigand chief and the pirate captain, brings the born boss to the top by a gravitation that ordinary people cannot resist.

The successful usurpers of thrones are not the worst cases. The political usurper may be an infernal scoundrel, ruthless in murder, treachery, and torture; but once his ambition is achieved and he has to rule a nation, the magnitude and difficulty of his job, and the knowledge that if he makes a mess of it he will fall as suddenly as he has risen, will civilize him with a ruthlessness greater than his own. When Henry IV usurped the English crown he certainly did not intend to die of political overwork; but that is what happened to him. No political ruler could possibly be as wickedly selfish and cruel as the tyrant of a private house. Queen Elizabeth was a *maîtresse femme;* but she could have had her own way much more completely as landlady of the Mermaid Tavern than she had as sovereign of England. Because Nero and Paul I of Russia could not be made to understand this, they were killed like mad dogs by their own courtiers. But our petty fireside tyrants are not killed. Christina of Sweden would not have had to abdicate if her realm had been a ten-roomed villa. Had Catherine II reigned over her husband only, she need not nor could not have had him murdered; but as Tsarina she was forced to liquidate poor Peter very much against her own easy good nature, which prevented her from scolding her maids properly.

Modern Liberal democracy claims unlimited opportunities for tyranny: qualification for rule by heredity and class narrows it and puts it in harness and blinkers. Especially does such democracy favor money rule. It is in fact not democracy at all, but unashamed plutocracy. And as the meanest creature can become rich if he devotes his life to it, and the people with wider and more generous interests become or remain poor with equal certainty, plutocracy is the very devil socially, because it creates a sort of Gresham law by which the baser human currency drives out the nobler coinage. This is quite different from the survival of the fittest in the contests of character and talent which are independent of money. If Moses is the only tribesman capable of making a code of laws, he inevitably becomes Lawgiver to all the tribes, and, equally inevitably, is forced to add to what he can understand of divine law a series of secular regulations designed to maintain his personal authority. If he finds that it is useless to expect the tribesmen to obey his laws as a matter of common sense, he must persuade them that his inspiration is the result of direct and miraculous communication with their deity. Moses and Mahomet and Joseph Smith the Mormon had to plead divine revelations to get them out of temporary and personal difficulties as well as out of eternal and impersonal ones. As long as an individual of their calibre remains the indispensable man (or woman) doing things that the common man can neither do without nor do for himself, he will be, up to a point, the master of the common man in spite of all the domocratic fudge that may be advanced to the contrary.

Of course there are limits. He cannot go to the lengths at which the common man will believe him to be insane or impious: when measures of that complexion are necessary, as they very often are, he must either conceal them or mask them as follies of the sort the common man thinks splendid. If the ruler thinks it well to begin a world war he must persuade his people that it is a war to end war, and that the people he wants them to kill are diabolical scoundrels; and if he is forced to suspend hostilities for a while, and does so by a treaty which contains the seeds of half a dozen new wars and is impossible enough in its conditions to make its violation certain, he must create a general belief that it is a charter of eternal peace and a monument of retributive justice.

In this way the most honest ruler becomes a tyrant and a fabricator of legends and falsehoods, not out of any devilment in himself, but because those whom he rules do not understand his business, and, if they did, would not sacrifice their own immediate interests to the permanent interests of the nation or the world. In short, a ruler must not only make laws, and rule from day to day: he must, by school instruction and printed propaganda, create and maintain an artificial mentality which will endorse his proceedings and obey his authority. This mentality becomes what we call Conservatism; and the revolt against it when it is abused oppressively or becomes obsolete as social conditions change, is classed as sedition, and reviled as Radicalism, Anarchism, Bolshevism, or what you please.

When a mentality is created and a code imposed, the born ruler, the Moses or Lenin, is no longer indispensable: routine government by dunderheads becomes possible and in fact preferable as long as the routine is fairly appropriate to the current phase of social development. The assumption of the more advanced spirits that revolutionists are always right is as questionable as the conservative assumption that they are always wrong. The industrious dunderhead who always does what was done last time because he is incapable of conceiving anything better, makes the best routineer. This explains the enormous part played by dunderheads as such in the history of all nations, provoking repeated explanations of surprise at the littleness of the wisdom with which the world is governed.

But what of the ambitious usurper? the person who has a capacity for kingship but has no kingdom and must therefore acquire a readymade one which is getting along in its own way very well without him? It cannot be contended with any plausibility that William the Conqueror was indispensable in England: he wanted England and grabbed it. He did this by virtue of his personal qualities, entirely against the will of the people of England, who, as far as they were politically conscious at all, would have greatly preferred Harold. But William had all the qualities that make an individual irresistible: the physical strength and ferocity of a king of beasts, the political genius of a king of men, the strategic cunning and tactical gumption of a military genius; and nothing that France or England could say or do prevailed against him. What are we to do with such people?

When an established political routine breaks down and produces political chaos, a combination of personal ambition with military genius and political capacity in a single individual gives that individual his opportunity. Napoleon, if he had been born a century earlier, would have had no more chance of becoming emperor of the French than Marshal Saxe had of supplanting Louis XV. In spite of the French Revolution, he was a very ordinary snob in his eighteenth-century social outlook. His assumption of the imperial diadem, his ridiculous attempt to establish the little Buonaparte family on all the thrones under his control, his remanufacture of a titular aristocracy to make a court for himself, his silly insistence on imperial etiquette when he was a dethroned and moribund prisoner in St Helena, shew that, for all his genius, he was and always had been behind the times. But he was for a time irresistible because, though he could fight battles on academic lines only, and was on that point a routineer soldier, he could play the war game on the established procedure so superbly that all the armies of Europe crumpled up before him. It was easy for anti-Bonapartist writers, from Taine to Mr H. G. Wells, to disparage him as a mere cad; but Goethe, who could face facts, and on occasion rub them in, said simply 'You shake your chains in vain.' Unfortunately for himself and Europe Napoleon was fundamentally a commonplace human fool. In spite of his early failure in the east he made a frightful draft on the manhood of France for his march to Moscow, only to hurry back leaving his legions dead in the snow, and thereafter go from disaster to disaster. Bernadotte, the lawyer's son who enlisted as a common soldier and ended unconquered on the throne of Sweden (his descendants still hold it), made a far better job of his affairs. When for the first time Napoleon came up against a really original commander at Waterloo, he still made all the textbook moves he had learnt at the military academy, and did not know when he was beaten until it was too late to do anything but run away. Instead of making for America at all hazards he threw himself on the magnanimity of the Prince Regent, who obviously could not have spared him even if he had wanted to. His attempt to wedge himself and his upstart family into the old dynasties by his divorce and his Austrian marriage ended in making him a notorious cuckold. But the vulgarer fool and the paltrier snob you prove Napoleon to have been, the more alarming becomes the fact that this shabby-genteel Corsican subaltern (and a very unsatisfactory subaltern at that) dominated Europe for years, and placed on his own head the crown of Charlemagne. Is there really nothing to be done with such men but submit to them until, having risen by their specialities, they ruin themselves by their vulgarities?

It was easy for Napoleon to make a better job of restoring

order after the French Revolution than Sieyès, who tried to do it by writing paper constitutions, or than a plucky bully like Barras, who cared for nothing except feathering his own nest. Any tidy and public spirited person could have done as much with the necessary prestige. Napoleon got that prestige by feeding the popular appetite for military glory. He could not create that natural appetite; but he could feed it by victories; and he could use all the devices of journalism and pageantry and patriotic braggadocio to make La Gloire glorious. And all this because, like William the Conqueror, he had the group of talents that make a successful general and democratic ruler. Had not the French Revolution so completely failed to produce a tolerable government to replace the monarchy it overthrew, and thereby reduced itself to desperation, Napoleon would have been only a famous general like Saxe or Wellington or Marlborough, who under similar circumstances could and indeed must have become kings if they had been ungovernable enough to desire it. Only the other day a man without any of the social advantages of these commanders made himself Shah of Iran.

Julius Caesar and Cromwell also mounted on the débris of collapsing political systems; and both of them refused crowns. But no crown could have added to the power their military capacity gave them. Caesar bribed enormously; but there were richer men than he in Rome to play that game. Only, they could not have won the battle of Pharsalia. Cromwell proved invincible in the field – such as it was.

It is not, however, these much hackneyed historical figures that trouble us now. Pharsalias and Dunbars and Waterloos are things of the past: battles nowadays last several months and then peter out on barbed wire under the fire of machine guns. Suppose Ludendorff had been a Napoleon, and Haig a Marlborough, Wellington, and Cromwell rolled into one, what more could they have done than either declare modern war impossible or else keep throwing masses of infantry in the old fashion against slaughtering machinery like pigs in

Chicago? Napoleon's booklearnt tactics and the columns that won so many battles for him would have no more chance nowadays than the ragged Irish pikemen on Vinegar Hill; and Wellington's thin red line and his squares would have vanished in the fumes of T.N.T. on the Somme. 'The Nelson touch' landed a section of the British fleet at the bottom of the Dardanelles. And yet this war, which, if it did not end civilized war (perhaps it did, by the way, though the War Office may not yet have realized it) at least made an end of the supremacy of the glory virtuoso who can play brilliant variations on the battle of Hastings, has been followed by such a group of upstart autocrats as the world had ceased to suppose possible. Mussolini, Hitler, Kemal and Riza Khan began in the ranks, and have no Marengos to their credit; yet there they are at the top!

Here again the circumstances gave the men their opportunity. Neither Mussolini nor Hitler could have achieved their present personal supremacy when I was born in the middle of the nineteenth century, because the prevailing mentality of that deluded time was still hopefully parliamentary. Democracy was a dream, an ideal. Everything would be well when all men had votes. Everything would be better than well when all women had votes. There was a great fear of public opinion because it was a dumb phantom which every statesman could identify with his own conscience and dread as the Nemesis of unscrupulous ambition. That was the golden age of democracy: the phantom was a real and beneficent force. Many delusions are. In those days even our Conservative rulers agreed that we were a liberty loving people: that, for instance, Englishmen would never tolerate compulsory military service as the slaves of foreign despots did.

It was part of the democratic dream that Parliament was an instrument for carrying out the wishes of the voters, absurdly called its constituents. And as, in the nineteenth century, it was still believed that British individual liberty forbad Parliament to do anything that it could possibly leave to private enterprise, Parliament was able to keep up its reputation by simply maintaining an effective police force and enforcing private contracts. Even Factory Acts and laws against adulteration and sweating were jealously resisted as interferences with the liberty of free Britons. If there was anything wrong, the remedy was an extension of the franchise. Like Hamlet, we lived on the chameleon's dish 'air, promise crammed.'

But you cannot create a mentality out of promises without having to face occasional demands for their materialization. The Treasury Bench was up for auction at every election, the bidding being in promises. The political parties, finding it much less troublesome to give the people votes than to carry out reforms, at last established adult suffrage.

The result was a colossal disappointment and disillusion. The phantom of Democracy, *alias* Public Opinion, which, acting as an artificial political conscience, had restrained Gladstone and Disraeli, vanished. The later parliamentary leaders soon learnt from experience that they might with perfect impunity tell the nation one thing on Tuesday and the opposite on Friday without anyone noticing the discrepancy. The donkey had overtaken the carrots at last; and instead of eating them he allowed them to be snatched away from him by any confidence trickster who told him to look up into the sky.

The diplomatists immediately indulged themselves with a prodigiously expensive war, after which the capitalist system, which had undertaken to find employment for everybody at subsistence wages, and which, though it had never fulfilled that undertaking, had at least found employment for enough of them to leave the rest too few to be dangerous, defaulted in respect of unprecedented millions of unemployed, who had to be bought off by doles administered with a meanness and cruelty which revived all the infamies of the Poor Law of a century ago (the days of Oliver Twist) and could not be administered in any kinder way without weakening the willingness of its recipients to prefer even the poorliest paid job to its humiliations.

The only way of escape was for the government to organize the labor of the unemployed for the supply of their own needs. But Parliament not only could not do this, but could and did prevent its being done. In vain did the voters use their votes to place a Labor Government, with a Cabinet of Socialists, on the Treasury Bench. Parliament took these men, who had been intransigent Socialists and revolutionists all their lives, and reduced them to a condition of political helplessness in which they were indistinguishable except by name from the most reactionary members of the House of Lords or the military clubs. A Socialist Prime Minister, after trying for years to get the parliamentary car into gear for a move forward, and finding that though it would work easily and smoothly in neutral the only gear that would engage was the reverse gear (popularly called 'the axe' because it could do nothing but cut down wages), first formed what he called a national government by a coalition of all parties, and then, having proved by this experiment that it did not make the smallest difference whether members of the Cabinet were the reddest of Bolsheviks or the bluest of Tories, made things easier by handing over his premiership to a colleague who, being a Conservative, and popular and amiable into the bargain, could steal a horse where a Socialist dare not look over a hedge. The voters rejected him at the next election; but he retained his membership of the Cabinet precisely as if he had been triumphantly returned. Bismarck could have done no more.

These events, helped by the terrific moral shock of war, and the subsequent exposure of the patriotic lying by which the workers of Europe had been provoked to slaughter one another, made an end of the nineteenth century democratic mentality. Parliament fell into contempt; ballot papers were less esteemed than toilet papers; the men from the trenches had no patience with the liberties that had not saved them from being driven like sheep to the shambles.

Of this change our parliamentarians and journalists had no suspicion. Creatures of habit, they went on as if nothing had occurred since Queen Victoria's death except a couple of extensions of the franchise and an epochmaking revolution in Russia which they poohpoohed as a transient outburst of hooliganism fomented by a few bloodthirsty scoundrels, exactly as the American revolution and the French revolution had been poohpoohed when they, too, were contemporary.

Here was clearly a big opportunity for a man psychologist enough to grasp the situation and bold enough to act on it. Such a man was Mussolini. He had become known as a journalist by championing the demobilized soldiers, who, after suffering all the horrors of the war, had returned to find that the men who had been kept at home in the factories comfortably earning good wages, had seized those factories according to the Syndicalist doctrine of 'workers' control', and were wrecking them in their helpless ignorance of business. As one indignant master-Fascist said to me 'They were listening to speeches round red flags and leaving the cows unmilked.'

The demobilized fell on the Syndicalists with sticks and stones. Some, more merciful, only dosed them with castor oil. They carried Mussolini to Rome with a rush. This gave him the chance of making an irreparable mistake and spending the next fifteen years in prison. It seemed just the occasion for a grand appeal for liberty, for democracy, for a parliament in which the people were supreme: in short, for nineteenth century resurrection pie. Mussolini did not make that mistake. With inspired precision he denounced Liberty as a putrefying corpse. He declared that what people needed was not liberty but discipline, the sterner the better. He said that he would not tolerate Oppositions: he called for action and silence. The people, instead of being shocked like good Liberals, rose to him. He was able to organize a special constabulary who wore black shirts and applied the necessary coercion.

Such improvised bodies attracted young men of military

tastes and old soldiers, inevitably including a percentage of ruffians and Sadists. This fringe of undesirables soon committed outrages and a couple of murders, whereupon all the Liberal newspapers in Europe shrieked with horror as if nothing else was happening in Italy. Mussolini refused to be turned aside from his work like a parliamentary man to discuss 'incidents.' All he said was 'I take the responsibility for everything that has happened.' When the Italian Liberals joined in the shrieking he seized the shriekers and transported them to the Lipari Isles. Parliament, openly flouted, chastised, and humiliated, could do nothing. The people were delighted; for that was just how they wanted to see Parliament treated. The doctrinaires of liberty fled to France and England, preferring them to Lipari, and wrote eloquent letters to the papers demanding whether every vestige of freedom, freedom of speech, freedom of the press, freedom of Parliament, was to be trampled under the heel of a ruthless dictator merely because the Italian trains were running punctually and travellers in Italy could depend on their luggage not being stolen without actually sitting on it. The English editors gave them plenty of space, and wrote sympathetic articles paraphrasing John Stuart Mill's Essay on Liberty. Mussolini, now Il Duce, never even looked round: he was busy sweeping up the elected municipalities, and replacing them with efficient commissioners of his own choice, who had to do their job or get out. The editors had finally to accord him a sort of Pragmatic Sanction by an admission that his plan worked better than the old plan; but they were still blind to the fact staring them in the face that Il Duce, knowing what the people wanted and giving it to them, was responding to the real democratic urge whilst the cold tealeaves of the nineteenth century were making them sick. It was evident that Mussolini was master of Italy as far as such mastership is possible; but what was not evident to Englishmen who had had their necks twisted the other way from their childhood was that even when he deliberately spat in the face of the

League of Nations at Corfu, and defiantly asked the Powers whether they had anything to say about it, he was delighting his own people by the spectacle of a great Italian bullying the world, and getting away with it triumphantly. Parliaments are supposed to have their fingers always on the people's pulse and to respond to its slightest throb. Mussolini proved that parliaments have not the slightest notion of how the people are feeling, and that he, being a good psychologist and a man of the people himself to boot, was a true organ of democracy.

I, being a bit of a psychologist myself, also understood the situation, and was immediately denounced by the refugees and their champions as an antidemocrat, a hero worshipper of tyrants, and all the rest of it.

Hitler's case was different; but he had only one quality in common with Il Duce: he knew what the victorious Allies would fight for and what they would only bluster about. They had already been forced to recognize that their demands for plunder had gone far beyond Germany's utmost resources. But there remained the clauses of the Versailles treaty by which Germany was to be kept in a condition of permanent, decisive, and humiliating military inferiority to the other Powers, and especially to France. Hitler was political psychologist enough to know that the time had arrived when it would be quite impossible for the Allies to begin the war over again to enforce these clauses. He saw his opportunity and took it. He violated the clauses, and declared that he was going to go on violating them until a fully re-armed Germany was on equal terms with the victors. He did not soften his defiance by any word of argument or diplomacy. He knew that his attitude was safe and sure of success; and he took care to make it as defiant as that of Ajax challenging the lightning. The Powers had either to renew the war or tear up the impossible clauses with a good grace. But they could not grasp the situation, and went on nagging pitifully about the wickedness of breaking a treaty. Hitler said that if they mentioned that subject again Germany would withdraw from the League of

Nations and cut the Powers dead. He bullied and snubbed as
the man who understands a situation can always bully and
snub the nincompoops who are only whining about it. He at
once became a popular idol, and had the regular executive
forces so completely devoted to him that he was able to dis-
band the brownshirted constabulary he had organized on the
Mussolini model. He met the conventional democratic challenge by plebiscites of ninety per cent in his favor. The myopia
of the Powers had put him in a position so far stronger than
Mussolini's that he was able to kill seventy-seven of his most
dangerous opponents at a blow and then justify himself completely before an assembly fully as representative as the British
Parliament, the climax being his appointment as absolute
dictator in Germany for life, a stretch of Caesarism no
nineteenth century Hohenzollern would have dreamt of
demanding.

Hitler was able to go further than Mussolini because he had
a defeated, plundered, humiliated nation to rescue and restore, whereas Mussolini had only an irritated but victorious
one. He carried out a persecution of the Jews which went to
the scandalous length of outlawing, plundering, and exiling
Albert Einstein, a much greater man than any politician, but
great in such a manner that he was quite above the heads of
the masses and therefore so utterly powerless economically
and militarily that he depended for his very existence on the
culture and conscience of the rulers of the earth. Hitler's
throwing Einstein to the Antisemite wolves was an appalling
breach of cultural faith. It raised the question which is the
root question of this preface: to wit, what safeguard have the
weaponless great against the great who have myrmidons at
their call? It is the most frightful betrayal of civilization for the
rulers who monopolize physical force to withhold their
protection from the pioneers in thought. Granted that they
are sometimes forced to do it because intellectual advances
may present themselves as quackery, sedition, obscenity, or
blasphemy, and always present themselves as heresies. Had

Einstein been formally prosecuted and sentenced by the German National Socialist State, as Galileo was prosecuted by the Church, for shaking the whole framework of established physical science by denying the infallibility of Newton, introducing fantastic factors into mathematics, destroying human faith in absolute measurement, and playing an incomprehensible trick with the sacred velocity of light, quite a strong case could have been made out by the public prosecutor. But to set the police on him because he was a Jew could be justified only on the ground that the Jews are the natural enemies of the rest of the human race, and that as a state of perpetual war necessarily exists between them any Gentile has the same reason for killing any Jew at sight as the Roman soldier had for killing Archimedes.

Now no doubt Jews are most obnoxious creatures. Any competent historian or psycho-analyst can bring a mass of incontrovertible evidence to prove that it would have been better for the world if the Jews had never existed. But I, as an Irishman, can, with patriotic relish, demonstrate the same of the English. Also of the Irish. If Herr Hitler would only consult the French and British newspapers and magazines of the latter half of 1914, he would learn that the Germans are a race of savage idolaters, murderers, liars, and fiends whose assumption of the human form is thinner than that of the wolf in Little Red Riding Hood.

We all live in glass houses. Is it wise to throw stones at the Jews? Is it wise to throw stones at all?

Herr Hitler is not only an Antisemite, but a believer in the possibility and desirability of a pure bred German race. I should like to ask him why. All Germans are not Mozarts, nor even Mendelssohns and Meyerbeers, both of whom, by the way, though exceptionally desirable Germans, were Jews. Surely the average German can be improved. I am told that children bred from Irish colleens and Chinese laundrymen are far superior to inbred Irish or Chinese. Herr Hitler is not a typical German. I should not be at all surprised if it were discovered that his very mixed blood (all our bloods today are hopelessly mixed) got fortified somewhere in the past by that of King David. He cannot get over the fact that the lost tribes of Israel expose us all to the suspicion (sometimes, as in Abyssinia, to the boast) that we are those lost tribes, or at least that we must have absorbed them.

One of my guesses in this matter is that Herr Hitler in his youth was fascinated by Houston Chamberlain's Foundations of the XIX Century, an interesting book which at the time of its appearance I recommended everybody to read. Its ethnology was not wholly imaginary. A smattering of Mendelism is all that one needs to know that the eternal fusion of races does not always blend them. The Jews will often throw up an apparently pure-bred Hittite or a pure-bred Philistine. The Germans throw up out-and-out blond beasts side by side with dark Saturnine types like the Führer himself. I am a blond, much less an antique Roman than a Dane. One of my sisters was a brunette: the other had hair of a flaming red seen only in the Scottish Highlands, to which my ancestry has been traced. All these types with which writers like Chamberlain play: the Teutons and Latins, the Apollonians and Dionysians, the Nordics and Southics, the Dominants and Recessives, have existed and keep cropping up as individuals, and exciting antipathies or affinities quite often enough to give substance to theories about them; but the notion that they can be segregated as races or species is bosh. We have nations with national characteristics (rapidly fading, by the way), national languages, and national customs. But they deteriorate without cross- fertilization; and if Herr Hitler could put a stop to cross fertilization in Germany and produce a population of brainless Bismarcks Germany would be subjugated by cross-fertilized aliens, possibly by cosmopolitan Jews. There is more difference between a Catholic Bavarian and a Lutheran Prussian, between a tall fair Saxon and a stocky Baltic Celt, than there is between a Frankfort Jew and a Frankfort Gentile. Even in Africa, where pink emigrants struggle with brown and black natives for possession of the land, and our Jamaican miscegenation shocks public sentiment, the sun sterilizes the pinks to such an extent that Cabinet ministers call for more emigration to maintain the pink population. They do not yet venture to suggest that the pinks had better darken their skins with a mixture of Bantu or Zulu blood; but that conclusion is obvious. In New Zealand, in Hawaii, there are pure-bred pinks and yellows; but there are hardly any pure-bred Maories or South Sea Islanders left. In Africa the intelligent pink native is a Fusionist as between Dutch and British stock. The intelligent Jew is a Fusionist as between Jew and Gentile stock, even when he is also a bit of a Zionist. Only the stupidest or craziest ultra-Nationalists believe that people corralled within the same political frontier are all exactly alike, and that they improve by continuous inbreeding.

Now Herr Hitler is not a stupid German. I therefore urge upon him that his Antisemitism and national exclusiveness must be pathological: a craze, a complex, a bee in his bonnet, a hole in his armor, a hitch in his statesmanship, one of those lesions which sometimes prove fatal. As it has no logical connection with Fascism or National Socialism, and has no effect on them except to bring them into disrepute, I doubt whether it can survive its momentary usefulness as an excuse for plundering raids and *coups d'état* against inconvenient Liberals or Marxists. A persecution is always a man hunt; and man hunting is not only a very horrible sport but socially a dangerous one, as it revives a primitive instinct incompatible with civilization: indeed civilization rests fundamentally on the compact that it shall be dropped.

And here comes the risk we run when we allow a dominant individual to become a despot. There is a story told of a pious man who was sustained through a lifetime of crushing misfortune by his steady belief that if he fought the good fight to the end he would at last stand in the presence of his God. In due course he died, and presented himself at the gates of heaven for his reward. St Peter, who was for some reason much worried, hastily admitted him and bade him go and enjoy himself. But the good man said that he did not want to enjoy himself: he wanted to stand in the presence of God. St Peter tried to evade the claim, dwelling on the other delights of heaven, coaxing, bullying, arguing. All in vain: he could not shake the claimant and could not deny his right. He sent for St Paul, who was as worried and as evasive as his colleague; but he also failed to induce the newcomer to forgo his promised privilege. At last they took him by the arms and led him to a mighty cathedral, where, entering by the west door, he saw the Ancient of Days seated in silent majesty on a throne in the choir. He sprang forward to prostrate himself at the divine feet, but was held back firmly by the apostles. 'Be quiet' said St Paul. 'He has gone mad; and we dont know what to do.' 'Dont tell anybody' added St Peter. And there the story ends.

But that is not how the story ends on earth. Make any common fellow an autocrat and at once you have the Beggar on Horseback riding to the devil. Even when, as the son of his father, he has been trained from infancy to behave well in harness and blinkers, he may go as mad sadistically as a Roman emperor or a Russian Tsar. But that is only the extreme case. Uncommon people, promoted on their merits, are by no means wholly exempt from megalomania. Morris's simple and profound saying that 'no man is good enough to be another man's master' holds good unless both master and man regard themselves as equally the fellow servants of God in States where God still reigns, or, in States where God is dead, as the subjects and agents of a political constitution applying humane principles which neither of them may violate. In that case autocrats are no longer autocrats. Failing any such religious or political creed all autocrats go more or less mad. That is a plain fact of political pathology.

Judged in this light our present predicament is lamentable. We no longer believe in the old 'sanctions' (as they are called nowadays) of heaven and hell; and except in Russia there is not in force a single political constitution that enables and enjoins the citizen to earn his own living as a matter of elementary honesty, or that does not exalt vast personal riches and the organization of slaughter and conquest above all conditions and activities. The financier and the soldier are the cocks of the walk; and democracy means that their parasites and worshippers carry all before them.

Thus when so many other tyrannies have been swept away by simple Liberalism, the tyranny of the talented individuals will remain. Again I ask what are we to do with them in self-defence? Mere liquidation would be disastrous, because at present only about five per cent of the population are capable of making decisions of any importance; and without many daily decisions civilization would go to pieces. The problem is how to make sure that the decisions shall be made in the general interest and not solely in the immediate personal interest of the decider. It was argued by our classical political economists that there is a divine harmony between these two interests of such a nature that if every decider does the best for himself the result will also be the best for everybody. In spite of a century of bitter experience of the adoption of these excuses for laziness in politics, shameless selfishness in industry, and glorification of idle uselessness in the face of the degrading misery of the masses, they are still taught in our universities, and, what is worse, broadcast by university professors by wireless, as authentic political economy instead of what they really are: that is, the special pleading put forward in defence of the speculators, exploiters, and parasitic property owners in whose grossly antisocial interests the country is misgoverned. Since Karl Marx and Friedrich Engels exposed the horrible condition of the working classes that underlies the pursepride and snobbery of the upper middle classes and the prestige of the landed gentry and peerage there has been no substantial excuse for believing in the alleged harmony of interests. Nothing more diabolical can be conceived than the destiny of a civilization in which the material sources of the people's subsistence are privately owned by a handful of persons taught from childhood that every penny they can extort from the propertyless is an addition to the prosperity of their country and an enrichment of the world at large.

But private property is not the subject of my demonstration in The Millionairess. Private property can be communized. Capitalists and landlords can be pressed into the service of the community, or, if they are idle or incorrigibly recalcitrant, handed over to the police. Under such circumstances the speculator would find his occupation gone. With him would disappear the routine exploiter. But the decider, the dominator, the organizer, the tactician, the mesmerizer would remain; and if they were still educated as ladies and gentlemen are educated today, and consequently had the same sort of consciences and ambitions, they would, if they had anything like our present proletariat to deal with, re-establish industrial anarchy and heritable private property in land with all their disastrous consequences and Gadarene destiny. And their rule, being that of able persons and not of nincompoops born with silver spoons in their mouths, would at first produce some striking improvements in the working of the public services, including the elimination of dud dignitaries and the general bracing up of plodders and slackers. But when dominators die, and are succeeded by persons who can only work a routine, a relapse is inevitable; and the destruction by the dominators of the organizations by which citizens defend themselves against oppression (trade unions, for example) may be found to leave society less organized than it was before the hand of the master had risen from the dust to which it has returned. For it is obvious that a business organized for control by an exceptionally omnipotent and omniscient head will go to pieces when that head is replaced by a commonplace numskull. We need not go back to Richard Cromwell or the Duke of Reichstadt to illustrate this. It is occurring every day in commercial business.

Now the remedy lies, not in the extermination of all dominators and deciders, but on the contrary in their multiplication to what may be called their natural minority limit, which will destroy their present scarcity value. But we must also eliminate the mass of ignorance, weakness, and timidity which force them to treat fools according to their folly. Armies, fanatical sects and mobs, and the blackshirts complained of today by their black and blue victims, have consisted hitherto mostly of people who should not exist in civilized society. Titus Oates and Lord George Gordon owed their vogue to the London mob. There should not have been any London mob. The soldiers of Marlborough and Wellington were never-do-wells, mental defectives, and laborers with the minds and habits of serfs. Military geniuses could hunt with such products more easily than with a pack of hounds. Our public school and university education equips armies of this kind with appropriate staffs of officers. When both are extinct we shall be able to breathe more freely.

Let us therefore assume that the soldier and his officer as we know them, the Orange and Papist rioters of Belfast, the Moslem and Hindu irreconcilables of the east and the Ku-Klux-Klans and lynching mobs of the west, have passed away as the less dangerous prehistoric monsters have passed, and that all men and women are meeting on equal terms as far as circumstances and education are concerned. Let us suppose that no man can starve or flog his fellows into obeying him, or force upon them the alternative of risking their lives for him in battle or being shot at dawn. Let us take for granted armies intelligent enough to present their officers at any moment with the alternative of organizing a return home or being superseded out of hand. Let us narrow the case to the mysterious precedence into which certain people get pushed even when they lack ambition and are far too intelligent to believe that eminence and its responsibilities are luxuries. To be 'greatest among you' is a distinction dearly bought at the price of being 'servant to all the rest.' Plato was quite right in

taking reluctance to govern as a leading symptom of supreme
fitness for it. But if we insisted on this qualification in all cases,
we should find ourselves as short of governors as the churches
would be if they insisted on all their parish priests or rectors
being saints. A great deal of the directing and organizing
work of the world will still have to be done by energetic and
capable careerists who are by no means void of vulgar ambition, and very little troubled by the responsibilities that
attend on power. When I said that Napoleon was fundamentally a fool and a snob I did not mean for a moment to question
his extraordinary capacity as a ruler of men. If we compare
him with his valet-secretary Bourrienne we find that there
were no external circumstances to prevent Bourrienne
becoming the emperor and Napoleon the valet. They quar-
relled and parted with an exchange of epithets unprintable in
polite English. Bourrienne was as much a Man of Destiny as
Buonaparte. But it was his destiny to be ruled and
Buonaparte's to rule; and so Buonaparte became Napoleon
Bonaparte, First Consul and Emperor, as inevitably as Bourrienne remained a speculator, litterateur and diplomatist. I
am not forgetting that Bourrienne saw Napoleon come and
go, and had a much more comfortable and finally a more
successful career than his quondam master; but the point is
that Napoleon was master whilst their personal relations las-
ted. And please note that Napoleon did not and could not
impose on Bourrienne and Talleyrand, nor even on the more
cultivated of his marshals (all planetary Napoleons) as he
could and did on the soldiery and peasantry. They turned
against him very promptly when his fortunes changed and he
could no longer be of any use to them.

Now if a ruler can command men only as long as he is
efficient and successful his rule is neither a tyranny nor a
calamity: it is a very valuable asset. But suppose the nation is
made up for the most part of people too ignorant to understand efficient government, and taught, as far as they are
taught at all, to measure greatness by pageantry and the

wholesale slaughter called military glory. It was this ignorance and idolatry that first exalted Napoleon and then
smashed him. From Toulon to Austerlitz Napoleon did what
good he did by stealth, and had no occasion to 'blush to find
it fame,' as nobody gave him the least credit for anything but
killing. When the glory turned to shame on the road back
from Moscow his good works availed him nothing, and the
way was open to St Helena. Catherine of Russia, when she
was faced with a revolt against the misery of her people, said,
not 'Let us relieve their misery by appropriate reforms,' but
'Let us give them a little war to amuse them.' Every tottering
regime tries to rally its subjects to its support in the last resort
by a war. It was not only the last card of Napoleon III before
he lost the game: it played a considerable part in the capitalist
support of Hohenzollern sabre rattling which made the desperate onslaught of Germany in 1914 possible. Patriotism,
roused to boiling point by an enemy at the gate, is not only
the last refuge of a scoundrel in Dr Johnson's sense, it is far
more dangerously the everyday resort of capitalism and
feudalism as a red herring across the scent of Communism.
Under such circumstances it is fortunate that war on the
modern scale is so completely beyond the capacity of private
capitalism that, as in 1915, it forces the belligerents into national factory production, public discipline, and rationed
distribution: in short into Socialism. Not only did national
factories spring up like mushrooms, but the private factories
had to be brought up to the mark by public control of prices
and dictation of scientific business methods, involving such an
exposure of the obsolescence and inefficiency of profitmonger-
ing methods that it took years of reckless lying from Press and
platform to make the silly public believe the contrary. For war
is like the seven magic bullets which the devil has ready to sell
for a human soul. Six of them may hit the glorymonger's mark
very triumphantly; but the seventh plays some unexpected
and unintended trick that upsets the gunman's apple cart. It
seemed an astute stroke of German imperial tactics to

send Lenin safely through Germany to Russia so that he might make trouble for the Tsar. But the bullet was a number seven: it killed the Tsar very efficiently; but it came back like a boomerang and laid the Hohenzollerns beside the Romanoffs.

Pageantry will lose its black magic when it becomes a local popular amusement; so that the countryside may come to know it from behind the scenes, when, though it will still please, it will no longer impose. For mere iconoclasm is a mistake: the Roundhead folly (really a Thickhead one) of destroying the power of the pageant by forbidding all theatrical displays and dressings-up, and making everybody wear ugly clothes, ended in the flamboyant profligacy of the Restoration; and the attempt to enforce the second commandment by smashing the images soon smashed the second commandment. Give away the secret that the dressed-up performers are only amateurs, and the images works of art, and the dupes and worshippers will become undeluded connoisseurs.

Unfortunately it is easier to produce a nation of artistic than of political connoisseurs. Our schools and universities do not concern themselves with fine art, which they despise as an unmanly pursuit. It is possible for a young gentleman to go through the whole educational mill of preparatory school, public school, and university with the highest academic honors without knowing the difference between a chanty and a symphony, a tavern sign and a portrait by Titian, a ballad by Macaulay and a stanza by Keats. But at least he is free to find out all this for himself if he has a fancy that way.

Not so in political science. Not so in religion. In these subjects he is proselytized from the beginning in the interests of established institutions so effectually that he remains all his life firmly convinced that his greatest contemporaries are rascally and venal agitators, villainous blasphemers, or at best seditious cads. He will listen to noodles' orations, read pompous leading articles, and worship the bloodthirsty tribal idols of Noah and Samuel with a gravity and sincerity that would make him infinitely pitiable if they did not also make him infinitely dangerous. He will feed his mind on empty phrases as Nebuchadnezzar fed his body on grass; and any boss who has mastered these phrases can become his dictator, his despot, his evangelist, and in effect his god-emperor.

Clearly we shall be bossridden in one form or another as long as education means being put through this process, or the best imitation of it that our children's parents can afford. The remedy is another Reformation, now long and perilously overdue, in the direction and instruction of our children's minds politically and religiously. We should begin well to the left of Russia, which is still encumbered with nineteenth century superstitions. Communism is the fairy godmother who can transform Bosses into 'servants to all the rest'; but only a creed of Creative Evolution can set the souls of the people free. Then the dominator will still find himself face to face with subordinates who can do nothing without him; but that will not give him the inside grip. A late rich shipowner, engaged in a quarrel with his workmen in which he assumed that I was on their side, rashly asked me what his men could do without him. Naturally I asked him what he could do without them, hoping to open his eyes to the fact that apart from the property rights he had bought or borrowed he was as dependent on them as they on him. But I fear I impressed him most by adding, quite untruly, that no gentleman would have asked that question.

Save for my allusion to the persecution and exile of Einstein I have not said a word here about the miserable plight of the great men neglected, insulted, starved, and occasionally put to death, sometimes horribly, by the little ones. Their case is helpless because nothing can defend them against the might of overwhelming numbers unless and until they develop the Vril imagined by Bulwer-Lytton which will enable one person to destroy a multitude, and thereby make us more particular than we are at present about the sort of persons we produce. I am confining myself to the power wielded by the moneymakers and military geniuses in political life and by the dominant personalities in private life. Lytton's Vril was a fiction only in respect of its being available for everybody, and therefore an infallible preventive of any attempt at oppression. For that individuals here and there possess a power of domination which others are unable to resist is undeniable; and since this power is as yet nameless we may as well call it Vril as anything else. It is the final reality of inequality. It is easy to equalize the dominators with the commonplacers economically: you just give one of them half-a-crown and the other two-and-sixpence. Nelson was paid no more than any other naval captain or admiral; and the poverty of Mozart or Marx was worse than the voluntary holy poverty of the great heads of the religious orders. Dominators and dominated are already equalized before the law: shall not I, a playwright of Shakesperean eminence, be hanged if I commit a murder precisely as if I were the most illiterate call boy? Politically we all have at least the symbol of equality in our votes, useless as they are to us under political and economic institutions made to encourage William the Conqueror to slay Harold and exploit Hodge. But, I repeat, when all these perfectly feasible equalizations are made real, there still remains Epifania, shorn of her millions and unable to replace them, but still as dominant as Saint Joan, Saint Clare, and Saint Teresa. The most complete Communism and Democracy can only give her her chance far more effectively than any feudal or capitalist society.

And this, I take it, is one of the highest claims of Communism and Democracy to our consideration, and the explanation of the apparently paradoxical fact that it is always the greatest spirits, from Jesus to Lenin, from St Thomas More to William Morris, who are communists and democrats, and always the commonplace people who weary us with their blitherings about the impossibility of equality when they are at a loss for any better excuse for keeping other people in the kitchen and themselves in the drawing room. I say cheerfully to the dominators· 'By all means dominate: it is up to us to so order our institutions that you shall not oppress us, nor bequeath any of your precedence to your commonplace children.' For when ambition and greed and mere brainless energy have been disabled, the way will be clear for inspiration and aspiration to save us from the fatheaded stagnation of the accursed Victorian snobbery which is bringing us to the verge of ruin.

Malvern, 28 August 1935

ACT I

Mr Julius Sagamore, a smart young solicitor, is in his office in Lincoln's Inn Fields. It is a fine morning in May. The room, an old panelled one, is so arranged that Mr Sagamore, whom we see sitting under the window in profile with his back to it and his left side presented to us, is fenced off by his writing table from excessive intimacy with emotional clients or possible assault by violent or insane ones. The door is on his right towards the farther end of the room. The faces of the clients are thus illuminated by the window whilst his own countenance is in shadow. The fireplace, of Adam design, is in the wall facing him. It is surmounted by a dingy portrait of a judge. In the wall on his right, near the corner farthest from him, is the door, with a cleft pediment enshrining a bust of some other judge. The rest of this wall is occupied by shelves of calf-bound law books. The wall behind Mr Sagamore has the big window as aforesaid, and beside it a stand of black tin boxes inscribed with clients' names.

So far, the place proclaims the eighteenth century; but as the year is 1935, and Mr Sagamore has no taste for dust and mould, and requires a room which suggests opulence, and in which lady clients will look their best, everything is well dusted and polished; the green carpet is new, rich, and thick; and the half dozen chairs, four of which are ranged under the bookshelves, are Chippendales of the very latest fake. Of the other two one is occupied by himself, and the other stands half way between his table and the fireplace for the accommodation of his clients.

The telephone, on the table at his elbow, rings.

SAGAMORE [*listening*] Yes? ... [*Impressed*] Oh! Send her up at once.

A tragic looking woman, athletically built and expensively dressed, storms into the room. He rises obsequiously.

THE LADY. Are you Julius Sagamore, the worthless nephew of my late solicitor Pontifex Sagamore?

SAGAMORE. I do not advertize myself as worthless; but Pontifex Sagamore was my uncle; and I have returned

245

from Australia to succeed to as much of his business as I can persuade his clients to trust me with.

THE LADY. I have heard him speak of you; and I naturally concluded that as you had been packed off to Australia you must be worthless. But it does not matter, as my business is very simple. I desire to make my will, leaving everything I possess to my husband. You can hardly go wrong about that, I suppose.

SAGAMORE. I shall do my best. Pray sit down.

THE LADY. No: I am restless. I shall sit down when I feel tired.

SAGAMORE. As you please. Before I draw up the will it will be necessary for me to know who your husband is.

THE LADY. My husband is a fool and a blackguard. You will state that fact in the will. You will add that it was his conduct that drove me to commit suicide.

SAGAMORE. But you have not committed suicide.

THE LADY. I shall have, when the will is signed.

SAGAMORE. Of course, quite so: stupid of me. And his name?

THE LADY. His name is Alastair Fitzfassenden.

SAGAMORE. What! The amateur tennis champion and heavy weight boxer?

THE LADY. Do you know him?

SAGAMORE. Every morning we swim together at the club.

THE LADY. The acquaintance does you little credit.

SAGAMORE. I had better tell you that he and I are great friends, Mrs Fitzfassen –

THE LADY. Do not call me by his detestable name. Put me in your books as Epifania Ognisanti di Parerga.

SAGAMORE [bowing] Oh! I am indeed honored. Pray be seated.

EPIFANIA. Sit down yourself; and dont fuss.

SAGAMORE. If you prefer it, certainly. [He sits] Your father was a very wonderful man, madam.

EPIFANIA. My father was the greatest man in the world.

And he died a pauper. I shall never forgive the world for that.

SAGAMORE. A pauper! You amaze me. It was reported that he left you, his only child, thirty millions.

EPIFANIA. Well, what was thirty millions to him? He lost a hundred and fifty millions. He had promised to leave me two hundred millions. I was left with a beggarly thirty. It broke his heart.

SAGAMORE. Still, an income of a million and a half —

EPIFANIA. Man: you forget the death duties. I have barely seven hundred thousand a year. Do you know what that means to a woman brought up on an income of seven figures? The humiliation of it!

SAGAMORE. You take away my breath, madam.

EPIFANIA. As I am about to take my own breath away, I have no time to attend to yours.

SAGAMORE. Oh, the suicide! I had forgotten that.

EPIFANIA. Had you indeed? Well, will you please give your mind to it for a moment, and draw up a will for me to sign, leaving everything to Alastair.

SAGAMORE. To humiliate him?

EPIFANIA. No. To ruin him. To destroy him. To make him a beggar on horseback so that he may ride to the devil. Money goes to his head. I have seen it at work on him.

SAGAMORE. I also have seen that happen. But you cannot be sure. He might marry some sensible woman.

EPIFANIA. You are right. Make it a condition of the inheritance that within a month from my funeral he marries a low female named Polly Seedystockings.

SAGAMORE [making a note of it] A funny name.

EPIFANIA. Her real name is Patricia Smith. But her letters to Alastair are signed Polly Seedystockings, as a hint, I suppose, that she wants him to buy her another dozen.

SAGAMORE [taking another sheet of paper and writing] I should like to know Polly.

EPIFANIA. Pray why?

SAGAMORE [*talking as he writes*] Well, if Alastair prefers her to you she must be indeed worth knowing. I shall certainly make him introduce me.

EPIFANIA. You are hardly tactful, Julius Sagamore.

SAGAMORE. That will not matter when you have taken this [*he hands her what he has written*].

EPIFANIA. Whats this?

SAGAMORE. For the suicide. You will have to sign the chemist's book for the cyanide. Say it is for a wasp's nest. The tartaric acid is harmless: the chemist will think you want it to make lemonade. Put the two separately in just enough water to dissolve them. When you mix the two solutions the tartaric and potash will combine and make tartrate of potash. This, being insoluble, will be precipitated at the bottom of the glass; and the supernatant fluid will be pure hydrocyanic acid, one sip of which will kill you like a thunderbolt.

EPIFANIA [*fingering the prescription rather disconcertedly*] You seem to take my death very coolly, Mr Sagamore.

SAGAMORE. I am used to it.

EPIFANIA. Do you mean to tell me that you have so many clients driven to despair that you keep a prescription for them?

SAGAMORE. I do. It's infallible.

EPIFANIA. You are sure that they have all died painlessly and instantaneously?

SAGAMORE. No. They are all alive.

EPIFANIA. Alive! The prescription is a harmless fraud!

SAGAMORE. No. It's a deadly poison. But they dont take it.

EPIFANIA. Why?

SAGAMORE. I dont know. But they never do.

EPIFANIA. I will. And I hope you will be hanged for giving it to me.

SAGAMORE. I am only acting as your solicitor. You say you are going to commit suicide; and you come to me for advice. I do my best for you, so that you can die without wasting 'a lot of gas or jumping into the Serpentine. Six and eight-pence I shall charge your executors.

EPIFANIA. For advising me how to kill myself?

SAGAMORE. Not today. Tomorrow.

EPIFANIA. Why put it off until tomorrow?

SAGAMORE. Well, it will do as well tomorrow as today. And something amusing may happen this evening. Or even tomorrow evening. Theres no hurry.

EPIFANIA. You are a brute, a beast, and a pig. My life is nothing to you: you do not even ask what has driven me to this. You make money out of the death of your clients.

SAGAMORE. I do. There will be a lot of business connected with your death. Alastair is sure to come to me to settle your affairs.

EPIFANIA. And you expect me to kill myself to make money for you?

SAGAMORE. Well, it is you who have raised my expectations, madam.

EPIFANIA. O God, listen to this man! Has it ever occurred to you that when a woman's life is wrecked she needs a little sympathy and not a bottle of poison?

SAGAMORE. I really cant sympathize with suicide. It doesnt appeal to me, somehow. Still, if it has to be done, it had better be done promptly and scientifically.

EPIFANIA. You dont even ask what Alastair has done to me?

SAGAMORE. It wont matter what he has done to you when you are dead. Why bother about it?

EPIFANIA. You are an unmitigated hog, Julius Sagamore.

SAGAMORE. Why worry about me? The prescription will cure everything.

EPIFANIA. Damn your prescription. There! [*She tears it up and throws the pieces in his face*].

SAGAMORE [*beaming*] It's infallible. And now that you have blown off steam, suppose you sit down and tell me all about it.

EPIFANIA. You call the outcry of an anguished heart blowing off steam, do you?

SAGAMORE. Well, what else would you call it?

EPIFANIA. You are not a man: you are a rhinoceros. You are also a fool.

SAGAMORE. I am only a solicitor.

EPIFANIA. You are a rotten solicitor. You are not a gentleman. You insult me in my distress. You back up my husband against me. You have no decency, no understanding. You are a fish with the soul of a blackbeetle. Do you hear?

SAGAMORE. Yes: I hear. And I congratulate myself on the number of actions for libel I shall have to defend if you do me the honor of making me your solicitor.

EPIFANIA. You are wrong. I never utter a libel. My father instructed me most carefully in the law of libel. If I questioned your solvency, that would be a libel. If I suggested that you are unfaithful to your wife, that would be a libel. But if I call you a rhinoceros – which you are: a most unmitigated rhinoceros – that is only vulgar abuse. I take good care to confine myself to vulgar abuse; and I have never had an action for libel taken against me. Is that the law, or is it not?

SAGAMORE. I really dont know. I will look it up in my law books.

EPIFANIA. You need not. I instruct you that it is the law. My father always had to instruct his lawyers in the law whenever he did anything except what everybody was doing every day. Solicitors know nothing of law: they are only good at practice, as they call it. My father was a great man: every day of his life he did things that nobody else ever dreamt of doing. I am not, perhaps, a great woman; but I am his daughter; and as such I am an unusual woman. You will take the law from me and do exactly what I tell you to do.

SAGAMORE. That will simplify our relations considerably, madam.

EPIFANIA. And remember this. I have no sense of humor. I will not be laughed at.

SAGAMORE. I should not dream of laughing at a client with an income of three quarters of a million.

EPIFANIA. Have you a sense of humor?

SAGAMORE. I try to keep it in check; but I am afraid I have a little. You appeal to it, somehow.

EPIFANIA. Then I tell you in cold blood, after the most careful consideration of my words, that you are a heartless blackguard. My distress, my disgrace, my humiliation, the horrible mess and failure I have made of my life seem to you merely funny. If it were not that my father warned me never to employ a solicitor who had no sense of humor I would walk out of this office and deprive you of a client whose business may prove a fortune to you.

SAGAMORE. But, my dear lady, I dont know anything about your distress, your disgrace, the mess you have made of your life and all the rest of it. How can I laugh at things I dont know? If I am laughing – and am I really laughing? – I assure you I am laughing, not at your misfortunes, but at you.

EPIFANIA. Indeed? Am I so comic a figure in my misery?

SAGAMORE. But what is your misery? Do, pray, sit down.

EPIFANIA. You seem to have one idea in your head, and that is to get your clients to sit down. Well, to oblige you. [*She sits down with a flounce. The back of the chair snaps off short with a loud crack. She springs up*]. Oh, I cannot even sit down in a chair without wrecking it. There is a curse on me.

SAGAMORE [*collapses on the table, shaking with uncontrollable laughter*]!!!!!

EPIFANIA. Ay: laugh, laugh, laugh. Fool! Clown!

SAGAMORE [*rising resolutely and fetching another chair from the wall*] My best faked Chippendale gone. It cost me four guineas. [*Placing the chair for her*] Now will you please sit down as gently as you can, and stop calling me names?

Then, if you wish, you can tell me what on earth is the matter. [*He picks up the broken-off back of the chair and puts it on the table*].

EPIFANIA [*sitting down with dignity*] The breaking of that chair has calmed and relieved me, somehow. I feel as if I had broken your neck, as I wanted to. Now listen to me. [*He comes to her and looks down gravely at her*]. And dont stand over me like that. Sit down on what is left of your sham Chippendale.

SAGAMORE. Certainly [*he sits*]. Now go ahead.

EPIFANIA. My father was the greatest man in the world. I was his only child. His one dread was that I should make a foolish marriage, and lose the little money he was able to leave me.

SAGAMORE. The thirty millions. Precisely.

EPIFANIA. Dont interrupt me. He made me promise that whenever a man asked me to marry him I should impose a condition on my consent.

SAGAMORE [*attentive*] So? What condition?

EPIFANIA. I was to give him one hundred and fifty pounds, and tell him that if within six months he had turned that hundred and fifty pounds into fifty thousand, I was his. If not, I was never to see him again. I saw the wisdom of this. Nobody but my father could have thought of such a real, infallible, unsentimental test. I gave him my sacred promise that I would carry it out faithfully.

SAGAMORE. And you broke that promise. I see.

EPIFANIA. What do you mean — broke that promise?

SAGAMORE. Well, you married Alastair. Now Alastair is a dear good fellow — one of the best in his way — but you are not going to persuade me that he made fifty thousand pounds in six months with a capital of one hundred and fifty.

EPIFANIA. He did. Wise as my father was, he sometimes forgot the wise things he said five minutes after he said them. He warned me that ninety per cent of our selfmade millionaires are criminals who have taken a five hundred to one chance and got away with it by pure luck. Well, Alastair was that sort of criminal.

SAGAMORE. No no: not a criminal. That is not like Alastair. A fool, perhaps, in business. But not a criminal.

EPIFANIA. Like all solicitors you think you know more about my husband than I do. Well, I tell you that Alastair came back to me after six months probation with fifty thousand pounds in his pocket instead of the penal servitude he richly deserved. That man's luck is extraordinary. He always wins. He wins at tennis. He wins at boxing. He won me, the richest heiress in England.

SAGAMORE. But you were a consenting party. If not, why did you put him to the test? Why did you give him the hundred and fifty to try his luck with?

EPIFANIA. Boxing.

SAGAMORE. Boxing?

EPIFANIA. His boxing fascinated me. My father held that women should be able to defend themselves. He made me study Judo.

SAGAMORE. Judo? Do you mean Hebrew?

EPIFANIA. Hebrew! Nonsense! Judo is what ignorant people call jujitsu. I could throw you through that window as easily as you handed me that rotten chair.

SAGAMORE. Oh! Japanese wrestling. Rather a rough sport for a lady, isnt it?

EPIFANIA. How dare you call Judo a sport? It is a religion.

SAGAMORE [collapsing] Forgive me. Go on with your story. And please break it to me as gently as you can. I have never had a client like you before.

EPIFANIA. You never will again.

SAGAMORE. I dont doubt it for a moment. Now tell me: where does Alastair come in?

EPIFANIA. I saw him win an amateur heavy weight championship. He has a solar plexus punch that no other boxer can withstand.

SAGAMORE. And you married a man because he had a superlative solar plexus punch!

EPIFANIA. Well, he was handsome. He stripped well, unlike many handsome men. I am not insusceptible to sex appeal, very far from it.

SAGAMORE [*hastily*] Oh quite, quite: you need not go into details.

EPIFANIA. I will if I like. It is your business as a solicitor to know the details. I made a very common mistake. I thought that this irresistible athlete would be an ardent lover. He was nothing of the kind. All his ardor was in his fists. Never shall I forget the day — it was during our honeymoon — when his coldness infuriated me to such a degree that I went for him with my fists. He knocked me out with that abominable punch in the first exchange. Have you ever been knocked out by a punch in the solar plexus?

SAGAMORE. No, thank heaven. I am not a pugilist.

EPIFANIA. It does not put you to sleep like a punch on the jaw. When he saw my face distorted with agony and my body writhing on the floor, he was horrified. He said he did it automatically — that he always countered that way, by instinct. I almost respected him for it.

SAGAMORE. Then why do you want to get rid of him?

EPIFANIA. I want to get rid of myself. I want to punish myself for making a mess of my life and marrying an imbecile. I, Epifania Ognisanti di Parerga, saw myself as the most wonderful woman in England marrying the most wonderful man. And I was only a goose marrying a buck rabbit. What was there for me but death? And now you have put me off it with your fooling; and I dont know what I want. That is a horrible state of mind. I am a woman who must always want something and always get it.

SAGAMORE. An acquisitive woman. Precisely. How splendid! [*The telephone rings. He rises*]. Excuse me. [*He goes to the table and listens*] Yes? ... [*Hastily*] One moment. Hold the line. [*To Epifania*] Your husband is downstairs, with a woman. They want to see me.

EPIFANIA [*rising*] That woman! Have them up at once.

SAGAMORE. But can I depend on you to control yourself?

EPIFANIA. You can depend on Alastair's fists. I must have a look at Seedystockings. Have them up I tell you.

SAGAMORE [*into the telephone*] Send Mr Fitzfassenden and the lady up.

EPIFANIA. We shall see now the sort of woman for whom he has deserted ME!

SAGAMORE. I am thrilled. I expect something marvellous.

EPIFANIA. Dont be a fool. Expect something utterly common.

Alastair Fitzfassenden and Patricia Smith come in. He is a splendid athlete, with most of his brains in his muscles. She is a pleasant quiet little woman of the self-supporting type. She makes placidly for the table, leaving Alastair to deal with his wife.

ALASTAIR. Eppy! What are you doing here? [*To Sagamore*] Why didnt you tell me?

EPIFANIA. Introduce the female.

PATRICIA. Patricia Smith is my name, Mrs Fitzfassenden.

EPIFANIA. That is not how you sign your letters, I think.

ALASTAIR. Look here, Eppy. Dont begin making a row –

EPIFANIA. I was not speaking to you. I was speaking to the woman.

ALASTAIR [*losing his temper*] You have no right to call her a woman.

PATRICIA. Now, now, Ally: you promised me –

EPIFANIA. Promised you! What right had he to promise you? How dare he promise you? How dare you make him promise you?

ALASTAIR. I wont have Polly insulted.

SAGAMORE [*goodhumoredly*] You dont mind, Miss Smith, do you?

PATRICIA [*unconcerned*] Oh, I dont mind. My sister goes on just like that.

EPIFANIA. Your sister! You presume to compare your sister to me!

PATRICIA. Only when she goes off at the deep end. You mustnt mind me: theres nothing like letting yourself go if you are built that way. Introduce me to the gentleman, Ally.

ALASTAIR. Oh, I forgot. Julius Sagamore, my solicitor. An old pal. Miss Smith.

EPIFANIA. Alias Polly Seedystockings.

PATRICIA. Thats only my pet name, Mr Sagamore. Smith is the patronymic, as dear wise old father says.

EPIFANIA. She sets up a wise father! This is the last straw.

SAGAMORE. Do sit down, Miss Smith, wont you? [*He goes to fetch a chair from the wall*].

PATRICIA [*contemplating the wrecked chair*] Hallo! Whats happened to the chair?

EPIFANIA. *I* have happened to the chair. Let it be a warning to you.

Sagamore places the chair for Patricia next the table. Alastair shoves the broken chair back out of the way with his foot; fetches another from the wall, and is about to sit on it next Patricia when Epifania sits on it and motions him to her own chair, so that she is seated between the two, Patricia on her left, Alastair on her right. Sagamore goes back to his official place at the table.

PATRICIA. You see, Mr Sagamore, it's like this. Alastair –

EPIFANIA. You need not explain. I have explained everything to Mr Sagamore. And you will please have the decency in his presence and in mine to speak of my husband as Mr Fitzfassenden. His Christian name is no business of yours.

ALASTAIR [*angry*] Of course, Eppy, if you wont let anybody speak –

EPIFANIA. I am not preventing you nor anybody from speaking. If you have anything to say for yourself, say it.

PATRICIA. I am sorry. But it's such a long name. In my little circle everyone calls him just Ally.

EPIFANIA [*her teeth on edge*] You hear this, Mr Sagamore! My husband is called 'Ally' by these third rate people!

What right have they to speak of him at all? Am I to endure this?

PATRICIA [*soothingly*] Yes: we know you have to put up with a lot, deary; –

EPIFANIA [*stamping*] Deary!!!

PATRICIA [*continuing*] – but thats what the world is like.

EPIFANIA. The world is like that to people who are like that. Your world is not my world. Every woman has her own world within her own soul. Listen to me, Mr Sagamore. I married this man. I admitted him to my world, the world which my imagination had peopled with heroes and saints. Never before had a real man been permitted to enter it. I took him to be hero, saint, lover all in one. What he really was you can see for yourself.

ALASTAIR [*jumping up with his fists clenched and his face red*] I am damned if I stand this.

EPIFANIA [*rising and facing him in the pose of a martyr*] Yes: strike me. Shew her your knock-out punch. Let her see how you treat women.

ALASTAIR [*baffled*] Damn! [*He sits down again*].

PATRICIA. Dont get rattled, Ally: you will only put yourself in the wrong before Mr Sagamore. I think youd better go home and leave me to have it out with her.

EPIFANIA. Will you have the goodness not to speak of me as 'her'? I am Mrs Fitzfassenden. I am not a pronoun. [*She resumes her seat haughtily*].

PATRICIA. Sorry; but your name is such a tongue-twister. Mr Sagamore: dont you think Ally had better go? It's not right that we should sit here arguing about him to his face. Besides, he's worn out: he's hardly slept all night.

EPIFANIA. How do you know that, pray?

PATRICIA. Never mind how I know it. I do.

ALASTAIR. It was quite innocent; but where could I go to when you drove me out of the house by your tantrums?

EPIFANIA [*most unexpectedly amused*] You went to her?

ALASTAIR. I went to Miss Smith: she's not a pronoun, you

know. I went where I could find peace and kindness, to my good sweet darling Polly. So there!

EPIFANIA. I have no sense of humor: but this strikes me as irresistibly funny. You actually left ME to spend the night in the arms of Miss Seedystockings!

ALASTAIR. No, I tell you. It was quite innocent.

EPIFANIA [to Patricia] Was he in your arms or was he not?

PATRICIA. Well, yes , of course he was for a while. But not in the way you mean.

EPIFANIA. Then he is even a more sexless fish than I took him for. But really a man capable of flouncing out of the house when I was on the point of pardoning him and giving him a night of legitimate bliss would be capable of any imbecility.

ALASTAIR. Pardoning me! Pardoning me for what? What had I done when you flew out at me?

EPIFANIA. I did not fly out at you. I have never lost my dignity even under the most insufferable wrongs.

ALASTAIR. You hadnt any wrongs. You drove me out of the house –

EPIFANIA. I did not. I never meant you to go. It was abominably selfish of you. You had your Seedystockings to go to; but I had nobody. Adrian was out of town.

SAGAMORE. Adrian! This is a new complication. Who is Adrian?

PATRICIA. Adrian is Mrs Fitzfassenden's Sunday husband, Mr Sagamore.

EPIFANIA. My what, did you say?

PATRICIA. Your Sunday husband. You understand. What Mr Adrian Blenderbland is to you, as it were. What Ally is to me.

SAGAMORE. I dont quite follow. What is Mr Blenderbland to you, Mrs Fitzfassenden, if I may ask?

EPIFANIA. Well, he is a gentleman with whom I discuss subjects that are beyond my husband's mental grasp, which is extremely limited.

ALASTAIR. A chap that sets up to be an intellectual because his father was a publisher! He makes up to Eppy and pretends to be in love with her because she has a good cook; but I tell her he cares for nothing but his food. He always calls at mealtimes. A bellygod, I call him. And I am expected to put up with him. But if I as much as look at Polly! Oh my!

EPIFANIA. The cases are quite different. Adrian worships the ground I tread on: that is quite true. But if you think that Seedystockings worships the ground you tread on, you flatter yourself grossly. She endures you and pets you because you buy stockings for her, and no doubt anything else she may be short of.

PATRICIA. Well, I never contradict anyone, because it only makes trouble. And I am afraid I do cost him a good deal; for he likes me to have nice things that I cant afford.

ALASTAIR [*affectionately*] No, Polly: you dont. Youre as good as gold. I'm always pressing things on you that you wont take. Youre a jolly sight more careful of my money that I am myself.

EPIFANIA. How touching! You are the Sunday wife, I suppose.

PATRICIA. No: I should say that you are the Sunday wife, Mrs Fitzfassenden. It's I that have to look after his clothes and make him get his hair cut.

EPIFANIA. Surely the creature is intelligent enough to do at least that much for himself.

PATRICIA. You dont understand men: they get interested in other things and neglect themselves unless they have a woman to look after them. You see, Mr Sagamore, it's like this. There are two sorts of people in the world: the people anyone can live with and the people that no one can live with. The people that no one can live with may be very goodlooking and vital and splendid and temperamental and romantic and all that; and they can make a man or woman happy for half an hour when they are pleased with

259

themselves and disposed to be agreeable; but if you try to
live with them they just eat up your whole life running after
them or quarrelling or attending to them one way or
another: you cant call your soul your own. As Sunday
husbands and wives, just to have a good tearing bit of
lovemaking with, or a blazing row, or mostly one on top of
the other, once a month or so, theyre all right. But as
everyday partners theyre just impossible.

EPIFANIA. So I am the Sunday wife. [*To Patricia, scornfully*]
And what are you, pray?

PATRICIA. Well, I am the angel in the house, if you follow
me.

ALASTAIR [*blubbering*] You are, dear: you are.

EPIFANIA [*to Patricia*] You are his doormat: thats what you
are.

PATRICIA. Doormats are very useful things if you want the
house kept tidy, dear.

The telephone rings. Sagamore attends to it.

SAGAMORE. Yes? ... Did you say Blenderbland?

EPIFANIA. Adrian! How did he know I was here?

SAGAMORE. Ask the gentleman to wait. [*He hangs up the
receiver*]. Perhaps you can tell me something about him,
Mrs Fitzfassenden. Is he the chairman of Blenderbland's
Literary Pennyworths?

EPIFANIA. No. That is his father, who created the business.
Adrian is on the board; but he has no business ability. He
is on fifteen boards of directors on the strength of his father's
reputation, and has never, as far as I know, contributed an
idea to any of them.

ALASTAIR. Be fair to him, Eppy. No man in London
knows how to order a dinner better. Thats what keeps him
at the top in the city.

SAGAMORE. Thank you: I think I have his measure sufficiently. Shall I have him up?

EPIFANIA. Certainly. I want to know what he is doing
here.

ALASTAIR. I dont mind. You understand, of course, that I am not supposed to know anything of his relations with my wife, whatever they may be.

EPIFANIA. They are perfectly innocent, so far. I am not quite convinced that I love Adrian. He makes himself agreeable: that is all.

SAGAMORE [*into the telephone*] Send Mr Blenderbland up. [*He hangs up the instrument*].

ALASTAIR [*to Patricia*] You will now see the blighter who has cut me out with Eppy.

PATRICIA. I cant imagine any man cutting you out with any woman, dear.

EPIFANIA. Will you be good enough to restrain your endearments when he comes in?

Adrian Blenderbland, an imposing man in the prime of life, bearded in the Victorian literary fashion, rather handsome, and well dressed, comes in. Sagamore rises. Adrian is startled when he sees the company, but recovers his aplomb at once, and advances smiling.

ADRIAN. Hallo! Where have we all come from? Good morning, Mrs Fitzfassenden. How do, Alastair? Mr Sagamore, I presume. I did not know you were engaged.

SAGAMORE. Your arrival is quite opportune, sir. Will you have the goodness to sit down? [*He takes a chair from the wall and places it at the table, on his own right and Patricia's left*].

ADRIAN [*sitting down*] Thank you. I hope I am not interrupting this lady.

PATRICIA. Not at all. Dont mind me.

SAGAMORE [*introducing*] Miss Smith, an intimate friend of Mr Fitzfassenden.

PATRICIA. Pleased to meet you, I'm sure.

Adrian bows to her; then turns to Sagamore.

ADRIAN. The fact is, Mrs Fitzfassenden mentioned your name to me in conversation as her choice of a new solicitor. So I thought I could not place myself in better hands.

SAGAMORE [*bowing*] Thank you, sir. But – excuse me – had you not a solicitor of your own?

ADRIAN. My dear Mr Sagamore: never be content with a single opinion. When I feel ill I always consult at least half a dozen doctors. The variety of their advice and prescriptions convinces me that I had better cure myself. When a legal point arises I consult six solicitors, with much the same –

EPIFANIA. Adrian: I have no sense of humor; and you know how it annoys me when you talk the sort of nonsense that is supposed to be funny. Did you come here to consult Mr Sagamore about me?

ADRIAN. I did. But of course I expected to find him alone.

SAGAMORE. Has the matter on which you wish to consult me any reference to Mr Fitzfassenden's family circle?

ADRIAN. It has.

SAGAMORE. Is it of such a nature that sooner or later it will have to be discussed with all the adult members of that circle?

ADRIAN. Well, yes: I suppose so. But hadnt we better talk it over a little in private first.

EPIFANIA. You shall do nothing of the sort. I will not have my affairs discussed by anybody in public or in private. They concern myself alone.

ADRIAN. May I not discuss my own affairs?

EPIFANIA. Not with my solicitor. I will not have it.

ALASTAIR. Now she is off at the deep end again. We may as well go home.

EPIFANIA [restlessly rising] Oh, the deep end! the deep end! What is life if it is not lived at the deep end? Alastair: you are a tadpole. [She seizes his head and ruffles his hair as she passes him].

ALASTAIR. Dont do that. [He tries to smooth his hair].

EPIFANIA [to Patricia] Smooth it for him, angel in the house.

PATRICIA [moving to Epifania's chair and doing so] You shouldnt make a sight of him like that.

SAGAMORE. Mr Fitzfassenden: why did you marry Mrs Fitzfassenden?

262

EPIFANIA. Why!!! Does that require any explanation? I have told you why *I* married him.

ALASTAIR. Well, though you mightnt think it, she can be frightfully fascinating when she really wants to be.

EPIFANIA. Why might he not think it? What do you mean?

ALASTAIR. He knows what I mean.

EPIFANIA. Some silly joke, I suppose.

ADRIAN. Dont be absurd, Fitzfassenden. Your wife is the most adorable woman on earth.

EPIFANIA. Not here, Adrian. If you are going to talk like that, take me away to some place where we can be alone.

ALASTAIR. Do, for heaven's sake, before she drives us all crazy.

SAGAMORE. Steady! steady! I hardly know where I am. You are all consulting me; but none of you has given me any instructions. Had you not better all be divorced?

EPIFANIA. What is the creature to live on? He has nothing: he would have had to become a professional boxer or tennis player if his uncle had not pushed him into an insurance office, where he was perfectly useless.

ALASTAIR. Look here, Eppy: Sagamore doesnt want to hear all this.

EPIFANIA. He does. He shall. Be silent. When Alastair proposed to me – he was too great an idiot to comprehend his own audacity – I kept my promise to my father. I handed him a cheque for a hundred and fifty pounds. 'Make that into fifty thousand within six months' I said 'and I am yours.'

ADRIAN. You never told me this.

EPIFANIA. Why should I? It is a revolting story.

ALASTAIR. What is there revolting about it? Did I make good or did I not? Did I go through hell to get that money and win you or did I not?

ADRIAN [*amazed*] Do I understand you to say, Alastair,

263

that you made fifty thousand pounds in six months?

ALASTAIR. Why not?

EPIFANIA. You may well look incredulous, Adrian. But he
did. Yes: this imbecile made fifty thousand pounds and won
Epifania Ognisanti di Parerga for his bride. You will not
believe me when I tell you that the possession of all that
money, and the consciousness of having made it himself,
gave him a sort of greatness. I am impulsive: I kept my
word and married him instantly. Then, too late, I found
out how he had made it.

ALASTAIR. Well, how did I make it? By my own brains.

EPIFANIA. Brains! By your own folly, your ignorance, your
criminal instincts, and the luck that attends the half-witted.
You won my hand, for which all Europe was on its knees
to me. What you deserved was five years penal servitude.

ALASTAIR. Five years! Fifteen, more likely. That was what
I risked for you. And what did I get by it? Life with you was
worse than any penal servitude.

EPIFANIA. It would have been heaven to you if Nature
had fitted you for such a companionship as mine. But what
was it for me? No man had been good enough for me. I was
like a princess in a fairy tale offering all men alive my hand
and fortune if they could turn my hundred and fifty pound
cheque into fifty thousand within six months. Able men,
brilliant men, younger sons of the noblest families either
refused the test or failed. Why? Because they were too
honest or too proud. This thing succeeded; and I found
myself tied for life to an insect.

ALASTAIR. You may say what you like; but you were just
as much in love with me as I was with you.

EPIFANIA. Well, you were young; you were well shaped;
your lawn tennis was outstanding; you were a magnificent
boxer; and I was excited by physical contact with you.

SAGAMORE. Is it necessary to be so very explicit, Mrs Fitzfassenden?

EPIFANIA. Julius Sagamore: you may be made of sawdust;

but I am made of flesh and blood. Alastair is physically attractive: that is my sole excuse for having married him. Will you have the face to pretend that he has any mental charm?

ADRIAN. But how did he make fifty thousand pounds? Was it on the Stock Exchange?

EPIFANIA. Nonsense! the creature does not know the difference between a cumulative preference and a deferred ordinary. He would not know even how to begin.

ADRIAN. But how did he begin? My bank balance at present is somewhere about a hundred and fifty. I should very much like to know how to make it up to fifty thousand. You are so rich, Epifania, that every decent man who approaches you feels like a needy adventurer. You dont know how a man to whom a hundred pounds is a considerable sum feels in the arms of a woman to whom a million is mere pin money.

EPIFANIA. Nor do you know what it feels like to be in the arms of a man and know that you could buy him up twenty times over and never miss the price.

ADRIAN. If I give you my hundred and fifty pounds, will you invest it for me?

EPIFANIA. It is not worth investing. You cannot make money on the Stock Exchange until your weekly account is at least seventy thousand. Do not meddle with money, Adrian: you do not understand it. I will give you all you need.

ADRIAN. No, thank you: I should lose my self-respect. I prefer the poor man's luxury of paying for your cabs and flowers and theatre tickets and lunches at the Ritz, and lending you all the little sums you have occasion for when we are together.

The rest all stare at this light on Epifania's habits.

EPIFANIA. It is quite true: I never have any pocket money: I must owe you millions in odd five pound notes. I will tell my bankers that you want a thousand on account.

ADRIAN. But I dont. I love lending you fivers. Only, as they run through my comparatively slender resources at an appalling rate, I should honestly like a few lessons from Alastair in the art of turning hundreds into tens of thousands.

EPIFANIA. His example would be useless to you, Adrian, because Alastair is one of Nature's marvels; and there is nothing marvellous about you except your appetite. Listen. On each of his birthdays his aunt had presented him with a gramophone record of the singing of the celebrated tenor Enrico Caruso. Now it so happens that Nature, in one of her most unaccountable caprices, has endowed Alastair with a startlingly loud singing voice of almost supernatural range. He can sing high notes never before attained by mortal man. He found that he could imitate gramophone records with the greatest facility; and he became convinced that he could make a fortune as an operatic tenor. The first use he made of my money was to give fifty pounds to the manager of some trumpery little opera company which was then on its last legs in the suburbs to allow him to appear for one night in one of Caruso's most popular roles. He actually took me to hear his performance.

ALASTAIR. It wasnt my fault. I can sing Caruso's head off. It was a plot. The regular tenor of the company: a swine that could hardly reach B flat without breaking his neck, paid a lot of blackguards to go into the gallery and boo me.

EPIFANIA. My dear Alastair, the simple truth is that Nature, when she endowed you with your amazing voice, unfortunately omitted to provide you with a musical ear. You can bellow loudly enough to drown ten thousand bulls; but you are always at least a quarter tone sharp or flat as the case may be. I laughed until I fell on the floor of my box in screaming hysterics. The audience hooted and booed; but they could not make themselves heard above your roaring. At last the chorus dragged you off the stage; and the regular tenor finished the performance only to find that the manager had absconded with my fifty pounds and left the whole company penniless. The prima donna was deaf in the left ear, into which you had sung with all your force. I had to pay all their salaries and send them home.

ALASTAIR. I tell you it was a plot. Why shouldnt people like my singing? I can sing louder than any tenor on the stage. I can sing higher.

EPIFANIA. Alastair: you cannot resist a plot when the whole world is a party to it.

ADRIAN. Still, this does not explain how Alastair made the fifty thousand pounds.

EPIFANIA. I leave him to tell that disgraceful tale himself. I believe he is proud of it. [*She sits down disdainfully in the vacant chair*].

ALASTAIR. Well, it worked out all right. But it was a near thing, I tell you. What I did was this. I had a hundred pounds left after the opera stunt. I met an American. I told him I was crazy about a woman who wouldnt marry me unless I made fifty thousand in six months, and that I had only a hundred pounds in the world. He jumped up and said 'Why, man alive, if you have a hundred you can open a bank account and get a cheque book.' I said 'What good is a cheque book?' He said 'Are we partners, fifty fifty?' So I said yes: what else could I say? That very day we started in. We lodged the money and got a book of a hundred cheques. We took a theatre. We engaged a first rate cast. We got a play. We got a splendid production: the scenery was lovely: the girls were lovely: the principal woman was an angry-eyed creature with a queer foreign voice and a Hollywood accent, just the sort the public loves. We never asked the price of anything: we just went in up to our necks for thousands and thousands.

ADRIAN. But how did you pay for all these things?

ALASTAIR. With our cheques, of course. Didnt I tell you we had a cheque book?

ADRIAN. But when the hundred was gone the cheques must have been dishonored.

ALASTAIR. Not one of them. We kited them all. But it was a heartbreaking job.

ADRIAN. I dont understand. What does kiting mean?

SAGAMORE. It is quite simple. You pay for something with a cheque after the banks have closed for the day: if on Saturday or just before bank holiday all the better. Say the cheque is for a hundred pounds and you have not a penny at the bank. You must then induce a friend or a hotel manager to cash another cheque for one hundred pounds for you. That provides for the previous cheque; but it obliges you, on pain of eighteen months hard labor, to induce another friend or hotel manager to cash another cheque for you for two hundred pounds. And so you go on spending and kiting from hundreds to thousands and from risks of eighteen months imprisonment to five years, ten years, fourteen years even.

ALASTAIR. If you think that was an easy job, just try it yourself: thats all. I dream of it sometimes: it's my worst nightmare. Why, my partner and I never saw that theatre! never saw the play! until the first night: we were signing cheques and kiting them all the time. Of course it was easier after a while, because as we paid our way all right we found it easier to get credit; and the biggest expenses didnt come until after the play was produced and the money was coming in. I could have done it for half the money; but the American could only keep himself up to the excitement of it by paying twice as much as we needed for everything and shoving shares in it on people for nothing but talk. But it didnt matter when the money began to come in. My! how it did come in! The whole town went mad about the angry-eyed woman. It rained money in bucketsful. It went to my head like drink. It went to the American's head. It went to the head of the American's American friends. They bought all the rights: the film rights, the translation rights, the touring rights, all sorts of rights that I never knew existed, and began selling them to one another until everybody in

London and New York and Hollywood had a rake-off on them. Then the American bought all the rights back for five hundred thousand dollars, and sold them to an American syndicate for a million. It took six more Americans to do it; and every one of them had to have a rake-off; but all I wanted was fifty thousand pounds; and I cleared out with that and came swanking back to claim Eppy's hand. She thought I was great. I was great: the money made me great: I tell you I was drunk with it: I was another man. You may believe it or not as you like; but my hats were really too small for me.

EPIFANIA. It is quite true. The creature was not used to money; and it transfigured him. I, poor innocent, had no suspicion that money could work such miracles; for I had possessed millions in my cradle; and it meant no more to me than the air I breathed.

SAGAMORE. But just now, when I suggested a divorce, you asked how he was to live. What has become of the fifty thousand pounds?

EPIFANIA. He lost it all in three weeks. He bought a circus with it. He thought everything he touched would turn into gold. I had to liquidate that circus a month later. He was about to turn the wild beasts loose and run away when I intervened. I was down four hundred and thirty pounds sixteen and sevenpence by the transaction.

ALASTAIR. Was it my fault? The elephant got influenza. The Ministry of Health closed me down and wouldnt let me move on because the animals might carry foot-and-mouth disease.

EPIFANIA. At all events, the net result was that instead of his being fifty thousand pounds to the good I was four hundred and thirty pounds to the bad. Instead of bringing me the revenues of a prince and a hero he cost me the allowance of a worm. And now he has the audacity to ask for a divorce.

ALASTAIR. No I dont. It was Sagamore who suggested

that. How can I afford to let you divorce me? As your husband I enjoy a good deal of social consideration; and the tradesmen give me unlimited credit.

EPIFANIA. For stockings, among other things.

PATRICIA. Oh [*she weeps*]! Does she pay for them, Ally?

ALASTAIR. Never mind, dear: I have shewn that I can make money when I am put to it; and I will make it again and buy you all the stockings you need out of my own earnings. [*He rises and goes behind her chair to take her cheeks in his hands*]. There, darling: dont cry.

EPIFANIA. There! They think they are married already!

SAGAMORE. But the matter is not in your hands, Mr Fitz-fassenden. Mrs Fitzfassenden can divorce you whether you like it or not. The evidence is that on a recent occasion you left your wife and took refuge in the arms of Miss Smith. The Court will give Mrs Fitzfassenden a decree on that.

PATRICIA [*consoled and plucky*] Well, let it. I can support Alastair until he has time to make another fortune. You all think him a fool; but he's a dear good boy; and it just disgusts me the way you all turn against him, and the way his wife treats him as if he were dirt under her feet. What would she be without her money, I'd like to know?

EPIFANIA. Nobody is anybody without money, Seedy-stockings. My dear old father taught me that. 'Stick to your money' he said 'and all the other things shall be added unto you.' He said it was in the Bible. I have never verified the quotation; but I have never forgotten it. I have stuck to my money; and I shall continue to stick to it. Rich as I am, I can hardly forgive Alastair for letting me down by four hundred and thirty pounds.

ALASTAIR. Sixteen and sevenpence! Stingy beast. But I will pay it.

PATRICIA. You shall, dear. I will sell out my insurance and give it to you.

EPIFANIA. May I have that in writing, Miss Smith?

ALASTAIR. Oh, you ought to be ashamed of yourself, you greedy pig. It was your own fault. Why did you let the elephant go for thirty pounds? He cost two hundred.

SAGAMORE. Do not let us wander from the point.

EPIFANIA. What is the point, pray?

SAGAMORE. The point is that you can obtain a divorce if you wish.

EPIFANIA. I dont wish. Do you think I am going to be dragged through the divorce court and have my picture in the papers with that thing? To have the story of my infatuation told in headlines in every rag in London! Besides, it is convenient to be married. It is respectable. It keeps other men off. It gives me a freedom that I could not enjoy as a single woman. I have become accustomed to a husband. No: decidedly I will not divorce Alastair – at least until I can find a substitute whom I really want.

PATRICIA. You couldnt divorce him unless he chose to let you. Alastair's too much the gentleman to mention it; but you know very well that your own behavior hasnt been so very nunlike that you dare have it shewn up in court.

EPIFANIA. Alastair was the first man I ever loved; and I hope he will not be the last. But legal difficulties do not exist for people with money. At all events, as Alastair cannot afford to divorce me, and I have no intention of divorcing him, the question does not arise. What o'clock is it?

ALASTAIR. I really think, Eppy, you might buy a wrist watch. I have told you so over and over again.

EPIFANIA. Why should I go to the expense of buying a wrist watch when everyone else has one; and I have nothing to do but ask? I have not carried a watch since I lost the key of my father's old repeater.

PATRICIA. It is ten minutes past twelve.

EPIFANIA. Gracious! I have missed my lesson. How annoying!

ALASTAIR. Your lesson? What are you learning now, may I ask?

EPIFANIA. All-in wrestling. When you next indulge in your favorite sport of wife beating, look out for a surprise. What did I come here for, Mr Sagamore?

SAGAMORE. To give me instructions about your will.

ALASTAIR. She makes a new will every time she loses her temper, Sagamore. Jolly good business for you.

EPIFANIA. Do be quiet, Alastair. You forget the dignity of your position as my husband. Mr Sagamore: I have changed my mind about my will. And I shall overlook your attempt to poison me.

SAGAMORE. Thank you.

EPIFANIA. What do I owe you for this abortive consultation?

SAGAMORE. Thirteen and fourpence, if you please.

EPIFANIA. I do not carry money about with me. Adrian: can you lend me thirteen and fourpence?

ADRIAN [*puts his hand in his pocket*] —

EPIFANIA. Stop. Mr Sagamore: your had better be my family solicitor and send me your bill at the end of the year.

ALASTAIR. Send a County Court summons with it, Sagamore; or you may go whistle for your money.

EPIFANIA. Do hold your tongue, Alastair. Of course I always wait for a summons. It is a simple precaution against paying bills sent in twice over.

SAGAMORE. Quite, Mrs Fitzfassenden. An excellent rule.

EPIFANIA. You are a man of sense, Mr Sagamore. And now I must have some fresh air: this orgy of domesticity has made the room stuffy. Come along, Adrian: we'll drive out into the country somewhere, and lunch there. I know the quaintest little place up the river. Goodbye, Mr Sagamore. Goodbye, Seedy: take care of Alastair for me. His good looks will give you a pleasing sensation down your spine. [*She goes out*].

SAGAMORE [*as Adrian is following her out*] By the way, Mr Blenderbland, what did you come for?

ADRIAN. I totally forget. I dont feel equal to any more this morning. [*He goes out without further salutations*].

SAGAMORE [*to Alastair*] Your wife is a most extraordinary lady.

ALASTAIR [*utters a stifled howl*]!

PATRICIA. He cant find words for her, poor dear.

SAGAMORE. And now, Mr Fitzfassenden, may I ask what you came to consult me about?

ALASTAIR. I dont know. After ten minutes of Eppy I never do know whether I am standing on my head or my heels.

PATRICIA. It was about a separation. Pull yourself together a bit, dear.

ALASTAIR. Separation! You might as well try to separate yourself from a hurricane. [*He becomes sententious*]. Listen to me, Sagamore. I am one of those unfortunate people – you must know a lot of them – I daresay many of them have sat in this chair and talked to you as I am talking to you –

SAGAMORE [*after waiting in vain for a completion of the sentence*] Yes? You were saying – ?

PATRICIA. Dont wander, Ally. Tell Mr Sagamore what sort of people.

ALASTAIR. The people that have bitten off more than they can chew. The ordinary chaps that have married extraordinary women. The commonplace women that have married extraordinary men. They all thought it was a splendid catch for them. Take my advice, Sagamore: marry in your own class. Dont misunderstand me: I dont mean rank or money. What I mean – what I mean –

PATRICIA [*coming to the rescue*] What he means is that people who marry should think about the same things and like the same things. They shouldnt be over oneanother's heads, if you follow me.

SAGAMORE. Perfectly. May I take it that Alastair made that mistake, and that later on (too late, unfortunately) he discovered in you a – shall I say a soul mate?

ALASTAIR. No: that sounds silly. Literary, you know.

PATRICIA. More of a mind mate, I should call it.

SAGAMORE. Precisely. Thank you. A mind mate with whom he could be thoroughly comfortable.

ALASTAIR [*grasping Sagamore's hand fervently*] Thank you, Sagamore: you are a real friend. Youve got it exactly. Think over it for us. Come on, Seedy darling: we mustnt waste a busy man's time.

He goes out, leaving Patricia and Sagamore alone together. She rises and goes to the table.

PATRICIA. Mr Sagamore: youll stand by us, wont you? Youll save Ally from that awful woman. Youll save him for me.

SAGAMORE. I'm afraid I cant control her, Miss Smith. Whats worse, I'm afraid she can control me. It's not only that I cant afford to offend so rich a client. It's that her will paralyzes mine. It's a sort of genius some people have.

PATRICIA. Dont you be afraid of her, Mr Sagamore. She has a genius for making money. It's in her family. Money comes to her. But I have my little bit of genius too; and she cant paralyze me.

SAGAMORE. And what have you a genius for, Miss Smith, if I may ask?

PATRICIA. For making people happy. Unhappy people come to me just as money comes to her.

SAGAMORE [*shaking his head*] I cant think that your will is stronger than hers, Miss Smith.

PATRICIA. It isnt, Mr Sagamore. I have no will at all. But I get what I want, somehow. Youll see.

ALASTAIR [*outside, shouting*] Seedy! Come on!

PATRICIA. Coming, darling. [*To Sagamore*] Goodbye, Mr Sagamore [*they shake hands quickly. She hurries to the door*]. Youll see. [*She goes out*].

SAGAMORE [*to himself*] I think I shall wait and see.

He resumes his morning's work.

ACT II

A dismal old coffee room in an ancient riverside inn. An immense and hideous sideboard of the murkiest mahogany stretches across the end wall. Above it hang, picturewise, two signboards, nearly black with age: one shewing the arms of the lord of the manor, and the other a sow standing upright and playing a flageolet. Underneath the sow is inscribed in tall letters The Pig and Whistle. Between these works of art is a glass case containing an enormous stuffed fish, certainly not less than a century old.

At right angles to the sideboard, and extending nearly the whole length of the room, are two separate long tables, laid for lunch for about a dozen people each. The chairs, too close together, are plain wooden ones, hard and uncomfortable. The cutlery is cheap kitchen ware, with rickety silver cruets and salt cellars to keep up appearances. The table cloths are coarse, and are not fresh from the laundry.

The walls are covered with an ugly Victorian paper which may have begun as a design of dull purple wreaths on a dark yellow background, but is now a flyblown muck of no describable color. On the floor a coarse drugget, very old. The door, which stands wide open and has COFFEE ROOM inscribed on it, is to the right of anyone contemplating the sideboard from the opposite end of the room. Next the door an old fashioned hatstand flattens itself against the wall; and on it hang the hat and light overcoat of Mr Adrian Blenderbland.

He, with Epifania, is seated at the end of the table farthest from the door. They have just finished a meal. The cheese and biscuits are still on the table. She looks interested and happy. He is in the worst of tempers.

EPIFANIA. How jolly!

ADRIAN [*looking round disparagingly*] I must be a very attractive man.

EPIFANIA [*opening her eyes wide*] Indeed! Not that I am denying it; but what has it to do with what I have just said?

ADRIAN. You said 'How jolly!' I look round at this rotten old inn trying to pretend that it's a riverside hotel. We have just had a horrible meal of tomato tea called soup, the remains of Sunday's joint, sprouts, potatoes, apple tart and stale American synthetic cheese. If you can suffer this and say 'How jolly!' there must be some irresistible attraction present; and I can see nothing that is not utterly repulsive except myself.

EPIFANIA. Dont you like these dear old-world places? I do.

ADRIAN. I dont. They ought all to be rooted up, pulled down, burnt to the ground. Your flat on the Embankment in London cost more to furnish than this place did to build from the cellar to the roof. You can get a decent lunch there, perfectly served, by a word through the telephone. Your luxurious car will whisk you out to one of a dozen first rate hotels in lovely scenery. And yet you choose this filthy old inn and say 'How jolly!' What is the use of being a millionairess on such terms?

EPIFANIA. Psha! When I was first let loose on the world with unlimited money, how long do you think it took me to get tired of shopping and sick of the luxuries you think so much of? About a fortnight. My father, when he had a hundred millions, travelled third class and never spent more than ten shillings a day on himself except when he was entertaining people who were useful to him. Why should he? He couldnt eat more than anyone else. He couldnt drink more than anyone else. He couldnt wear more than anyone else. Neither can I.

ADRIAN. Then why do you love money and hate spending it?

EPIFANIA. Because money is power. Money is security. Money is freedom. It's the difference between living on the slope of a volcano and being safe in the garden of the Hesperides. And there is the continual pleasure of making more of it, which is quite easy if you have plenty to start with. I can turn a million into two million much more easily than a poor woman can turn five pounds into ten, even if she could get the five pounds to begin with. It turns itself, in fact.

ADRIAN. To me money is a vulgar bore and a soul destroying worry. I need it, of course; but I dont like it. I never think of it when I can possibly help it.

EPIFANIA. If you dont think about money what do you think about? Women?

ADRIAN. Yes, of course; but not exclusively.

EPIFANIA. Food?

ADRIAN. Well, I am not always thinking about my food; but I am rather particular about it. I confess I looked forward to a better lunch than [*indicating the table*] that.

EPIFANIA. Oho! So that is what has put you out of temper, is it?

ADRIAN [*annoyed*] I am not out of temper, I hope. But you promised me a very special treat. You said you had found out the most wonderful place on the river, where we could be ourselves and have a delicious cottage meal in primitive happiness. Where is the charm of this dismal hole? Have you ever eaten a viler lunch? There is not even a private sitting room: anybody can walk in here at any moment. We should have been much more comfortable at Richmond or Maidenhead. And I believe it is raining.

EPIFANIA. Is that my fault?

ADRIAN. It completes your notion of a happy day up the river. Why is it that the people who know how to enjoy themselves never have any money, and the people who have money never know how to enjoy themselves?

EPIFANIA. You are not making yourself agreeable, Adrian.

ADRIAN. You are not entertaining me very munificently, Epifania. For heaven's sake let us get into the car and drive about the country. It is much more luxurious than this hideous coffee room, and more private.

EPIFANIA. I am tired of my car.

ADRIAN. I am not. I wish I could afford one like it.

EPIFANIA. I thought you would enjoy sitting in this crazy out-of-way place talking to me. But I find you are a spoilt old bachelor: you care about nothing but your food and

277

your little comforts. You are worse than Alastair; for at least he could talk about boxing and tennis.

ADRIAN. And you can talk about nothing but money.

EPIFANIA. And you think money uninteresting! Oh, you should have known my father!

ADRIAN. I am very glad I did not.

EPIFANIA [*suddenly dangerous*] Whats that you say?

ADRIAN. My dear Epifania, if we are to remain friends, I may as well be quite frank with you. Everything you have told me about your father convinces me that though he was no doubt an affectionate parent and amiable enough to explain your rather tiresome father fixation, as Dr Freud would call it, he must have been quite the most appalling bore that ever devastated even a Rotary club.

EPIFANIA [*stunned for a moment by this blasphemy*] My father! You infinite nothingness! My father made a hundred and fifty millions. You never made even half a million.

ADRIAN. My good girl, your father never made anything. I have not the slightest notion of how he contrived to get a legal claim on so much of what other people made; but I do know that he lost four fifths of it by being far enough behind the times to buy up the properties of the Russian nobility in the belief that England would squash the Soviet revolution in three weeks or so. Could anyone have made a stupider mistake? Not I.

EPIFANIA [*springing up*] You rotten thing. [*He rises apprehensively*]. Take that for calling my father a bore. [*She throws him*].

ADRIAN [*picking himself up painfully*] Oh! Restrain yourself. You might hurt me very seriously.

EPIFANIA. I will hurt you until you wish yourself dead. Scum! Filth! Take that for saying he never made anything. [*She throws him again*].

ADRIAN. Help! help! There is a madwoman here: I shall not be able to hold her single handed. Help! [*He comes behind her and seizes her round the waist*].

EPIFANIA. Vermin! [*She throws him over her shoulder*].

ADRIAN. Police! She is murdering me. She is mad. Help! help! [*He scrambles up and is flying to the door when she overtakes him*].

EPIFANIA. Dirt! Carrion! [*She throws him out head over heels and flings his hat and overcoat after him*].

ADRIAN [*outside, rolling downstairs with appalling bumps*] Oh! Oh! Help! Murder! Police! Oh! [*He faints. Silence*].

EPIFANIA. You brute! You have killed me. [*She totters to the nearest chair and sinks into it, scattering the crockery as she clutches the table with her outstretched arms and sprawls on it in convulsions*].

A serious looking middleaged Egyptian gentleman in an old black frock coat and a tarboosh, speaking English too well to be mistaken for a native, hurries in.

THE EGYPTIAN [*peremptorily*] Whats the matter? What is going on here?

EPIFANIA [*raising her head slowly and gazing at him*] Who the devil are you?

THE EGYPTIAN. I am an Egyptian doctor. I hear a great disturbance. I hasten to ascertain the cause. I find you here in convulsions. Can I help?

EPIFANIA. I am dying.

THE DOCTOR. Nonsense! You can swear. The fit has subsided. You can sit up now: you are quite well. Good afternoon.

EPIFANIA. Stop. I am not quite well: I am on the point of death. I need a doctor. I am a rich woman.

THE DOCTOR. In that case you will have no difficulty in finding an English doctor. Is there anyone else who needs my help? I was upstairs. The noise was of somebody falling downstairs. He may have broken some bones. [*He goes out promptly*].

EPIFANIA [*struggling to her feet and calling after him*] Never mind him: if he has broken every bone in his body it is no more than he deserves. Come back instantly. I want you.

Come back. Come back.

THE DOCTOR [*returning*] The landlord is taking the gentleman to the Cottage Hospital in your car.

EPIFANIA. In my car! I will not permit it. Let them get an ambulance.

THE DOCTOR. The car has gone. You should be very glad that it is being so useful.

EPIFANIA. It is your business to doctor me, not to lecture me.

THE DOCTOR. I am not your doctor: I am not in general practice. I keep a clinic for penniless Mahometan refugees; and I work in the hospital. I cannot attend to you.

EPIFANIA. You can attend to me. You must attend to me. Are you going to leave me here to die?

THE DOCTOR. You are not dying. Not yet, at least. Your own doctor will attend to you.

EPIFANIA. You are my own doctor. I tell you I am a rich woman: doctors' fees are nothing to me: charge me what you please. But you must and shall attend to me. You are abominably rude; but you inspire confidence as a doctor.

THE DOCTOR. If I attended all those in whom I inspire confidence I should be worn out in a week. I have to reserve myself for poor and useful people.

EPIFANIA. Then you are either a fool or a Bolshevik.

THE DOCTOR. I am nothing but a servant of Allah.

EPIFANIA. You are not: you are my doctor: do you hear? I am a sick woman: you cannot abandon me to die in this wretched place.

THE DOCTOR. I see no symptoms of any sickness about you. Are you in pain?

EPIFANIA. Yes. Horrible pain.

THE DOCTOR. Where?

EPIFANIA. Dont cross-examine me as if you didnt believe me. I must have sprained my wrist throwing that beast all over the place.

THE DOCTOR. Which hand?

EPIFANIA [*presenting a hand*] This.

THE DOCTOR [*taking her hand in a businesslike way, and pulling and turning the fingers and wrist*] Nothing whatever the matter.

EPIFANIA. How do you know? It's my hand, not yours.

THE DOCTOR. You would scream the house down if your wrist were sprained. You are shamming. Lying. Why? Is it to make yourself interesting?

EPIFANIA. Make myself interesting! Man: I am interesting.

THE DOCTOR. Not in the least, medically. Are you interesting in any other way?

EPIFANIA. I am the most interesting woman in England. I am Epifania Ognisanti di Parerga.

THE DOCTOR. Never heard of her. Italian aristocrat, I presume.

EPIFANIA. Aristocrat! Do you take me for a fool? My ancestors were moneylenders to all Europe five hundred years ago: we are now bankers to all the world.

THE DOCTOR. Jewess, eh?

EPIFANIA. Christian, to the last drop of my blood. Jews throw half their money away on charities and fancies like Zionism. The stupidest di Parerga can just walk round the cleverest Jew when it comes to moneymaking. We are the only real aristocracy in the world: the aristocracy of money.

THE DOCTOR. The plutocracy, in fact.

EPIFANIA. If you like. I am a plutocrat of the plutocrats.

THE DOCTOR. Well, that is a disease for which I do not prescribe. The only known cure is a revolution; but the mortality rate is high; and sometimes, if it is the wrong sort of revolution, it intensifies the disease. I can do nothing for you. I must go back to my work. Good morning.

EPIFANIA [*holding him*] But this is your work. What else have you to do?

THE DOCTOR. There is a good deal to be done in the world besides attending the rich imaginary invalids.

EPIFANIA. But if you are well paid?

THE DOCTOR. I make the little money I need by work which I venture to think more important.

EPIFANIA [*throwing him away and moving about distractedly*] You are a pig and a beast and a Bolshevik. It is the most abominable thing of you to leave me here in my distress. My car is gone. I have no money. I never carry money about.

THE DOCTOR. I have none to carry. Your car will return presently. You can borrow money from your chauffeur.

EPIFANIA. You are an unmitigated hippopotamus. You are a Bashibazouk. I might have known it from your ridiculous tarboosh. You should take it off in my presence. [*She snatches it from his head and holds it behind her back*]. At least have the manners to stay with me until my chauffeur comes back.

The motor horn is heard honking.

THE DOCTOR. He has come back.

EPIFANIA. Damn! Cant you wait until he has had his tea and a cigaret?

THE DOCTOR. No. Be good enough to give me back my fez.

EPIFANIA. I wanted to see what you looked like without it. [*She puts it tenderly on his head*]. Listen to me. You are having an adventure. Have you no romance in you? Havnt you even common curiosity? Dont you want to know why I threw that beast downstairs? Dont you want to throw your wretched work to the devil for once and have an afternoon on the river with an interesting and attractive woman?

THE DOCTOR. Women are neither interesting nor attractive to me except when they are ill. I know too much about them, inside and out. You are perfectly well.

EPIFANIA. Liar. Nobody is perfectly well, nor ever has been, nor ever will be. [*She sits down, sulking*].

THE DOCTOR. That is true. You must have brains of a sort. [*He sits down opposite to her*]. I remember when I began as a young surgeon I killed several patients by my operations because I had been taught that I must go on cutting until there was nothing left but perfectly healthy tissue. As there is no such thing as perfectly healthy tissue I should have cut my patients entirely away if the nurse had not stopped me before they died on the table. They died after they left the hospital; but as they were carried away from the table alive I was able to claim a successful operation. Are you married?

EPIFANIA. Yes. But you need not be afraid. My husband is openly unfaithful to me and cannot take you into court if you make love to me. I can divorce him if necessary.

THE DOCTOR. And the man you threw downstairs: who was he? One does not throw one's husband downstairs. Did he make love to you?

EPIFANIA. No. He insulted my father's memory because he was disappointed with his lunch here. When I think of my father all ordinary men seem to me the merest trash. You are not an ordinary man. I should like to see some more of you. Now that you have asked me confidential questions about my family, and I have answered them, you can no longer pretend that you are not my family doctor. So that is settled.

THE DOCTOR. A father fixation, did you say?

EPIFANIA [nods]!

THE DOCTOR. And an excess of money?

EPIFANIA. Only a beggarly thirty millions.

THE DOCTOR. A psychological curiosity. I will consider it.

EPIFANIA. Consider it! You will feel honored, gratified, delighted.

THE DOCTOR. I see. Enormous self-confidence. Reckless audacity. Insane egotism. Apparently sexless.

EPIFANIA. Sexless! Who told you that I am sexless?

THE DOCTOR. You talk to me as if you were a man. There is no mystery, no separateness, no sacredness about men to you. A man to you is only a male of your species.

EPIFANIA. My species indeed! Men are a different and very inferior species. Five minutes conversation with my husband will convince you that he and I do not belong to the same species. But there are some great men, like my father. And there are some good doctors, like you.

THE DOCTOR. Thank you. What does your regular doctor say about you?

EPIFANIA. I have no regular doctor. If I had I should have an operation a week until there was nothing left of me or of my bank balance. I shall not expect you to maul me about with a stethoscope, if that is what you are afraid of. I have the lungs of a whale and the digestion of an ostrich. I have a clockwork inside. I sleep eight hours like a log. When I want anything I lose my head so completely about it that I always get it.

THE DOCTOR. What things do you want mostly?

EPIFANIA. Everything. Anything. Like a lightning flash. And then there is no stopping me.

THE DOCTOR. Everything and anything is nothing.

EPIFANIA. Five minutes ago I wanted you. Now I have got you.

THE DOCTOR. Come! You cannot bluff a doctor. You may want the sun and the moon and the stars; but you cannot get them.

EPIFANIA. That is why I take good care not to want them. I want only what I can get.

THE DOCTOR. Good. A practical intellect. And what do you want at present, for instance?

EPIFANIA. That is the devil of it. There is nothing one can get except more money.

THE DOCTOR. What about more men?

EPIFANIA. More Alastairs! More Blenderblands! Those are not deep wants. At present I want a motor launch.

THE DOCTOR. There is no such thing in this little place.

EPIFANIA. Tell the landlord to stop the first one that comes along and buy it.

THE DOCTOR. Tcha! People will not sell their boats like that.

EPIFANIA. Have you ever tried?

THE DOCTOR. No.

EPIFANIA. I have. When I need a car or a motor boat or a launch or anything like that I buy straight off the road or off the river or out of the harbor. These things cost thousands when they are new; but next day you cannot get fifty pounds for them. Offer £300 for any of them, and the owner dare not refuse: he knows he will never get such an offer again.

THE DOCTOR. Aha! You are a psychologist. This is very interesting.

EPIFANIA. Nonsense! I know how to buy and sell, if that is what you mean.

THE DOCTOR. That is how good psychologists make money.

EPIFANIA. Have you made any?

THE DOCTOR. No. I do not care for money: I care for knowledge.

EPIFANIA. Knowledge is no use without money. Are you married?

THE DOCTOR. I am married to Science. One wife is enough for me, though by my religion I am allowed four.

EPIFANIA. Four! What do you mean?

THE DOCTOR. I am what you call a Mahometan.

EPIFANIA. Well, you will have to be content with two wives if you marry me.

THE DOCTOR. Oh! Is there any question of that between us?

EPIFANIA. Yes. I want to marry you.

THE DOCTOR. Nothing doing, lady. Science is my bride.

EPIFANIA. You can have Science as well: I shall not be jealous of her. But I made a solemn promise to my father on his deathbed –

THE DOCTOR [interrupting] Stop. I had better tell you that

I made a solemn promise to my mother on her deathbed.

EPIFANIA. What!!!

THE DOCTOR. My mother was a very wise woman. She made me swear to her that if any woman wanted to marry me, and I felt tempted, I would hand the woman two hundred piastres and tell her unless she would go out into the world with nothing but that and the clothes she stood in, and earn her living alone and unaided for six months, I would never speak to her again.

EPIFANIA. And if she stood the test?

THE DOCTOR. Then I must marry her even if she were the ugliest devil on earth.

EPIFANIA. And you dare ask me – me, Epifania Ognisanti di Parerga! to submit myself to this test – to any test!

THE DOCTOR. I swore. I have a mother fixation. Allah has willed it so. I cannot help myself.

EPIFANIA. What was your mother?

THE DOCTOR. A washerwoman. A widow. She brought up eleven children. I was the youngest, the Benjamin. The other ten are honest working folk. With their help she made me a man of learning. It was her ambition to have a son who could read and write. She prayed to Allah; and he endowed me with the necessary talent.

EPIFANIA. And you think I will allow myself to be beaten by an old washerwoman?

THE DOCTOR. I am afraid so. You could never pass the test.

EPIFANIA. Indeed! And my father's test for a husband worthy of me?

THE DOCTOR. Oh! The husband is to be tested! That never occurred to me.

EPIFANIA. Nor to your mother either, it seems. Well, you know better now. I am to give you a hundred and fifty pounds. In six months you are to increase it to fifty thousand. How is that for a test?

THE DOCTOR. Quite conclusive. At the end of the six

months I shall not have a penny of it left, praise be to Allah.

EPIFANIA. You confess yourself beaten?

THE DOCTOR. Absolutely. Completely.

EPIFANIA. And you think I am beaten too.

THE DOCTOR. Hopelessly. You do not know what homeless poverty is; and Allah the Compassionate will take care that you never do.

EPIFANIA. How much is two hundred piastres?

THE DOCTOR. At the rate of exchange contemplated by my mother, about thirtyfive shillings.

EPIFANIA. Hand it over.

THE DOCTOR. Unfortunately my mother forgot to provide for this contingency. I have not got thirtyfive shillings. I must borrow them from you.

EPIFANIA. I have not a penny on me. No matter: I will borrow it from the chauffeur. He will lend you a hundred and fifty pounds on my account if you dare ask him. Goodbye for six months. [*She goes out*].

THE DOCTOR. There is no might and no majesty save in Thee, O Allah; but, oh! most Great and Glorious, is this another of Thy terrible jokes?

ACT III

A basement in the Commercial Road. An elderly man, anxious, poor, and ratlike, sits at a table with his wife. He is poring over his accounts. She, on his left, is sewing buttons on a coat, working very fast. There is a pile of coats on the table to her right waiting to have buttons sewn on, and another to her left which she has finished. The table is draped down to the ground with an old cloth. Some daylight comes in down the stone stairs; but does not extend to the side where the couple sit, which is lighted by a small electric bulb on a wire. Between the stairs and the table a dirty old patched curtain hangs in front of an opening into a farther compartment.

A bell tinkles. The woman instantly stops sewing and conceals the piles of coats under the table. Epifania, her dress covered by an old waterproof, and wearing an elaborately damaged hat, comes down the stairs. She looks at the pair; then looks round her; then goes to the curtain and looks through. The old man makes a dash to prevent her, but is too late. He snatches the curtain from her and bars her passage.

THE MAN. What do you want? What are you doing here?

EPIFANIA. I want employment. A woman told me I should find it here. I am destitute.

THE MAN. Thats not the way to get employment: poking your nose into places that dont concern you. Get out. There are no women employed here.

EPIFANIA. You lie. There are six women working in there. Who employs them?

THE MAN. Is that the way to talk to me? You think a lot of yourself, dont you? What do you take me for?

EPIFANIA. A worm.

THE MAN [*making a violent demonstration*]!!

EPIFANIA. Take care. I can use my fists. I can shoot, if necessary.

THE WOMAN [*hurrying to the man and holding him*] Take care, Joe. She's an inspector. Look at her shoes.

EPIFANIA. I am not an inspector. And what is the matter with my shoes, pray?

THE WOMAN [*respectfully*] Well maam, could a woman looking for work at tuppence hapeny an hour afford a west end shoe like that? I assure you we dont employ any women here. We're only caretakers.

EPIFANIA. But I saw six women –

THE MAN [*throwing open the curtain*] Where? Not a soul. Search the whole bloody basement.

THE WOMAN. Hush, hush, Joe: dont speak to the lady like that. You see, maam: theres not a soul.

EPIFANIA. Theres a smell. You have given them a signal to hide. You are breaking the law. Give me some work or I will send a postcard to the Home Office.

THE MAN. Look here, lady. Cant we arrange this? What good will it do you to get me into trouble and shut up my little shop?

EPIFANIA. What good will it do me to say nothing?

THE MAN. Well, what about half a crown a week?

EPIFANIA. I cannot live on half a crown a week.

THE MAN. You can if you look round a bit. There are others, you know.

EPIFANIA. Give me the address of the others. If I am to live by blackmail I must have an extended practice.

THE MAN. Well, if I have to pay I dont see why the others shouldnt too. Will you take half a crown? [*He holds up half a crown*]. Look here! Look at it! Listen to it! [*He rings it on the table*]. It's yours, and another every Wednesday if you keep the inspector off me.

EPIFANIA. It's no use ringing half crowns at me: I am accustomed to them. And I feel convinced that you will pay five shillings if I insist.

THE WOMAN. Oh, maam, have some feeling for us. You dont know the struggle we have to live.

THE MAN [*roughly*] Here: we're not beggars. I'll pay what the business can afford and not a penny more. You seem to know that it can afford five shillings. Well, if you know that, you know that it cant afford any more. Take your five shillings and be damned to you. [*He flings two half crowns on the table*].

THE WOMAN. Oh, Joe, dont be so hasty.

THE MAN. You shut up. You think you can beg a shilling or two off: but you cant. I can size up a tough lot without looking at her shoes. She's got us; and she knows she's got us.

EPIFANIA. I do not like this blackmailing business. Of course if I must I must; but can you not give me some manual work?

THE MAN. You want to get a little deeper into our business, dont you?

EPIFANIA. I am as deep as I can go already. You are employing six women in there. The thing in the corner is a gas engine: that makes you a workshop under the Act. Except that the sanitary arrangements are probably abominable, there is nothing more for me to know. I have you in the hollow of my hand. Give me some work that I can live by or I will have you cleared out like a wasp's nest.

THE MAN. I have a good mind to clear out now and take some place where you wont find me so easy. I am used to changing my address.

EPIFANIA. That is the best card in your hand. You have some business ability. Tell me why you cannot give me work to live by just as you give it, I suppose, to the women I saw in there.

THE MAN. I dont like the people I employ to know too much.

EPIFANIA. I see. They might call in the inspector.

THE MAN. Call in the inspector! What sort of fool are you? They dread the inspector more than I do.

EPIFANIA. Why? Dont they want to be protected?

THE WOMAN. The inspector wouldnt protect them, maam: he'd only shut up the place and take away their job from them. If they thought youd be so cruel as to report them theyd go down on their knees to you to spare them.

THE MAN. You that know such a lot ought to know that a business like this cant afford any luxuries. It's a cheap labor business. As long as I get women to work for their natural wage, I can get along; but no luxuries, mind you. No trade union wages. No sanitary arrangements as you call them. No limewashings every six months. No separate rooms to eat in. No fencing in of dangerous machinery or the like of that: not that I care; for I have nothing but the old gas engine that wouldnt hurt a fly, though it brings me under the blasted Workshop Act as you spotted all right. I have no big machinery; but I have to undersell those that have it. If I put up my prices by a farthing theyd set their machinery going and drop me. You might as well ask me to pay trade union wages as do all that the inspector wants: I should be out of business in a week.

EPIFANIA. And what is a woman's natural wage?

THE MAN. Tuppence hapeny an hour for twelve hours a day.

EPIFANIA. Slavery!

THE WOMAN. Oh no, maam: nobody could call that slavery. A good worker can make from twelve to fifteen shillings a week at it, week in and week out.

THE MAN. Isnt it what the Government paid at the beginning of the war when all the women were called on to do their bit? Do you expect me to pay more than the British Government?

THE WOMAN. I assure you it's the regular and proper wage and always has been, maam.

THE MAN. Like five per cent at the Bank of England it is. This is a respectable business, whatever your inspectors may say.

EPIFANIA. Can a woman live on twelve shillings a week?

THE MAN. Of course she can. Whats to prevent her?

THE WOMAN. Why, maam, when I was a girl in a match

factory I had five shillings a week; and it was a godsend to my mother. And a girl who had no family of her own could always find a family to take her in for four and sixpence, and treat her better than if she had been in her father's house.

THE MAN. I can find you a family what'll do it today, in spite of all the damned doles and wages boards that have upset everything and given girls ideas above their station without giving them the means to pamper themselves.

EPIFANIA. Well, I will work even for that, to prove that I can work and support myself. So give me work and have done talking.

THE MAN. Who started talking? You or I?

EPIFANIA. I did. I thank you for the information you have given me: it has been instructive and to the point. Is that a sufficient apology? And now to work, to work. I am in a hurry to get to work.

THE MAN. Well, what work can you do?

THE WOMAN. Can you sew? Can you make buttonholes?

EPIFANIA. Certainly not. I dont call that work.

THE MAN. Well, what sort of work are you looking for?

EPIFANIA. Brain work.

THE MAN. She's dotty!

EPIFANIA. Your work. Managing work. Planning work. Driving work. Let me see what you make here. Tell me how you dispose of it.

THE MAN [to his wife] You had better get on with your work. Let her see it. [To Epifania, whilst the woman pulls out the pile of coats from under the table and sits down resignedly to her sewing] And when youve quite satisfied your curiosity, perhaps youll take that five shillings and go.

EPIFANIA. Why? Dont you find my arrival a pleasant sort of adventure in this den?

THE MAN. I never heard the like of your cheek, not from nobody. [He sits down to his accounts].

EPIFANIA [*to the woman, indicating the pile of coats*] What do you do with these when they are finished?

THE WOMAN [*going on with her work*] The man comes with his lorry and takes them away.

EPIFANIA. Does he pay you for them?

THE WOMAN. Oh no. He gives us a receipt for them. Mr Superflew pays us for the receipts at the end of the week.

EPIFANIA. And what does Mr Superflew do with the coats?

THE WOMAN. He takes them to the wholesaler that supplies him with the cloth. The lorry brings us the cloth when it takes away the finished clothes.

EPIFANIA. Why dont you deal directly with the wholesalers?

THE WOMAN. Oh no: that wouldnt be right. We dont know who they are; and Mr Superflew does. Besides, we couldnt afford a lorry.

EPIFANIA. Does Mr Superflew own the lorry?

THE WOMAN. Oh no: that wouldnt be right. He hires it by the hour from Bolton's.

EPIFANIA. Is the driver always the same man?

THE WOMAN. Yes, of course: always old Tim Goodenough.

EPIFANIA [*to the man*] Write those names for me: Superflew, Bolton's, Goodenough.

THE MAN. Here! I'm not your clerk, you know.

EPIFANIA. You will be, soon. Do as I tell you.

THE MAN. Well of all the cheek – ! [*He obeys*].

EPIFANIA. When Goodenough comes round next tell him to tell Bolton's that he has found somebody who will buy the lorry for fourteen pounds. Tell him that if he can induce Bolton's to part from it at that figure you will give him a pound for himself and engage him at half a crown advance on his present wages to drive it just the same old round to the same places. He knows the wholesalers. Mr Superflew is superfluous. We shall collect not only our own stuff but that of all the other sweaters.

THE MAN. Sweaters! Who are you calling sweaters?

EPIFANIA. Man, know thyself. You sweat yourself; you sweat your wife; you sweat those women in there; you live on sweat.

THE MAN. Thats no way to talk about it. It isnt civil. I pay the right wages, same as everybody pays. I give employment that the like of them couldnt make for themselves.

EPIFANIA. You are sensitive about it. I am not. I am going to sweat Mr Superflew out of existence. I am going to sweat Mr Timothy Goodenough instead of allowing Mr Superflew to sweat him.

THE MAN. See here. Does this business belong to me or to you?

EPIFANIA. We shall see. Dare you buy the lorry?

THE MAN. Wheres the money to come from?

EPIFANIA. Where does all money come from? From the bank.

THE MAN. You got to put it there first, havnt you?

EPIFANIA. Not in the least. Other people put it there; and the bank lends it to you if it thinks you know how to extend your business.

THE WOMAN [terrified] Oh, Joe, dont trust your money in a bank. No good ever comes out of banks for the likes of us. Dont let her tempt you, Joe.

EPIFANIA. When had you last a holiday?

THE WOMAN. Me! A holiday! We cant afford holidays. I had one on Armistice Day, eighteen years ago.

EPIFANIA. Then it cost a world war and the slaughter of twenty millions of your fellow creatures to give you one holiday in your lifetime. I can do better for you than that.

THE WOMAN. We dont understand that sort of talk here. Weve no time for it. Will you please take our little present and go away?

The bell tinkles.

THE MAN [rising] Thats Tim, for the clothes.

EPIFANIA [masterfully] Sit down. I will deal with Tim.

She goes out. The man, after a moment of irresolution, sits down helplessly.

THE WOMAN [*crying*] Oh, Joe, dont listen to her: dont let her meddle with us. That woman would spend our little savings in a week, and leave us to slave to the end of our days to make it up again. I cant go on slaving for ever: we're neither of us as young as we were.

THE MAN [*sullen*] What sort of wife are you for a man? You take the pluck out of me every time. Dont I see other men swanking round and throwing money about that they get out of the banks? In and out of banks they are, all day. What do they do but smoke cigars and drink champagne? A five pound note is to them what a penny is to me. Why shouldnt I try their game instead of slaving here for pence and hapence?

THE WOMAN. Cause you dont understand it, Joe. We know our own ways; and though we're poor our ways have never let us down; and they never will if we stick to them. And who would speak to us? who would know us or give us a helping hand in hard times if we began doing things that nobody else does? How would you like to walk down Commercial Road and get nothing but black looks from all your friends and be refused a week's credit in the shops? Joe: Ive gone on in our natural ways all these years without a word of complaint; and I can go on long enough still to make us comfortable when we're too old to see what I'm sewing or you to count the pence. But if youre going to risk everything and put our money in a bank and change our ways I cant go on: I cant go on: itll kill me. Go up and stop her, Joe. Dont let her talk: just put her out. Be a man, darling: dont be afraid of her. Dont break my heart and ruin yourself. Oh, dont sit there dithering: you dont know what she may be doing. Oh! oh! oh! [*She can say no more for sobbing*].

THE MAN [*rising, but not very resolutely*] There! there! Hold your noise: I'm not going to let her interfere with us. I'll put her out all right. [*He goes to the stairs. Epifania comes down*].

Now, missis: lets have an understanding.

EPIFANIA. No understanding is necessary. Tim is sure that Bolton's will take ten pounds for the lorry. Tim is my devoted slave. Make that poor woman stop howling if you can. I am going now. There is not enough work here for me: I can do it all in half a day every week. I shall take a job as scullery maid at a hotel to fill up my time. But first I must go round to the address Tim has given me and arrange that we send them our stuff direct and collect just as Superflew did. When I have arranged everything with them I will come back and arrange everything for you. Meanwhile, carry on as usual. Good morning. [*She goes out*].

THE MAN [*stupefied*] It seems to me like a sort of dream. What could I do?

THE WOMAN [*who has stopped crying on hearing Epifania's allusion to her*] Do what she tells us, Joe. We're like children – [*She begins crying again softly*].

There is nothing more to be said.

ACT IV

The coffee room of The Pig & Whistle, now transmogrified into the lounge of The Cardinal's Hat, a very attractive riverside hotel. The long tables are gone, replaced by several tea-tables with luxurious chairs round them. The old sideboard, the stuffed fish, the signboards are no more: instead there is an elegant double writing desk for two sitters, divided by stationery cases and electric lamps with dainty shades. Near it is a table with all the illustrated papers and magazines to hand. Farther down the room, towards the side next the door, there is a long well cushioned seat, capable of accommodating three persons. With three chairs at the other side it forms a fireside circle. The old hatstand has gone to its grave with the sideboard. The newly painted walls present an attractive color scheme. The floor is parquetted and liberally supplied with oriental rugs. All the appurtenances of a brand new first class hotel lounge are in evidence.

Alastair, in boating flannels, is sprawling happily on the long seat, reading an illustrated magazine. Patricia, in her gladdest summer rags, is knitting in the middle chair opposite, full of quiet enjoyment.

It is a fine summer afternoon; and the general effect is that of a bank holiday paradise.

ALASTAIR. I say, Seedy, isnt this jolly?

PATRICIA. Yes, darling: it's lovely.

ALASTAIR. Nothing beats a fine week-end on the river. A pull on the water in the morning to give one a good stretch and a good appetite. A good lunch, and then a good laze. What more can any man desire on earth?

PATRICIA. You row so beautifully, Ally. I love to see you sculling. And punting too. You look so well standing up in the punt.

ALASTAIR. It's the quiet of it, the blessed quiet. You are so quiet: I'm never afraid of your kicking up a row about nothing. The river is so smooth. I dont know which is more comforting, you or the river, when I think of myself shooting Niagara three or four times a day at home.

PATRICIA. Dont think of it, darling. It isnt home: this is home.

ALASTAIR. Yes, dear: youre right: this is what home ought to be, though it's only a hotel.

PATRICIA. Well, what more could anyone ask but a nice hotel? All the housekeeping done for us: no trouble with the servants: no rates nor taxes. I have never had any peace except in a hotel. But perhaps a man doesnt feel that way.

The manager of the hotel, a young man, smartly dressed, enters. He carries the hotel register, which he opens and places on the newspaper table. He then comes obsequiously to his two guests.

THE MANAGER [*between them*] Good afternoon, sir. I hope you find everything here to your liking.

ALASTAIR. Yes, thanks. But what have you done to the old place? When I was here last, a year ago, it was a common pub called The Pig and Whistle.

THE MANAGER. It was so until quite lately, sir. My father kept The Pig and Whistle. So did his forefathers right back to the reign of William the Conqueror. Cardinal Wolsey stopped once for an hour at The Pig and Whistle when his mule cast a shoe and had to go to the blacksmith's. I assure you my forefathers thought a lot of themselves. But they were uneducated men, and ruined the old place by trying to improve it by getting rid of the old things in it. It was on its last legs when you saw it, sir. I was ashamed of it.

ALASTAIR. Well, you have made a first rate job of it now.

THE MANAGER. Oh, it was not my doing, sir: I am only the manager. You would hardly believe it if I were to tell you the story of it. Much more romantic, to my mind, than the old tale about Wolsey. But I mustnt disturb you talking. You will let me know if theres anything I can do to make you quite comfortable.

PATRICIA. I should like to know about the old Pig if it's romantic. If you can spare the time, of course.

THE MANAGER. I am at your service, madam, always.

ALASTAIR. Fire ahead, old man.

THE MANAGER. Well, madam, one day a woman came here and asked for a job as a scullery maid. My poor old father hadnt the nerve to turn her out: he said she might just try for a day or two. So she started in. She washed two dishes and broke six. My poor old mother was furious: she thought the world of her dishes. She had no suspicion, poor soul, that they were ugly and common and old and cheap and altogether out of date. She said that as the girl had broken them she should pay for them if she had to stay for a month and have the price stopped out of her wages. Off went the girl to Reading and came back with a load of crockery that made my mother cry: she said we should be disgraced for ever if we served a meal on such old fashioned things. But the very next day an American lady with a boating party bought them right off the table for three times what they cost; and my poor mother never dared say another word. The scullery maid took things into her own hands in a way we could never have done. It was cruel for us; but we couldnt deny that she was always right.

PATRICIA. Cruel! What was there cruel in getting nice crockery for you?

THE MANAGER. Oh, it wasnt only that, madam: that part of it was easy and pleasant enough. You see all she had to do with the old crockery was to break it and throw the bits into the dustbin. But what was the matter with the old Pig and Whistle was not the old thick plates that took away your appetite. It was the old people it had gathered about itself that were past their work and had never been up to much according to modern ideas. They had to be thrown into the street to wander about for a few days and then go into the workhouse. There was the bar that was served by father and mother: she dressed up to the nines, as she thought, poor old dear, never dreaming that the world was a day older than when she was married. The scullery maid told them the truth about themselves; and it just cut them to pieces; for it was the truth; and I couldnt deny it. The old man had to give in, because he had raised money on his freehold and was at his wits' end to pay the mortgage interest. The next thing we knew, the girl had paid off the mortgage and got the whip hand of us completely. 'It's time for you two to sell your freehold and retire: you are doing no good here' she said.

PATRICIA. But that was dreadful, to root them up like that.

THE MANAGER. It was hard; but it was the truth. We should have had the brokers in sooner or later if we had gone on. Business is business; and theres no room for sentiment in it. And then, think of the good she did. My parents would never have got the price for the freehold that she gave them. Here was I, ashamed of the place, tied to the old Pig and Whistle by my feeling for my parents, with no prospects. Now the house is a credit to the neighborhood and gives more employment than the poor old Pig did in its best days; and I am the manager of it with a salary and a percentage beyond anything I could have dreamt of.

ALASTAIR. Then she didnt chuck you, old man.

THE MANAGER. No, sir. You see, though I could never have made the change myself, I was intelligent enough to see that she was right. I backed her up all through. I have such faith in that woman, sir, that if she told me to burn down the hotel tonight I'd do it without a moment's hesitation. When she puts her finger on a thing it turns to gold every time. The bank would remind my father if he overdrew by five pounds; but the manager keeps pressing overdrafts on her: it makes him miserable when she has a penny to her credit. A wonderful woman, sir: one day a scullery maid, and the next the proprietress of a first class hotel.

PATRICIA. And are the old people satisfied and happy?

THE MANAGER. Well, no: the change was too much for them at their age. My father had a stroke and wont last long, I'm afraid. And my mother has gone a bit silly. Still, it was best for them; and they have all the comforts they care for.

ALASTAIR. Well, thats a very moving tale: more so than you think, old boy, because I happen to know a woman of that stamp. By the way, I telegraphed for a friend of mine to come and spend the week-end with us here: a Mr Sagamore. I suppose you can find a room for him.

THE MANAGER. That will be quite all right, sir, thank you.

PATRICIA. Have you many people in the house this week-end?

THE MANAGER. Less than usual, madam. We have an Egyptian doctor who takes his meals here: a very learned man I should think: very quiet: not a word to anybody. Then there is another gentleman, an invalid, only just discharged from the Cottage Hospital. The Egyptian doctor recommended our chef to him; and he takes his meals here too. And that is all, madam, unless some fresh visitors arrive.

ALASTAIR. Well, we must put up with them.

THE MANAGER. By the way, sir, I am sorry to trouble you; but you came up this morning without signing the register. I have brought it up. Would you be so good? [*He fetches the register from the table and presents it to Alastair with his fountain pen*].

ALASTAIR [*sitting up and taking it on his knees*] Oh, I am sorry: I forgot. [*He signs*]. There you are. [*He puts up his legs again*].

THE MANAGER. Thanks very much, sir. [*He glances at the register before shutting it. The signature surprises him*]. Oh, indeed, sir! We are honored.

ALASTAIR. Anything wrong?

THE MANAGER. Oh no, sir, nothing wrong: quite the contrary. Mr and Mrs Fitzfassenden. The name is so unusual. Have I the honor of entertaining the celebrated —

ALASTAIR [*interrupting*] Yes: it's all right: I am the tennis champion and the boxing champion and all the rest of it; but I am here for a holiday and I dont want to hear anything more about it.

THE MANAGER [*shutting the book*] I quite understand, sir. I should not have said anything if it were not that the proprietress of this hotel, the lady I told you of, is a Mrs Fitzfassenden.

ALASTAIR [*rising with a yell*] What! Let me out of this. Pack up, Seedy. My bill, please, instantly.

THE MANAGER. Certainly, sir. But may I say that she is not on the premises at present and that I do not expect her this week-end.

PATRICIA. Dont fuss, darling. Weve a perfect right to be in her hotel if we pay our way just like anybody else.

ALASTAIR. Very well: have it your own way. But my week-end is spoilt.

THE MANAGER. Depend on it, she wont come, sir. She is getting tired of paying us unexpected visits now that she knows she can depend on me. [*He goes out, but immediately looks in again to say*] Your friend Mr Sagamore, sir, coming up with the invalid gentleman. [*He holds the door open for Sagamore and Adrian, who come in. Then he goes out, taking the register with him*].

Adrian, who comes first, limps badly on two walking sticks; and his head is bandaged. He is disagreeably surprised at seeing Fitz-fassenden and Patricia.

ADRIAN. Alastair! Miss Smith! What does this mean, Sagamore? You never told me who you were bringing me to see: you said two friends. Alastair: I assure you I did not know you were here. Sagamore said some friends who would be glad to see me.

PATRICIA. Well, we are glad to see you, Mr Blenderbland. Wont you sit down?

ALASTAIR. But whats happened to you, old chap? What on earth have you done to yourself?

ADRIAN [*exasperated*] Everyone asks me what I have done to myself. I havnt done anything to myself. I suppose you mean this and this [*he indicates his injuries*]. Well, they are what your wife has done to me. That is why Sagamore should not have brought me here.

ALASTAIR. I say: I am frightfully sorry, old chap.

PATRICIA [*rising solicitously*] Do sit down, Mr Blenderbland. Rest yourself on that couch. [*Arranging cushions*] Dear! dear!

ALASTAIR. Eppy is like that, you know.

ADRIAN. Yes: I know now. But I ought not to be here: Sagamore should not have brought me here.

PATRICIA. But why not? I assure you we're delighted to ·see you. We dont mind what Mrs Fitzfassenden does.

ADRIAN. But I do. You are most kind; but I cannot claim the privilege of a friend and at the same time be the plaintiff in an action for assault and battery.

ALASTAIR. Yes you can, old chap. The situation is not new. The victims always come to us for sympathy. Make yourself comfortable.

ADRIAN [*reluctantly sitting down and disposing his damaged limbs along the couch*] Well, it's most kind of you; and I really cant stand any longer. But I dont understand why Sagamore should have played such a trick on me. And, of course, on you too.

Patricia returns to her chair, and resumes her knitting.

SAGAMORE [*taking a chair next Patricia on her left*] Well, the truth of the matter is that Blenderbland wont be reasonable; and I thought you two might help me to bring him to his senses.

ADRIAN [*obstinately*] It's no use, Sagamore. Two thousand five hundred. And costs. Not a penny less.

SAGAMORE. Too much. Ridiculous. A jury might give five hundred if there was a clear disablement from earning, or if the defendant had done something really womanly, like throwing vitriol. But you are only a sleeping partner in the firm your father founded: you dont really earn your income. Besides, hang it all! a man accusing a woman of assault!

ALASTAIR. Why didnt you give her a punch in the solar plexus?

ADRIAN. Strike a woman! Impossible.

ALASTAIR. Rot! If a woman starts fighting she must take what she gets and deserves.

PATRICIA. Look at the marks she's left on you, Mr Blenderbland! You shouldnt have put up with it: it only encourages her.

ALASTAIR. Search me for marks: you wont find any. Youd have found a big mark on her this first time she tried it on me. There was no second time.

ADRIAN. Unfortunately I have neither your muscle nor your knowledge of how to punch. But I will take lessons when I get well. And she shall pay for them. Two thousand five hundred. And medical expenses. And costs.

SAGAMORE. And cab fare to the Cottage Hospital, I suppose.

ADRIAN. No; I went in her own car. But now you remind me, I tipped the chauffeur. Now dont misunderstand me. It is not the money. But I wont be beaten by a woman. It's a point of honor: of self-respect.

SAGAMORE. Yes; but how do you arrive at the figure? Why is your honor and self-respect worth two thousand five hundred pounds and not two thousand five hundred millions?

ADRIAN. My brother got two thousand five hundred from the railway company when an electric truck butted into him on the platform at Paddington. I will not let Epifania off with less. It was an unprovoked, brutal, cowardly assault.

SAGAMORE. Was it quite unprovoked? You will not get a jury to swallow that without a peck of salt!

ADRIAN. I have told you over and over again that it was absolutely unprovoked. But the concussion from which I suffered obliterated all consciousness of what happened immediately before the assault: the last thing I can recollect was a quiet ordinary conversation about her father's money.

SAGAMORE. So much the worse for you. She can accuse you of anything she likes. And remember: no man can get damages out of a British jury unless he goes into court as a moral man.

ADRIAN. Do you suggest that I am not a moral man?

SAGAMORE. No; but Mrs Fitzfassenden's counsel will if you take her into court.

ADRIAN. Stuff! Would any jury believe that she and I were lovers on the strength of a sprained ankle, a dislocated knee, and a lump on my head the size of an ostrich's egg?

SAGAMORE. The best of evidence against you. It's only lovers that have lovers' quarrels. And suppose she pleads self-defence against a criminal assault!

ADRIAN. She dare not swear to such a lie.

SAGAMORE. How do you know it's a lie? You dont know what happened at the end. You had concussion of the brain.

ADRIAN. Yes: after the assault.

SAGAMORE. But it obliterated your consciousness of what happened before the assault. How do you know what you did in those moments?

ADRIAN. Look here. Are you my solicitor or hers?

SAGAMORE. Fate seems to have made me the solicitor of everybody in this case. If I am forced to throw up either her case or yours, I must throw up yours. How can I afford to lose a client with such an income and such a temper? Her tantrums are worth two or three thousand a year to any solicitor.

ADRIAN. Very well, Sagamore. You see my condition: you know that right and justice are on my side. I shall not forget this.

The manager enters, looking very serious.

THE MANAGER [*to Alastair*] I am extremely sorry, sir. Mrs Fitzfassenden is downstairs with the Egyptian doctor.

I really did not expect her.

EPIFANIA [*dashing into the room and addressing herself fiercely to the manager*] You have allowed my husband to bring a woman to my hotel and register her in my name. You are fired. [*She is behind the couch and does not see Adrian. Sagamore rises*].

THE MANAGER. I am sorry, madam: I did not know that the gentleman was your husband. However, you are always right. Do you wish me to go at once or to carry on until you have replaced me?

EPIFANIA. I do not wish you to go at all: you are re-engaged. Throw them both out, instantly.

ALASTAIR. Ha ha ha!

SAGAMORE. Your manager cannot throw Alastair out: Alastair can throw all of us out, if it comes to that. As to Miss Smith, this is a licensed house; and she has as much right to be here as you or I.

EPIFANIA. I will set fire to the hotel if necessary. [*She sees Adrian*] Hallo! What is this? Adrian here too! What has happened to your head? What are those sticks for? [*To the manager*] Send the doctor here at once. [*To Adrian*] Have you hurt yourself?

The manager hurries out, glad to escape from the mêlée.

ADRIAN. Hurt myself! Hurt myself!!

EPIFANIA. Has he been run over?

ADRIAN. This woman has half killed me; and she asks have I hurt myself! I fell down the whole flight of stairs. My ankle was sprained. My knee was twisted. The small bone of my leg was broken. I ricked my spine. I had to give them a subscription at the Cottage Hospital, where your man took me. I had to go from there to a nursing home: twelve guineas a week. I had to call in three Harley Street surgeons; and none of them knew anything about dislocated knees: they wanted to cut my knee open to see what was the matter with it. I had to take it to a bonesetter; and he charged me fifty guineas.

EPIFANIA. Well, why did you not walk downstairs properly? Were you drunk?

ADRIAN [*suffocating*] I —

SAGAMORE [*cutting in quickly*] He declares that his injuries were inflicted by you when you last met, Mrs Fitzfassenden.

EPIFANIA. By me! Am I a prizefighter? Am I a coalheaver?

ADRIAN. Both.

SAGAMORE. Do you deny that you assaulted him?

EPIFANIA. Of course I deny it. Anything more monstrous I never heard. What happened was that he insulted my father grossly, without the slightest provocation, at a moment when I had every reason to expect the utmost tenderness from him. The blood rushed to my head: the next thing I remember is that I was lying across the table, trembling, dying. The doctor who found me can tell you what my condition was.

ADRIAN. I dont care what your condition was. What condition did your chauffeur find me in?

SAGAMORE. Then neither of you has the least notion of how this affair ended.

ADRIAN. I have medical evidence.

EPIFANIA. So have I.

ADRIAN. Well, we shall see. I am not going to be talked out of my case.

EPIFANIA. What do you mean by your case?

SAGAMORE. He is taking an action against you.

EPIFANIA. An ·action! very well: you know my invariable rule. Fight him to the last ditch, no matter what it costs. Take him to the House of Lords if necessary. We shall see whose purse will hold out longest. I will not be blackmailed.

ADRIAN. You think your father's money places you above the law?

EPIFANIA [*flushing*] Again!

She makes for him. Alastair seizes her from behind and whirls her away towards Sagamore; then places himself on guard between her and the couch, balancing his fist warningly.

307

ALASTAIR. Now! now! now! None of that. Toko, my girl, toko.

SAGAMORE. Toko! What is toko?

ALASTAIR. She knows. Toko is an infallible medicine for calming the nerves. A punch in the solar plexus and a day in bed: thats toko.

EPIFANIA. You are my witness, Mr Sagamore, how I go in fear of my husband's brutal violence. He is stronger than I am: he can batter me, torture me, kill me. It is the last argument of the lower nature against the higher. My innocence is helpless. Do your worst. [*She sits down in Sagamore's chair with great dignity*].

ALASTAIR. Quite safe now, ladies and gentlemen. [*He picks up his illustrated paper, and retires with it to one of the remoter tea-tables, where he sits down to read as quietly as may be*].

ADRIAN [*to Epifania*] Now you know what I felt. It serves you right.

EPIFANIA. Yes: go on. Insult me. Threaten me. Blackmail me. You can all do it with impunity now.

SAGAMORE [*behind her chair*] Dont take it that way, Mrs Fitzfassenden. There is no question of blackmailing or insulting you. I only want to settle this business of Mr Blenderbland's injuries before we go into the matrimonial question.

EPIFANIA. I want to hear no more of Mr Blenderbland and his ridiculous injuries.

SAGAMORE. Do be a little reasonable, Mrs Fitzfassenden. How are we to discuss the compensation due to Mr Blenderbland without mentioning his injuries?

EPIFANIA. There is no compensation due to Mr Blenderbland. He deserved what he got, whatever that was.

SAGAMORE. But he will take an action against you.

EPIFANIA. Take one against him first.

SAGAMORE. What for?

EPIFANIA. For anything; only dont bother me about it. Claim twenty thousand pounds damages. I tell you I will not be blackmailed.

ADRIAN. Neither will I. I am entitled to compensation and I mean to have it.

SAGAMORE [*coming between them*] Steady! steady! please. I cannot advise either of you to go to law; but quite seriously, Mrs Fitzfassenden, Mr Blenderbland is entitled to some compensation. You can afford it.

EPIFANIA. Mr Sagamore: a woman as rich as I am cannot afford anything. I have to fight to keep every penny I possess. Every beggar, every blackmailer, every swindler, every charity, every testimonial, every political cause, every league and brotherhood and sisterhood, every church and chapel, every institution of every kind on earth is busy from morning to night trying to bleed me to death. If I weaken for a moment, if I let a farthing go, I shall be destitute by the end of the month. I subscribe a guinea a year to the Income Tax Payers' Defence League; but that is all: absolutely all. My standing instructions to you are to defend every action and to forestall every claim for damages by a counterclaim for ten times the amount. That is the only way in which I can write across the sky 'Hands off My Money.'

SAGAMORE. You see, Mr Blenderbland, it's no use. You must withdraw your threat of an action.

ADRIAN. I wont.

SAGAMORE. You will. You must. Mrs Fitzfassenden: he can do nothing against you. Let me make an appeal on his behalf ad misericordiam.

EPIFANIA [*impatiently*] Oh, we are wasting time; and I have more important business to settle. Give him a ten pound note and have done with it.

ADRIAN. A ten pound note!!!

SAGAMORE [*remonstrant*] Oh, Mrs Fitzfassenden!

EPIFANIA. Yes: a ten pound note. No man can refuse a ten pound note if you crackle it under his nose.

SAGAMORE. But he wants two thousand five hundred.

EPIFANIA [*rising stupefied*] Two thou – [*She gasps*].

309

ADRIAN. Not a penny less.

EPIFANIA [*going past Sagamore to the couch*] Adrian, my child, I have underrated you. Your cheek, your gluttony, your obstinacy impose respect on me. I threw a half baked gentleman downstairs: and my chauffeur picked him up on the mat a magnificently complete Skunk.

ADRIAN [*furious*] Five thousand for that, Sagamore, do you hear?

SAGAMORE. Please! please! Do keep your temper.

ADRIAN. Keep your own temper. Has she lamed you for life? Has she raised a bump on your head? Has she called you a skunk?

SAGAMORE. No; but she may at any moment.

EPIFANIA [*flinging her arms round him with a whoop of delight*] Ha ha! Ha ha! My Sagamore! My treasure! Shall I give him five thousand on condition that he turns it into a million in six months?

ADRIAN. I will do what I like with it. I will have it unconditionally.

SAGAMORE [*extricating himself gently from Epifania's hug*] Mr Blenderbland: it is a mistake to go into court in the character of a man who has been called a skunk. It makes the jury see you in that light from the start. It is also very difficult for a plaintiff to get sympathy in the character of a man who has been thrashed by a woman. If Mrs Fitzfassenden had stabbed you, or shot you, or poisoned you, that would have been quite in order: your dignity would not have been compromised. But Mrs Fitzfassenden knows better. She knows the privileges of her sex to a hair's breadth and never oversteps them. She would come into court beautifully dressed and looking her best. No woman can be more ladylike – more feminine – when it is her cue to play the perfect lady. Long before we can get the case into the lists the bump on your head will have subsided; your broken bone will have set; and the color will have come back to your cheeks. Unless you can provoke Mrs Fitzfassenden to assault you again the day before the trial – and she is far too clever for that – the chances are a million to one against you.

ALASTAIR [*rising and coming from the other end of the room*] That is so, Blenderbland. You havnt a dog's chance. Next time you see her fist coming in your direction, duck and counter. If you dont get that satisfaction you wont get any. [*He sits down next Patricia, on her right*].

PATRICIA. Yes, Mr Blenderbland: Alastair's right. Ask her nicely, and perhaps she'll pay your expenses.

ADRIAN [*sitting up and taking his head in his hands, shaken, almost lachrymose*] Is there any justice for a man against a woman?

SAGAMORE [*sitting beside him to console him*] Believe me: no. Not against a millionairess.

EPIFANIA. And what justice is there for a millionairess, I should like to know?

SAGAMORE. In the courts –

EPIFANIA. I am not thinking of the courts: there is little justice there for anybody. My millions are in themselves an injustice. I speak of the justice of heaven.

ALASTAIR. Oh Lord! Now we're for it. [*He deliberately puts his arm round Patricia's waist*].

EPIFANIA. Alastair: how can you jeer at me? Is it just that I, because I am a millionairess, cannot keep my husband, cannot keep even a lover, cannot keep anything but my money? There you sit before my very eyes, snuggling up to that insignificant little nothingness who cannot afford to pay for her own stockings; and you are happy and she is happy. [*She turns to Adrian*] Here is this suit of clothes on two sticks. What does it contain?

ADRIAN [*broken*] Let me alone, will you?

EPIFANIA. Something that once resembled a man, something that liked lending me five pound notes and never asked me to repay them. Why? Kindness to me? Love of me? No: the swank of a poor man lending to a millionairess. In my divine wrath I smashed him as a child smashes a disappointing toy; and when he was beaten down to his real self I found I was not a woman to him but a bank account with a good cook.

PATRICIA. Thats all very fine, deary; but the truth is that no one can live with you.

EPIFANIA. And anyone can live with you. And apparently you can live with anybody.

ALASTAIR. What Seedy says is God's truth. Nobody could live with you.

EPIFANIA. But why? Why? Why?

SAGAMORE. Do be reasonable, Mrs Fitzfassenden. Can one live with a tornado? with an earthquake? with an avalanche?

EPIFANIA. Yes. Thousands of people live on the slopes of volcanoes, in the track of avalanches, on land thrown up only yesterday by earthquakes. But with a millionairess who can rise to her destiny and wield the power her money gives her, no. Well, be it so. I shall sit in my lonely house, and be myself, and pile up millions until I find a man good enough to be to me what Alastair is to Seedy-stockings.

PATRICIA. Well, I hope you wont have to wait too long.

EPIFANIA. I never wait. I march on; and when I come upon the things I need I grab them. I grabbed your Alastair. I find that he does not suit me: he beats me –

ALASTAIR. In self-defence. I never raised a hand to you except in self-defence.

EPIFANIA. Yes: you are like the great European Powers: you never fight except in self-defence. But you are two stone heavier than I; and I cannot keep my head at infighting as you can. You do not suit. I throw you to Greedy-Seedy-Stockings: you can punch her to your heart's content. Mr Sagamore: arrange the divorce. Cruelty and adultery.

PATRICIA. But I dont like this: it's not fair to Alastair. Why is he to be divorced instead of you?

EPIFANIA. Mr Sagamore: take an action against Patricia

Smith for alienating my husband's affections. Damages twenty thousand pounds.

PATRICIA. Oh! Is such a thing possible, Mr Sagamore?

SAGAMORE. I am afraid it is, Miss Smith. Quite possible.

PATRICIA. Well, my dear old father used to say that in the law courts there is only one way to beat the people who have unlimited money; and that is to have no money at all. You cant get twenty thousand out of me. And call it vanity if you will; but I should rather like the world to know that in my little way I was able to take the best and dearest man in England from the richest woman.

EPIFANIA. Damn your dear old father!

ALASTAIR [*laughing boisterously*] Ha ha! One for you, Eppy. [*He kisses Patricia*].

SAGAMORE [*smiling*] I am afraid the laugh is with old Mr Smith, Mrs Fitzfassenden. Where there is nothing, the king loses his rights.

EPIFANIA. Oh, I can bear no more of this. I will not have my life dragged down to planes of vulgarity on which I cannot breathe. I will live in utter loneliness and keep myself sacred until I find the right man – the man who can stand with me on the utmost heights and not lose his head – the mate created for me in heaven. He must be somewhere.

THE DOCTOR [*appearing at the door*] The manager says I am wanted here. Who wants me?

EPIFANIA. *I* want you. Come here [*she stretches out her hand to him imperiously*].

THE DOCTOR [*coming to her and feeling her pulse*] Something wrong with your blood pressure, eh? [*Amazed*] Ooooh! I have never felt such a pulse. It is like a slow sledge hammer.

EPIFANIA. Well, is my pulse my fault?

THE DOCTOR. No. It is the will of Allah. All our pulses are part of the will of Allah.

ALASTAIR. Look here, you know, Doc: that wont go down in this country. We dont believe in Allah.

THE DOCTOR. That does not disconcert Allah in the least, my friend. The pulse beats still, slow, strong. [*To Epifania*] You are a terrible woman; but I love your pulse. I have never felt anything like it before.

PATRICIA. Well, just fancy that! He loves her pulse.

THE DOCTOR. I am a doctor. Women as you fancy them are nothing to me but bundles of ailments. But the life! the pulse! is the heartbeat of Allah, save in Whom there is no majesty and no might. [*He drops her hand*].

EPIFANIA. My pulse will never change: this is the love I crave for. I will marry you. Mr Sagamore: see about a special licence the moment you have got rid of Alastair.

THE DOCTOR. It is not possible. We are bound by our vows.

EPIFANIA. Well, have I not passed your mother's test? You shall have an accountant's certificate. I learned in the first half hour of my search for employment that the living wage for a single woman is five shillings a week. Before the end of the week I had made enough to support me for a hundred years. I did it honestly and legitimately. I explained the way in which it was done.

THE DOCTOR. It was not the way of Allah, the Merciful, the Compassionate. Had you added a farthing an hour to the wages of those sweated women, that wicked business would have crashed on your head. You sold it to the man Superflew for the last penny of his savings; and the women still slave for him at one piastre an hour.

EPIFANIA. You cannot change the market price of labor: not Allah himself can do that. But I came to this hotel as a scullery maid: the most incompetent scullery maid that ever broke a dinner service. I am now its owner; and there is no tuppencehapeny an hour here.

THE DOCTOR. The hotel looks well in photographs; and the wages you pay would be a fortune to a laborer on the Nile. But what of the old people whose natural home this place had become? the old man with his paralytic stroke?

the old woman gone mad? the cast out creatures in the workhouse? Was not this preying on the poverty of the poor? Shall I, the servant of Allah, live on such gains? Shall I, the healer, the helper, the guardian of life and the counsellor of health, unite with the exploiter of misery?

EPIFANIA. I have to take the world as I find it.

THE DOCTOR. The wrath of Allah shall overtake those who leave the world no better than they found it.

EPIFANIA. I think Allah loves those who make money.

SAGAMORE. All the evidence is that way, certainly.

THE DOCTOR. I do not see it so. I see that riches are a curse; poverty is a curse; only in the service of Allah is there justice, righteousness, and happiness. But all this talk is idle. This lady has easily fulfilled the condition imposed by my mother. But I have not fulfilled the condition imposed by the lady's father.

EPIFANIA. You need not trouble about that. The six months have not expired. I will shew you how to turn your hundred and fifty pounds into fifty thousand.

THE DOCTOR. You cannot. It is gone.

EPIFANIA. Oh, you cannot have spent it all: you who live like a mouse. There must be some of it left.

THE DOCTOR. Not a penny. Not a piastre. Allah –

EPIFANIA. Oh, bother Allah! What did you do with it?

THE DOCTOR. Allah is never bothered. On that afternoon when you left me to earn your own living I called upon the Merciful, the Compassionate, to reveal to me whether you were not one of the strokes of his infinite humor. Then I sat down and took up a newspaper. And behold! a paragraph headed Wills and Bequests. I read a name that I cannot remember: Mrs Somebody of Clapham Park, one hundred and twenty-two thousand pounds. She had never done anything but live in Clapham Park; and she left £122,000. But what was the next name? It was that of the teacher who changed my whole life and gave me a new soul by opening the world of science to me. I was his assistant for four years.

He used to make his own apparatus for his experiments; and one day he needed a filament of metal that would resist a temperature that melted platinum like sealing wax.

EPIFANIA. Buy his patent for me if it has not been snapped up.

THE DOCTOR. He never took out a patent. He believed that knowledge is no man's property. And he had neither time nor money to waste in patent offices. Millions have been made out of that discovery of his by people who care nothing about science and everything about money. He left four hundred pounds and a widow: the good woman who had been a second mother to me. A shilling a day for her at most: not even one piastre an hour.

EPIFANIA. That comes of marrying an incompetent dreamer. Are you going to beg for her? I warn you I am tired of destitute widows. I should be a beggar myself if I took them all on my shoulders.

THE DOCTOR. Have no fear. The Merciful, the Compassionate heard the prayer of the widow. Listen. I once cured a Prime Minister when he imagined himself to be ill. I went to him and told him that it was the will of Allah that the widow should have a civil list pension. She received it: a hundred pounds a year. I went to the great Metallurgical Trust which exploits his discovery, and told them that her poverty was a scandal in the face of Allah. They were rich and generous: they made a special issue of founders' shares for her, worth three hundred a year to her. They called it letting her in on the ground floor. May her prayers win them favor from Him save in whom there is no might and no majesty! But all this took time. The illness, the nurse, the funeral, the disposal of the laboratory, the change to a cheaper lodging, had left her without a penny, though no doctor and lawyer took a farthing, and the shopkeepers were patient; for the spirit of Allah worked more strongly upon them than on the British Treasury, which clamored for its little death duty. Between the death and the pensions there was a gap exactly one hundred and fifty pounds wide. He who is just and exact supplied that sum by your chauffeur's hands and by mine. It rejoiced my heart as money had never rejoiced it before. But instead of coming to you with fifty thousand pounds I am in arrear with my bill for my daily bread in your hotel, and am expecting every day to be told by your manager that this cannot go on: I must settle.

ALASTAIR. Well, old man, you may not have done a lot for yourself; but you have done damned well for the widow. And you have escaped Eppy. She wont marry you with your pockets empty.

EPIFANIA. Pray why? Fifty thousand pounds must have been made out of that discovery ten times over. The doctor, in putting my money into the widow's necessary expenses, may be said to have made a retrospective investment in the discovery. And he has shewn the greatest ability in the affair: has he not, Mr Sagamore?

SAGAMORE. Unquestionably. He has bowled out the Prime Minister. He has bowled out the Imperial Metallurgical Trust. He has settled the widow's affairs to perfection.

THE DOCTOR. But not my own affairs. I am in debt for my food.

EPIFANIA. Well, if you come to that, *I* am in debt for my food. I got a letter this morning from my purveyors to say that I have paid them nothing for two years, and unless I let them have something on account they will be obliged to resort to the premises.

THE DOCTOR. What does that mean?

EPIFANIA. Sell my furniture.

THE DOCTOR. You cannot sell mine, I am afraid. I have hardly any.

BLENDERBLAND. If you have a stick she will sell it. She is the meanest woman in England.

EPIFANIA. That is why I am also the richest. Mr Sagamore: my mind is made up: I will marry this doctor.

Ascertain his name and make the necessary arrangements.

BLENDERBLAND. You take care, doctor. She is unfaithful to her husband in wanting to marry you. She flirted with me: took me down the river and made me believe I was to be Alastair's successor before ever she saw you. See what she has done to me! She will do it to you when the next man takes her fancy.

THE DOCTOR [to Epifania] What have you to say to that?

EPIFANIA. You must learn to take chances in this world. This disappointed philanderer tries to frighten you with my unfaithfulness. He has never been married: I have. And I tell you that in the very happiest marriages not a day passes without a thousand moments of unfaithfulness. You begin by thinking you have only one husband: you find you have a dozen. There is a creature you hate and despise and are tied to for life; and before breakfast is over the fool says something nice and becomes a man whom you admire and love; and between these extremes there are a thousand degrees with a different man and woman at each of them. A wife is all women to one man: she is everything that is devilish: the thorn in his flesh, the jealous termagant, the detective dogging all his movements, the nagger, the scolder, the worrier. He has only to tell her an affectionate lie and she is his comfort, his helper, at best his greatest treasure, at worst his troublesome but beloved child. All wives are all these women in one, all husbands all these men in one. What do the unmarried know of this infinitely dangerous heart tearing everchanging life of adventure that we call marriage? Face it as you would face a dangerous operation: have you not performed hundreds of them?

THE DOCTOR. Of a surety there is no wit and no wisdom like that of a woman ensnaring the mate chosen for her by Allah. Yet I am very well as I am. Why should I change? I shall be very happy as an old bachelor.

EPIFANIA [flinging out her wrists at him] Can you feel my pulse every day as an old bachelor?

THE DOCTOR [*taking her wrist and mechanically taking out his watch at the same time*] Ah! I had forgotten the pulse. One, two, three: it is irresistible: it is a pulse in a hundred thousand. I love it: I cannot give it up.

BLENDERBLAND. You will regret it to the last day of your life.

EPIFANIA. Mr Sagamore: you have your instructions.

SAGAMORE [*bows*].

PATRICIA. Congratulations, darling.

And that is how the story ends in capitalist countries. In Russia, however, and in countries with Communist sympathies, the people demand that the tale shall have an edifying moral. Accordingly, when the doctor, feeling Epifania's pulse, says that he loves it and cannot give it up, Blenderbland continues the conversation as follows.

BLENDERBLAND. Take care. Her hand is accursed. It is the hand of Midas: it turns everything it touches to gold.

THE DOCTOR. My hand is more deeply accursed. Gold flies away from it. Why am I always poor? I do not like being poor.

EPIFANIA. Why am I always rich? I do not like being rich.

ALASTAIR. Youd better both go to Russia, where there are neither rich nor poor.

EPIFANIA. Why not? I buy nothing but Russian stock now.

BLENDERBLAND. The Russians would shoot you as they would a mad dog. You are a bloated capitalist, you know.

EPIFANIA. I am a capitalist here; but in Russia I should be a worker. And what a worker! My brains are wasted here: the wealth they create is thrown away on idlers and their parasites, whilst poverty, dirt, disease, misery and slavery surround me like a black sea in which I may be engulfed at any moment by a turn of the money market. Russia needs managing women like me. In Moscow I shall not be a millionairess; but I shall be in the Sovnarkom within six months and in the Politbureau before the end of the year.

Here I have no real power, no real freedom, and no security at all: we may all die in the workhouse. In Russia I shall have such authority! such scope for my natural powers! as the Empress Catharine never enjoyed. I swear that before I have been twenty years in Russia every Russian baby shall weigh five pounds heavier and every Russian man and woman live ten years longer. I shall not be an empress; and I may work myself to death; but in a thousand years from now holy Russia shall again have a patron saint, and her name shall be Saint Epifania.

BLENDERBLAND. The egotism of that woman!!

SAGAMORE. I am afraid there are no saints now in Russia.

THE DOCTOR. There are saints everywhere: they are the one species you cannot liquidate. Kings, emperors, conquerors, pontiffs and all the other idols are swept away sooner or later; and all the king's horses and all the king's men cannot set them up again; but the saints shall reign for ever and ever in the temple of the hammer and the sickle. But we must not go to Russia, because the Russians do not need us: they have stayed at home and saved their own souls. Ought not we to stay at home and save ours? Why not make the British Empire a Soviet republic?

EPIFANIA. By all means; but we shall have to liquidate all the adult inhabitants and begin with the newly born. And the first step to that is to get married. Mr Sagamore: make the necessary arrangements.

SAGAMORE [bows].

PATRICIA. Congratulations, darling.